The Catholic Church
and Social Change
in Nicaragua

The Catholic Church and Social Change in Nicaragua

MANZAR FOROOHAR

State University of New York Press

Published by
State University of New York Press, Albany

© 1989 State University of New York

For information, address State University of New York Press,
State University Plaza, Albany, N.Y., 12246

Library of Congress Cataloging-in-Publication Data

Foroohar, Manzar, 1948–
    The Catholic Church and social change in Nicaragua.

    Bibliography: p.
    Includes index.
    1. Catholic Church — Nicaragua.   2. Liberation
theology.   3. Church and state — Nicaragua.
4. Nicaragua — Church history — 20th century.
5. Nicaragua — Politics and government.   I. Title.
BX1442.2.F67   1988   282'.7285   88-2144
ISBN 0-88706-864-2
ISBN 0-88706-865-0 (pbk.)

10 9 8 7 6 5 4 3 2 1

Contents

Introduction   ix

1. The Catholic Church in Nicaragua   1
   Historical Background   1
   The Nicaraguan Catholic Church and the
   Independence Movement   3
   Conservative-Liberal Conflict and Foreign
   Intervention   6
   Expulsion of Jesuits   9
   Political Development and the Church   10
   Zelaya and the United States   11
   North American Direct Intervention   13
   The Church and the North American
   Intervention   16
   Sandino's Struggle   17
   The Catholic Church and Sandino   21
   The Liberal Government   22
   The Catholic Church and Liberal Governments   24

2. Economic Formation and Sociopolitical Conflict   27
   Agriculture   27
   Industrial System   31
   Sociopolitical Conflict   36
   Political Opposition   43

3. The Response of Latin American Catholics to
   Socioeconomic Problems   45
   Liberation Theology   50

The Church and Politics   51
Catholicism and Class Struggle   53
The Latin American Church and Class Struggle   55
The Catholic Church and Socialism   61
Conclusion   66

4. Implementation of Liberation Theology in
   Nicaragua, 1968–72   67
      A Conservative Hierarchy   67
      Radical Clergy   67
      First National Pastoral Meeting   71
      Public Expression of New Ideas   73
      New Leadership in the Catholic Church   80

5. The 1972 Earthquake and the Aftermath   87
      Growing Political Opposition   91
      The Catholic Church and the Opposition   94
      Unión Democrática de Liberación (UDEL)   98
      Dissident Liberals   98
      The Social Christian Party   99
      The Conservative Opposition   101
      The Socialists   101
      Workers' Unions   102
      UDEL's Program   104

6. The FSLN and the Progressive Church   111
      Frente Sandinista de Liberación Nacional   112
      The Student Movement and the FSLN   113
      The Political Opposition and the Reforms
      of the 1960s   115
      FSLN and the Catholic Church   117
      Military and Political Work   119
      The FSLN in the 1970s   120
      Radicalization of the Christian Base
      Communities in Managua   124
      The Process of Radicalization in Barrio
      Riguero, 1972–77   127
      The Process of Radicalization in Barrio OPEN
      3, 1972–77   135

Radicalization in San Pablo Parish 141
Rural Population and the Catholic Church 142
The Capuchin Fathers in Zelaya 147
Repression in Zelaya 148
Repression in Other Rural Communities 149
Transformation of the Peasantry and the
Rural Church 152
Public Condemnation of the Repression 155

7. Intensification of the Political Conflict and
Clarification of the Sociopolitical Alliance 159
 The October Offensive, National Dialogue, and
 the Role of the Church 163
 The Assassination of Pedro Joaquin Chamorro
 and the General Strike 176
 Collapse of the Bourgeois Leadership 183
 The FSLN and the Bourgeoisie 187
 The Last Attempt to Stop the Revolution: the
 United States, the Nicaraguan Bourgeoisie, and
 the Catholic Hierarchy 193

Epilogue 199

Notes 213

Bibliography 239

Index 255

Introduction

The role of the Catholic Church in the contemporary sociopolitical upheaval in Nicaragua has been a highly controversial issue. Some have called the Church a revolutionary institution supporting a leftist movement with strong Marxist tendencies and a declared plan for socialization of the country. Others have called it a conservative establishment standing in the way of social change and the radicalization of the revolutionary process. Both analyses share a fundamental misconception in viewing the Church as a monolithic institution with internal cohesion and a well-defined political line. A brief look at the history of the Church in Nicaragua, and its development within a concrete social and political framework in any given historical period, provides a different picture; the Church, as any other institution in the society, has been affected by its surrounding environment and has reflected the social divisions and political conflicts in its own structure and ideology.

At the beginning of its history in Nicaragua, the Church, as a Spanish institution, clearly took sides with the colonial power, and it acted in close collaboration with the conquerors to convert the indigenous population to faithful vassals of the Catholic monarchs. The first conflict and internal division in the Nicaraguan Catholic Church was a clear reflection of the political conflict among the colonialists, the Spanish monarchs seeking to consolidate their direct power over their new subjects, and the encomenderos trying to maintain their absolute power over the indigenous population entrusted to them for exploitation. The power struggle dictating the political events in the colonies deeply affected the Church. The majority of the clergy — some of whom were themselves encomenderos, while others were employed in encomiendas — closed their eyes to the cruelty of the system and took sides with the encomenderos to defend the institution against the wishes of the crown. On the other hand, a few priests and bishops, including Bishop Antonio Valdivieso, took sides with the crown, and strongly opposed the abusive, cruel, and inhumane encomienda system.

During the rest of the colonial period, the strength of the colonial government was reflected in the continuous activities of the Church to fulfill its mission to Christianize the natives, and, by preaching fatalism, to prepare them for a total submission to the colonial system.

In the early nineteenth century, when the legitimacy of colonial power came under question, and the Nicaraguans began to plan a future free of Spanish domination, the Church once more became involved in a division between those priests who supported the independence movement and those who remained faithful to the Spanish crown.

For more than a century after independence, Nicaragua was torn apart by constant fighting between the Liberals and Conservatives, and by foreign interventions on behalf of one group or the other. Throughout this period, the Catholic Church, threatened by the anticlerical policies of the Liberals, chiefly supported the Conservative side in the political conflict. However, the foreign interventions, first by William Walker in the 1850s and later by the U.S. Marines from 1912 to 1933, divided the clergy and caused a political clash in the Church.

One important social element common during the colonial period and the first century of independence was the total absence of the Nicaraguan masses as conscious agents in the historical development of the country. Lacking valuable mineral resources and suitable soil and climate for profitable export agriculture, most of Nicaragua was abandoned by the colonial power; thus, the majority of native Nicaraguans continued to live in their ancient social structures — for the most part, isolated in remote areas with no communication system — and totally out of the mainstream of the sociopolitical life of the country. The primitive economy and a precapitalist social structure were the main hindrance to development of a clear class stratification and class consciousness in Nicaragua. On the other hand, the absence of the majority of the people in the national life had limited the political development to a few urban centers, and had reduced the sociopolitical conflict to a power struggle between the Liberals and the Conservatives. The simplicity in social structure and the reduction of the conflict to a factional power struggle with occasional foreign intervention was reflected in the division within the Church, which was chiefly political rather than social.

In the 1950s and 1960s, however, social and economic developments converted the majority of Nicaraguans from subsistence farmers to seasonal plantation workers or wage laborers concentrated in working-class neighborhoods. Many joined the marginal population in the slum areas of the large cities. The new social stratification and the gradual awareness of emerging realities culminated in the creation of political groups proclaiming class representation. Terms such as popular classes, proletariat, bourgeoisie, and class struggle entered the Nicaraguan political vocabulary.

Although independent from the changes in Nicaragua, profound innovations in the ideology and structure of the Catholic Church were introduced by Pope John XXIII and by the Second Vatican Council in the 1960s. In Latin America, the new social teachings of the Catholic Church came into a head-on clash with repressive military governments of the 1960s. The result was a sharp radicalization of the Catholic Church in Latin America which culminated in deepening the new social commitments of the Church at the Second Conference of the Latin American bishops at Medellín in 1968, and in the development of liberation theology.

The Nicaraguan Catholic Church, led by an ultraconservative hierarchy, was shocked by the social developments in Nicaragua and by the structural and theological innovations in European and Latin American Catholicism. The wave was rapid and sweeping. The younger generation of priests and nuns, affected by the poverty and misery of the lower classes, angered by political repression, and aroused by new theological directions, revolted against the Church hierarchy and its close relations with the rich and the powerful. Once more the Nicaraguan Church was divided; this time the issue was not only political but social. The focus of the debate was the class option and the future direction of the Church. The progressive clergy which was taking sides with the poor and which was participating in the social conflict, felt closer to those political groups that represented the poor than to the Church hierarchy that supported the rich. The division was real and deep.

However, in the 1970s, high-level government corruption and an intensified repression which drove almost every social sector, including the bourgeoisie, into the camp of the political opposition, blurred the lines between class struggle and an antidictatorial movement. Both the bourgeois dissidents and the radical opposition called for the overthrow of Somoza. The lines became even more obscure in religious circles when a new archbishop was assigned to Managua in 1970. Archbishop Miguel Obando y Bravo, a vocal critic of the repression and violation of human rights, led the conservative hierarchy as it distanced itself from the dictator. The Catholic hierarchy for the first time in Nicaraguan history appeared to be taking sides with the people against the repressive government. Obando's early statements as archbishop, in which he quoted extensively with Medellín documents, created high hopes among the Nicaraguan people, and particularly the progressive clergy, for implementation of the Medellín teachings urging a preferential option for the poor on the part of the Church.

The intensified armed struggle in the 1977–78 period, led by the *Frente Sandinista de Liberación Nacional*, added a new dimension to the political picture: a feasible triumph for the radical opposition, targeting both the dictatorial regime and the economic structure of dependent capitalism. The reformist bourgeoisie, hoping for a termination of the Somoza's personal rule in a rapid and peaceful manner which would leave the basic structures of the regime intact, clashed with the revolutionaries. The lines began to become distinct between the two groups and the two programs; and the people, in their daily political behavior, began to choose between the two alternatives.

The Catholic Church did not remain unaffected by the tremendous social movement and political debate. Indeed, the progressive clergy, deeply committed to liberation theology, became an important factor and an active participant in the ongoing struggle. Many priests, nuns, and lay persons increasingly allied themselves with the radical forces opting for the poor and aiming at the destruction of the existing structures through a revolutionary process. They advocated the creation of a totally new order that included the participation of the poor. On the other hand, the hierarchy, still highly critical of the dictatorship, followed the lead of the reformist bourgeoisie, and saved a major part of its political attacks for the radical movement. The public statements and the documents issued by the Church hierarchy in the 1977-79 period manifest an amazing similarity with the statements and the documents of the bourgeois opposition.

Somoza's intransigence in the face of the compromise proposals of the bourgeoisie, on the one hand, and the National Guard's savagery in crushing all forms of opposition, on the other hand, forced many reformists away from their illusion about the possibility of a peaceful removal of Somoza. The split in the bourgeois opposition was inevitable. An increasing number of organizations and individuals left the reformist camp and began backing the FSLN.

The new political support made the possibility of revolutionary triumph even greater, and this resulted in a growing fear among the reformists. This fear was the cause of a sharp move toward ultraconservatism and an alliance with the North American government to stop the revolution. In the intense planning and attempts to reach a compromise with Somoza, the Church hierarchy, particularly Archbishop Obando, had an important, if not leading, role. However, the popular upheaval was strong enough to survive the orchestrated attempt by the ultraconservative bourgeoisie, the North American government, and the antirevolutionary Catholic hierarchy to crush the movement.

To understand the present-day involvement of the Nicaraguan Church in politics, and the sharp internal divisions in its ranks, we have to study the history of the Church in the social and political context of the country. Since the triumph of the revolution in 1979, many scholars have devoted their time to the study of Church-State relations in revolutionary Nicaragua. However, there is a lack of scholarly inquiry into the historical development of the subject. The present book is an attempt to fill the void and to provide a historical depth to the ongoing discussion of the Church-State relations in Nicaragua. I have focused on the period prior to the establishment of the revolutionary government. In the epilogue, I will briefly discuss some of the developments that followed the triumph to show the continuity in the historical pattern of the Church's involvement in politics, and the ongoing conflict inside the Church over political and social issues.

While analyzing the Catholic Church institution from a historical perspective, I have also extended my analysis to the development of new elements in Catholic thought, known as liberation theology. This is a very important and a difficult subject to study. Largely a product of Latin American social and political development, liberation theology is a subject open to scientific historical inquiry. However, the nature of the subject, a theology based on a belief in forces beyond human history which transcend socioeconomic and political structures of human society, creates a strong obstacle to a thorough analysis based on historical methodology. To understand liberation theology as a historical force we have to overcome this obstacle by demythologizing religious terminology and by placing theological categories in their social and political context within human history. With an unprecedented openness to some tenets of non-Catholic theologies and nonreligious philosophies, liberation theologians have opened the way to secular historians and social scientists for a scientific study of the subject.

Throughout the present work, I have treated theology from a historical point of view. The use of social science categories for clarifying religious terms is not owing to any disrespect for religious beliefs; rather, it is an attempt to explain their historical, social, and political importance to readers who do not necessarily share the same beliefs.

CHAPTER 1

The Catholic Church in Nicaragua

Historical Background

As in most of the rest of Latin America, Catholic priests arrived in Nicaragua almost simultaneously with Spanish conquerors. The first priest, Father Diego de Agüero, reached the area with Captain González Dávila in 1523.

The role of the Catholic Church in colonial Latin America has been generally interpreted as that of providing an ideological justification for the conquest of the New World. The priests, especially the high-ranking clergy who were appointed to their holy offices by the Iberian kings in accordance with the Royal Patronage,[1] were generally faithful to the monarchs. However, from the beginning, the social and political conflicts in Spain and its colonies in Latin America were reflected in the Catholic Church.

A major political conflict in Spain at the time of the conquest of Latin America was the rivalry between the local rulers who were striving to maintain their political and economic independence, and the absolute monarchs who were trying to increase their political power and to establish a central government. In this power struggle, the kings were supported by the emerging capitalist class. In the new colonies, this rivalry was manifested by the attempts of the encomenderos to maintain the quasi-feudal encomienda system, and by the efforts of the kings to impose their total political power and to put the indigenous population under the direct control of the state.

In this political struggle, the high-ranking clergy was divided between those who took sides with the encomenderos, closing their eyes to the social ills of the system and the inhumane treatment of the indigenous population (as previously mentioned, some of the high clergy were themselves encomenderos), and those who voiced their opposition to the existing structure and took sides with the kings for abolition of the encomienda system. In Central America, the most famous champion of the indigenous rights was Friar Bartolome de las Casas, who denounced the brutality of the conquerors as early as 1533.

The political conflict between the Spanish kings and the encomenderos finally resulted in the declaration of the New Laws (Leyes Nuevas) by the monarch in 1542, which provided for the gradual abolition of the encomienda system. It also prohibited the enslavement of the indigenous population. At the time of the declaration of the New Laws, Nicaragua was governed by Rodrigo de Contreras. An encomendero, Contreras joined the other encomenderos in Nicaragua in opposition to the New Laws.

In 1543, a Spanish Dominican bishop, Antonio de Valdivieso, was appointed bishop of León. He was another famous champion of the rights of the indigenous population, and his beliefs and his activities brought him into a sharp conflict with Contreras. Following an unsuccessful attempt to oblige the governor to obey the New Laws, Bishop Valdivieso took his grievances to the Spanish authorities and asked for an investigation of the abuses committed by the encomenderos, including Governor Contreras.[2]

On July 15, 1545, the bishop wrote to the king, once again complaining about the continuation of Indian slavery in Nicaragua and the lack of justice because of corrupt administration by Contreras. In addition, on October 19, 1545, Valdivieso joined Fray Bartolomé de las Casas to publish a document defending the poor and condemning the lack of justice in Central America.[3] The constant pressure from Valdivieso to implement the New Laws created a high tension between the bishop and the governor.

To defend himself against the Bishop's charges, Contreras travelled to Spain and took his case to the Council of the Indies.

Following an investigation and a hearing, the Council ruled against Contreras. When the news reached Nicaragua, encomenderos, led by Contreras's sons, Pedro and Hernando, rebelled against the Spanish authorities. They assassinated Bishop Valdivieso, and looted the city of León. One of the participants in the assassination was a former Dominican friar, Pedro de Castañeda.[4]

The revolt did not last long and the official government institutions consolidated their power and gradually implemented colonial laws. The consolidation of the government was reflected in the smooth operation of the Church, which continued to Christianize the natives and to prepare them for the acceptance of the system.

The Nicaraguan Catholic Church and the Independence Movement

By the beginning of the movement for independence in Latin America, the Nicaraguan Church was divided once again over political issues. The high-ranking Catholic clergy took sides with the Spanish rulers, while some of the low-ranking priests actively participated in the movement.

In December 1811, Nicaraguans, especially in León, were demanding change. The provincial governor, José Salvador, who had governed León for eighteen years, was no longer able to control the opposition, among them Father José Antonio Moñino, a Franciscan friar, and Father Benito Miguelena of the Merced order.[5]

On December 13, the people of León rebelled against the governor, demanding a change in the authorities, cuts in taxes, suppression of monopolies, abolition of slavery, and freedom for prisoners. The rebels submitted their demands to the bishop of León, Monsignor Nicolás García Jerez, in a letter written by Father Miguelena, whose residence had been converted to a meeting place and storage house of arms for the rebels. Father Miguelena also played an important role in spreading the movement to other parts of Nicaragua, including Granada, Chontales, and Segovia.[6]

The rebellion in León was strong and Bishop García Jerez, a Spanish monarchist, had to agree to the demands of the rebels. Astutely, he proposed an election in each barrio to choose deputies in order to form a junta to deal with the new situation. As he hoped, the majority of the elected deputies were priests under his control, and he was chosen as the head of the new junta as a substitute for the governor. When the movement lost its initial fervor, Bishop Jerez dissolved the junta, proclaimed himself governor, and issued a decree establishing the death penalty for rebellion. He sent Father Miguelena to El Salvador, where he was arrested and taken to a jail in Guatemala.[7]

Another rebellion began in Granada on December 22, 1811. The rebels of Granada were Conservative and in favor of the preservation of the colonial structure. However, they were strongly against the peninsulars (Spanish-born officials) and wanted to replace them in the government. The first act of the *Cabildo Abierto* (Open Town Council) of Granada was the ousting of all Spaniards from government positions. Among the creole deputies of the *cabildo* was a priest, Benito Soto, who proposed the abolition of slavery on January 10, 1812. Influenced by Bishop Jerez, Soto later changed his position and joined the monarchists against the movement. He was sent to Masaya by Jerez as the commander of the army to pacify the rebellion.[8]

Although the rebels of Granada had accepted the new authority in León under the leadership of Bishop Nicolás García Jerez, the Bishop sent troops to Granada to break the rebellion. When they reached Masaya, the soldiers, most of them creoles, refused to ally with the peninsulars against the creole rebels of Granada.

The uprising spread to other cities, and in many of them the same pattern of Church division between the supporters of independence and the royalists was repeated. In 1812, the vicar of Granada, José Antonio Chamorro, issued a proclamation against the popular revolt and denounced the antimonarchist rebels as anti-Christian.

> The people have disobeyed the Spaniards. The kings of Spain are Spaniards. Therefore, the people have disobeyed the kings of Spain, and in this manner, they have been violators and offenders of all laws. The people have removed the employees without due process, and promulgated absolute laws. Therefore, the people conceive that they have more power than God, the Church, and the King. We can conclude that the insurgents are traitors to God, to the religion, and to the King of the country.[9]

Facing the rising level of the rebellion in Nicaragua, José

Bustamante y Guerra, Captain General of Guatemala, ordered his troops to march to Nicaragua to crush the movement. He punished the arrested leaders of the rebellion, including the rebellious clergy.

Some of the movement's leaders who had fled the persecution met in December 1813 in the convent of Belén to organize the struggle for independence. This new wave mainly consisted of the urban middle class: small merchants, lower army officers, lower public workers, and enlightened priests. They were the sectors which did not have any hope for progress in a colonial society, and they were prepared to change the situation, even by violent actions. One of the organizers of the Belén meeting was Tomás Ruíz, the first Nicaraguan Indian to obtain a doctorate in theology and to be ordained as a priest.

The movement was betrayed, and on December 23, 1813, most of the leaders, including Father Miguelena and Father Ruíz, were captured by Captain General Bustamante y Guerra. Most of the captured remained in jail until 1819.

Even after the achievement of independence, the Nicaraguan Church remained divided among those who supported independence and worked in its favor, and those who were against independence and favored the return of the Spanish monarch.

For a few years following independence from Spain, Nicaragua was a part of the United Provinces of Central America, whose Constitution of 1824 recognized Catholicism as the official religion and forbade others from publicly exercising their faith. However, when the Liberal president Francisco Morazán took power in January 1830, the Church-State relationship changed profoundly. On February 8, the Legislative Assembly passed a law affirming that "all monastery establishments belonging to San Francisco, Merced, and Recollección orders will be permanently abolished in the country."[10] The Assembly passed another law, on March 5 of the same year, declaring, "All the properties of extinguished monasteries in the country belong to the state."[11]

During Morazán's rule the traditional hegemony of Catholicism suffered all over Central America, but it proved strong enough to survive the difficult times.

On November 17, 1838, the first constitution of the state of Nicaragua ratified articles similar to previous legislations of Morazan's regime concerning the Church, and established religious freedom, as stated in Article 53: "The Roman Catholic religion professed by the country is protected by the government, but public practice of other religions is not prohibited."[12] However, religious freedom only lasted until 1854, when the Conservative president Fruto Chamorro wrote another constitution and returned the old privileges to the Catholic Church.

Conservative-Liberal Conflict and Foreign Intervention

Throughout the nineteenth century, the main internal conflict in Nicaragua was between two ruling circles, the Conservatives, mainly representatives of dominant merchants and cattle-raising groups based in Granada, and the Liberals, advocates for the interests of the artisans and landowners of León. The political conflict often resulted in armed struggle. From 1824 to 1842, seventeen major battles occurred between the two groups.

The turbulent political situation did not prevent foreign powers from developing strong interests in the economic affairs of the country. From the early nineteenth century, the commercial and strategic importance of Nicaragua was known to the great powers, and by the 1840s both the United States and Great Britain were trying to obtain the right for their citizens to build an interoceanic canal in Nicaragua. The discovery of gold in California in 1848 made the route through the lakes of Nicaragua even more important to the Americans. The Clayton-Bulwer Treaty of 1850 temporarily reduced the tension between the rival powers, by giving the right to use the route to both British and American governments.

In 1849, prior to the ratification of the Clayton-Bulwer Treaty, a North American businessman, Cornelius Vanderbilt, formed a firm, Accessory Transit Company, to establish a transit route across the isthmus via the Río San Juan and Lake Nicaragua. By the early 1850s the new company was transporting two thousand passengers per month. Unsuccessful in obtaining enough money in the United States to expand his business, Vanderbilt turned to British financiers, which resulted in a confrontation within the Accessory Transit Company. The company manager in San Francisco, Cornelius Garrison, conspired with some New York financiers to obtain control of the company, and to stop the advancement of the rival British bankers in Central America.

About the same time, Liberals in Nicaragua, unable to defeat the Conservatives, were looking for outside help to obtain power. They offered a North American adventurer, William Walker, a large land grant in return for his help in ousting the Conservatives. Walker accepted the offer, and with the financial support of Cornelius Garrison, Vanderbilt's rival, landed at Realejo in June of 1855, accompanied by fifty-seven other Californians.

Walker took over the Conservatives' stronghold, Granada, in October, and put a Nicaraguan, President Rivas, in power. The puppet regime of Rivas was recognized by the United States, an act which added to Central Americans' fear of Washington expansionist complicity in the intervention.

Receiving additional help from New York and San Francisco, Walker's army grew to 2,500 men. An "election" in June 1856 made Walker the President of Nicaragua. The new President declared English the official language of the country and legalized slavery. However, Walker's rule did not last very long. The conservative governments of other Central American countries, encouraged and armed by the British government, and helped by Vanderbilt's agents, opposed Walker. Following a destructive war, Walker was defeated, and took refuge on an American vessel, sent by President Buchanan to take back the "hero" to New Orleans, where an enthusiastic welcome was awaiting him. Walker was killed by a Honduran firing squad on September 12, 1861, after he made another attempt to invade Central America.

Prior to William Walker's intervention the constant shift of power between the Conservatives and the Liberals, each with its own constitution and laws for regulating religious affairs, had left the Catholic Church in an extremely unstable position, with no clear direction. Consequently, when William Walker invaded Nicaragua, individual priests reacted differently to the new situation. For instance, the vicar-general of Granada bishopric, José Hilario Herdocia, extended his congratulations to William Walker for the conquest. In return, Walker wrote him a letter on November 27, 1855, expressing gratitude for receiving the Church's support for his rule in Nicaragua.

> It is very acceptable for me to hear that the authority of the Church will be used in favor of the existing government. Without

the aid of religious sentiments and religious teachers there can be
no good government; for the fear of God is the foundation of all
social and political organizations.[13]

Another strong supporter of Walker among the Nicaraguan clergy
was Father Agustín Vigil of Granada, who exhausted his vocabulary
of flattery to praise Walker and his rule in the country. On different
occasions, Father Vigil called Walker, "Protective Angel," and "Star
of the North."[14]

Church support for the North Americans went beyond verbal
praises, and the money and valuable jewels donated to Walker's army
were later used to provide war materials. On February 26, 1856, the
Church of Granada was approached by the new government for a
loan, and Father Vigil donated the parish funds and 963 ounces of
silver taken from the Altar of the Merced Church and the statue of
the Virgin of Mercedes.[15]

Being aware of the importance of the Church's support, Walker
named Father Agustín Vigil as the Nicaraguan plenipotentiary
Minister in the United States. The North American government,
following the recognition of the new administration in Nicaragua, on
May 4, 1856, officially received Father Vigil as the Nicaraguan
Minister.

Father Vigil's support for Walker's government was so strong
that even Walker's plans to conquer all of Central America and to
reintroduce slavery in Nicaragua did not change his loyalty.

In contrast to the priests supporting Walker, there were others
who actively participated in the anti-interventionist struggle. An
example was Father Rafael Villavicencio from León, who joined
a small group of priests to fight against slavery and for "defense
of faith" and the country. He was encouraged by the bishop of
Costa Rica.

By the end of the National War, the new Constitution of 1858
established a good relationship between the state and the Church by
protecting Catholicism, and demanding that every civil and military
functionary be sworn in for God and "Santos Evangelios." The new
friendship between the Conservative government and the Church
culminated in the signing of a Concordat with the Holy See in 1862,
regulating the Church-State relationship. The Concordat had

twenty-eight articles addressing issues such as recognition of Catholicism as the official religion of Nicaragua and the Church's right to supervise the education system and to censor books and other publications. The Concordat also obliged the government to sustain the Church economically. In return, the state obtained the right to present candidates for bishoprics.[16]

Expulsion of Jesuits

Expelled from Guatemala by the Liberal government of Justo Rufino Barrios, more than sixty Jesuits entered the port of Corinto on September 15, 1871, during the administration of Vincente Quadra. Three weeks later, the Nicaraguan government gave them conditional asylum, limiting them by an 1830 law, under which they were prohibited from establishing any centers or institutions in Nicaragua. However, before the end of the year, some of them became involved in the educational system in León, while others established a hospital in Rivas, a residence in León, a parish in Granada, and different missions almost all over the country. The intense activities of the Jesuits caused protest among liberal groups and also among liberal elements in the Conservative Party.

Simultaneously, although unrelated to the arrival of the Jesuits in Nicaragua, was the expansion of coffee production and the growing socioeconomic power of liberal circles based on coffee exports. President Joaquín Zavala, a member of the Conservative Party, was himself a coffee grower with strong inclinations toward liberal principles of economic expansion and capitalist renovation. The new ideas and profound changes in the economic and political life of the country were not only opposed by the traditional oligarchy and the Church, who were fearful of losing their privileged status, but also by the indigenous population, most of whom were afraid of losing their communal lands to the expanding coffee plantations. A manifestation of this fear was a rebellion in Matagalpa on May 30, 1881. The rebellion began as a protest against the inhumane treatment of the indigenous population by the superintendents, which included forced labor, forced sale of their communal land to private parties, forced military registration, and nonpayment for construction of roads and public buildings. Peasants, armed with old rifles and machetes, attacked and destroyed telegraph lines, the symbol of modernization in the area, then retreated to the mountains. The Jesuits living in the area tried to mediate between the leaders of the rebellion and the government officials, but the government considered this a sign of Jesuits meddling in politics and destabilizing the peace. President Zavala ordered the expulsion of all Jesuits from Nicaragua. Although their supporters protested against the government's action, and a fight broke out in León between the soldiers and the supporters of the Jesuits, the authorities finally expelled the Jesuits from Nicaragua in July 1881.[17]

Political Development and the Church

The Conservative regime allowed the political opposition to share in economic opportunities, but the groups and individuals closer to the ruling circle enjoyed much better chances at prosperity. Economic rivalries resulted in political unrest. The increasing cost of maintaining internal peace and order added to the problems of the already financially troubled government. Taking advantage of the turbulent political situation, the Liberals conspired unsuccessfully against the government several times. Finally, in 1893, a coup toppled the Conservative regime of Roberto Sacasa, and brought the Liberals, led by General José Santos Zelaya, to power.

The main objective of the new government was economic expansion. To create a strong central government to carry out the economic policies, the Liberals sought to terminate the internal conflict by allowing the Conservatives to participate in the new economic upsurge. Zelaya was so successful in integrating his opponents in the regime that for the first time in Nicaragua a class interest transcended a factional power struggle and became the major force behind Zelaya's long rule.

However, the Church-State conflict reached its peak during the government of President Zelaya. The new Liberal government was committed to destroying the traditional hegemony of the Church, and it attempted to use liberalism as an ideological tool.

Zelaya initiated the Constitution of 1893, in which the separation of the Church and state was emphasized. Nullifying the Concordat of 1862, this Constitution established freedom of education, and its secular character. It also secularized cemeteries and marriage ceremonies. On May 14, 1899, Zelaya passed another law taking over the property of many religious associations, and passing them to the hands of the local governments. According to the text,

> the real estates, furniture, livestock, and other valuables belonging to the *Cofradías*, are the property of the people of that locality. These properties shall be administered by the municipality for the use of local development.[18]

Despite the protest of the Church, the law was implemented, and it succeeded in undermining the economic basis of the Church's power.

Zelaya exiled many priests and nuns, and also opened the country to members of other religions (e.g., Moravians and Lutherans). He also closed the *Colegio de Sagrado Corazón* in Granada, accusing the nuns of preparing an antigovernment demonstration. Finally, Bishop Pereira y Castellón excommunicated the president, and Zelaya's response was to send the Bishop into exile.

Zelaya and the United States

In the beginning, the Zelaya administration maintained friendly relations with the United States. The first problem between the two governments occurred in 1901, during negotiations for constructing a canal in Nicaragua. Zelaya refused to give the United States extraterritorial rights, such as establishing American courts in the canal zone. The United States shifted its attention to the Panama route.

The decision to build the canal in Panama resulted in a steady decline in relations between the United States and Nicaragua. Zelaya cancelled some of the concessions given to U.S. citizens by the previous Nicaraguan administrations. Finally, when in May 1909, Zelaya negotiated a loan with the Ethelburg Syndicate of London for £1,250,000 to provide funds for a railroad to the Atlantic Coast, the U.S. government, disturbed by Zelaya's friendly gestures toward the United States' old rival in the region, Great Britain, backed the opposition to his regime. Zelaya's opponents were led by the Bluefields' governor, General Juan J. Estrada, a liberal officer who allied with the conservative opposition led by General Emiliano Chamorro and Adolfo Díaz, a secretary in the American-owned Rosario and Light Mines Company.

The U.S. policy toward Nicaragua was actively supported by North American private capital, which contributed $1 million to finance the rebellion. Among the contributors was the Rosario and Light Mines Company, for whom Secretary of State Knox was legal counsel.[19] In a later interview with the *New York Times*, the leader of the anti-Zelaya rebellion, General Juan Estrada, admitted that his forces had received about $1,000,000 from certain American Companies, including "the house of Joseph W. Beers . . . for $200,000, and that of Samuel Well for about $150,000."[20] Whatever the motivations were, the United States sent four hundred American marines to Nicaragua and imposed a new government, which, following a short interim period, was handed over to Adolfo Díaz, the former secretary of the Rosario and Light Mines Company, who did "everything the State Department suggested. . . ."[21]

Following the overthrow of Zelaya, the new Conservative government reestablished a good relationship with the Catholic Church, and the Church regained its ideological hegemony. Most of the religious individuals and orders previously expelled from Nicaragua, including the Jesuits, came back and established their centers and schools.

The Conservative government's first Constitution of 1911 stressed, in Article 6, that the religion of the republic was Roman Catholicism. However, the pressure of the Liberals in the Congress marked the second Constitution of 1911, in which Article 5 read as follows:

> The majority of the Nicaraguan population believe in Roman Apostolic Catholicism. The state guarantees the free exercise of this religion, and also of the other religions not opposing the Christian morality and public order. It is prohibited to favor or restrict any determined religion.[22]

This article permitted open admission of Protestants who, since 1900, had established themselves in the Pacific zone.

In this Conservative period, 1910–23, a structural change occurred in the Catholic Church of Nicaragua. Until 1913, the

Diocese of Nicaragua had been a part of Guatemala. The Bull of Pio X, *Quam luxta apistolicum ejjetum*, dated December 2, 1913, established the Archdiocese of Managua, the dioceses of León and Granada, and the Apostolic Vicarate of Bluefields. The first archbishop assigned to Managua was José Antonio Lezcano y Ortega.

North American Direct Intervention

The overthrow of Zelaya was the beginning of a period of political instability in Nicaragua, marked by short-lived governments, rivalry and hostility between the Liberals and Conservatives, and internal conflict in each group. The rebels looted the treasury and public wealth.

> Each person who had taken part in the revolt received fifty hectars (about 123 acres) of the national lands, and vast sums were awarded to prominent members of the Conservative Party who had suffered under the Zelaya regime from confiscation or forced loans, or even from 'moral' injuries. . . .[23]

To control the situation, the United States resorted to a full occupation in 1912. Except for a few months in the period 1925–26, the occupation continued until January 1933. In this period, the Conservative government heavily relied on the U.S. marines for its protection. As Munro suggested, "the Government of Nicaragua [had] practically been maintained in office by the support of the United States."[24] The North Americans took full advantage of the situation to obtain economic and political privileges in Nicaragua. For instance, the customs collection was reorganized under the direction of U.S. Colonel Clifford D. Ham. The Collector General, in his own words, regarded himself

> not so much as an employee of the Nicaraguan Government as a trustee, with obligations to four parties — the Republic of Nicaragua, the Secretary of State of the United States, and certain citizens of the United States, and certain citizens of England.[25]

Another indicator of North American control was the Bryan-Chamorro Treaty negotiated on August 5, 1914.

By this treaty, Nicaragua granted in perpetuity to the United States the right to construct an interoceanic canal, leased for 99 years the right to construct a naval base on Fonseca Bay, in exchange for which the United States agreed to pay Nicaragua $3,000,000.[26]

In 1917, General Chamorro became the president of Nicaragua, and he soon signed another agreement with the United States, known as the Lansing Plan. A High Commission, consisting of Nicaragua's finance minister, a resident American commissioner, and a third member appointed by the Secretary of State, was established. The Commission controlled all Nicaraguan revenues in excess of $95,999 each month, and used these funds to pay off foreign creditors.[27]

U.S. troops left Nicaragua in August 1926, but not for long. Almost immediately, the Liberals, led by Sacasa, revolted against the Conservative president, General Chamorro, who had obtained the presidency in a coup against the Conservative Solorzano's coalition administration. The Liberals were supported by the Mexican government. General Chamorro resigned under the pressure of the Nicaraguan Congress and the U.S. government. The new president, Adolfo Díaz, asked for the return of American troops. His request was accepted, and on January 6, 1927, American soldiers entered Managua. This new intervention was justified by the State Department as necessary to prevent the victory of Liberals supported by Mexicans and, supposedly, "Communists." However, as Dana Munro observed:

> The Nicaraguan Liberals and most thinking people in other parts of the Isthmus feel that the intervention of American marines in the revolution of 1912 and the subsequent maintenance of the administration by armed force have reduced Nicaragua to the position of a subject country and have gravely jeopardized the independence of the other republics. . . . Both the contracts with the American bankers and the canal convention are regarded as evidences of intention in the State Department to exploit the present situation for the benefit of American capitalists and for the promotion of an aggressive policy of political expansion.[28]

Apparently, the State Department policy makers were not concerned with public sentiment in Central America. They based their policy on other considerations, best summarized by the Under-Secretary of State, Robert Olds, in a confidential memorandum on January 2, 1927.

> We do control the destinies of Central America and we do so for the simple reason that the national interest absolutely dictates such a course. There is no room for any outside influence other than ours in this region. . . . At this moment a deliberate attempt to undermine our position and set aside our special relationship in Central America is being made. The action of Mexico in the Nicaraguan crisis is a direct challenge to the United States. . . . We must decide whether we shall tolerate the interference of any other power (i.e., Mexico) in Central America affairs or insist upon our own dominant position. If this Mexican maneuver succeeds it will take many years to recover the ground we shall have lost. . . . Until now Central America has always understood that governments which we recognize and support stay in power, while those which we do not recognize and support fall. Nicaragua has become a test case. It is difficult to see how we can afford to be defeated.[29]

Pursuing this policy, the United States tried to put down the Liberal rebellion by sending two thousand sailors and marines to Nicaragua. The United States also tried to bring a settlement through political channels and negotiation. The State Department's attempts finally culminated in the signing of an agreement by both Liberals and Conservatives on May 12, 1927, in Tipitapa, a small town east of Managua. The pact called for a general amnesty and the disarming of both armies by the Americans. Both groups agreed to accept the results of a general election to be held under American supervision. The marines were to remain in Nicaragua until a new U.S.-trained constabulary was ready to keep order.

The Tipitapa Pact, although carefully planned, did not work well because of its failure to recognize the growing nationalist sentiment of the urban middle class, and the revolutionary potential of the rural poor who rallied behind the nationalist and anti-interventionist struggle led by Augusto César Sandino. Sandino's decision to reject the U.S.-proposed solution resulted in six years of anti-guerrilla warfare by the U.S. marines in Nicaragua.

The Church and the North American Intervention

Facing a clear domination by the North Americans, the Nicaraguan Church as an institution, remained silent. The individual members of the hierarchy, however, took sides in the political conflict and caused another clash inside the Church. For instance, in mid-February 1928, Bishop Canuto Reyes y Valladares of Granada blessed the arms of the U.S. battalion that was marching "to finish off the bandit Sandino."[30]

In contrast to Bishop Reyes's support for the American marines, Bishop Simeón Pereira y Castellón voiced his opposition to the United States' occupation of Nicaragua from the beginning. In a letter to a high dignitary of the U.S. Catholic Church, Cardinal James Gibbons, dated October 9, 1912, Pereira y Castellón opposed the intervention and its impact on Nicaragua.

> Your great people, Dear Brother, have brought to our small country the weight of their millions and their men. Your powerful country has dominated our weak country and with its battleships, powerful cannons and treasures of the bankers of the North, who strengthen themselves every day and exhaust our treasury with large loans, unjust treaties and unequal contracts.[31]

The bishop's condemnation of the intervention was not only because of the military, political, and financial domination of Nicaragua by the United States, but also because of the fear of imposition of Protestantism on the Catholic people of Nicaragua.

> The conquest extends not only to the finance and the politics of our country, but also invades the serene areas of conscience. The wave of Protestantism seeks to advance by first opening a road with dollars throughout our countryside and towns which are, unfortunately, susceptible to the attraction of money. For development of such a wicked plan, it has used the impoverishment and the misery of our suffering people, who have maintained their dignity, although at the high cost of sacrifices.[32]

The overwhelming silence of most of the Catholic hierarchy in the face of the American invasion can be attributed to the close alliance of the hierarchy and the Conservative faction of the ruling class. During the presidency of Zelaya, the Church experienced political, economic, and social decline as a result of the anticlerical policies of a strong Liberal government. When Zelaya was ousted by an opposition supported by U.S. troops, and a Conservative government was installed in the country, again under total protection of the United States government, the Church hierarchy regained its hopes to revive its old privileges and social status. Naturally, the hierarchy supported the new government against any danger of a Liberal revolt. Knowing that the Conservatives could not stay in power in the absence of the U.S. marines, the hierarchy extended its support to the United States' occupation of Nicaragua.

The Catholic authorities' decision to support the American intervention was clear evidence of the predominance of sociopolitical considerations over religious values. The ultraconservative Catholic hierarchy, with its traditional hostility toward Protestantism, supported the subordination of Catholic Nicaraguans to a Protestant army as long as that army would keep the Conservatives, the Catholic hierarchy's sociopolitical ally, in power.

Sandino's Struggle

In 1927, when the Tipitapa Pact was signed by the Liberals, the Conservatives, and the United States government, one of the Liberal officers, Augusto César Sandino, denounced the agreement and refused to lay down arms.

Sandino's war was basically a nationalist and anti-interventionist struggle. However, both Sandino's own experience and the development of Nicaraguan agricultural capitalism, along with the emergence of new social classes, gave a component of class conflict to this nationalist struggle.

Augusto César Sandino was an illegitimate son of Don Gregorio Sandino, a Nicaraguan Liberal landowner, and Margarita Calderón, an Indian girl who had been a worker on the Sandino's coffee plantation. Augusto spent his early childhood with his mother, experiencing poverty and social injustices in his daily life. When he was nine, he spent time in jail with his mother, who was arrested because of her inability to pay back a loan.

The peasants and the urban poor, trapped in an unjust social structure, had a profound impact on the development of Sandino's later sociopolitical ideology as well as his religious beliefs. Describing his traumatic jail experience, Sandino later remembered his thoughts:

> Why is God like this? Why do they say that the authority is the arm of law? And what is law? If law is God's voice to protect the people, as the priest says, why instead of helping us, the poor, it favors the parasites?[33]

Although later accepted in his father's family, Augusto was always conscious of his different background and was always loyal to the poor and oppressed classes.

Still in his early twenties, Sandino had to flee the country following a personal fight. Leaving Nicaragua, Sandino crossed the border into Honduras, where he worked in gold mines and on sugar and banana plantations. Later, he found a job with an American company in Guatemala, and subsequently he worked for an American oil company in Tampico, Mexico. In Tampico, Sandino adopted some elements of Mexican radical nationalism, and also became familiar with the Mexican labor movement, which was influenced by socialist, syndicalist, anarchist, and communist organizers.

Sandino also acquired elements of Mexican Freemasonry ideas and Mexican spiritualism. As Donald C. Hodges, a social and political philosopher observed:

> From Mexican Freemasonry Sandino acquired a belief in an impersonal God who supervises human destinies from afar. . . . Through Mexican spiritualism he came to believe in communication with the spirits of the dead, in a cycle of birth and rebirth, in extrasensory perception, in the power of prophecy, and in the continuing struggle between good and evil spirits for control of universe.[34]

Sandino also studied theosophical ideas, and later he joined the Magnetic-Spiritual School, a theosophical school founded by Joaquín Trincado (1866–1935), an Argentinian immigrant of Basque descent. The Magnetic-Spiritual School was heavily influenced by the Zoroastrian doctrine of constant struggle between the forces of an Evil Spirit and the Holy Spirit, and the free choice in choosing one over the other. As Hodges observes, "Basic to Sandino's theosophy was the struggle between the forces of light and darkness, between good and evil. . . ."[35]

Sandino's theosophical beliefs corresponded with his sociopolitical role as the leader of the army of the poor and the oppressed against the rich, the oppressors, and their North American supporters.[36]

After three years in Mexico, Sandino returned to his homeland in 1926. Following a short period of working at the American owned San Albino gold mine of Nueva Segovia, Sandino gathered and armed a group of twenty-nine men, and joined the Liberal rebellion of General Moncada against General Chamorro's Conservative government.

In 1927, when Moncada reached an agreement with the American occupying forces and the Conservatives, Sandino was the only leader of the rebel army who refused to sign the pact, and continued fighting. His guerrilla army was the first Nicaraguan group fighting against both Conservatives and Liberals. Another distinguishing element in Sandino's struggle was the popular support that his fighters received among the Nicaraguan people.

Since the majority of the Nicaraguans had never consciously participated in the political life of the country and the long conflict between the Liberals and the Conservatives, their voices were not heard in the new political arrangement. However, when American marines began policing the country after the confirmation of the Tipitapa Pact, a general anti-interventionist sentiment grew among the people, especially in León and Chinandega. Several incidents of hostility and clashes between the people and the marines were reported. This nationalist sentiment was manifested in an emotional support for Sandino among popular classes, and in the large number of volunteers participating in the fight. The number of Sandino's guerrillas rose to six thousand in 1931–32.[37]

Historically, in Nicaragua, whenever there was a battle between the Conservatives and the Liberals, the soldiers of both sides were often poor agricultural laborers, forced into different armies by the politicians of the upper class. In contrast to this background,

Sandino's men were volunteers, most of whom believed in the cause and fought faithfully to the end. None of the historians writing about Sandino's struggle has reported any significant desertion among his men or any major betrayal by local supporters. The main element responsible for the change in the Nicaraguan attitude in this war can be attributed to changing social alliances. Unlike the previous internal conflicts between the Liberals and the Conservatives, two factions of the same oligarchy, Sandino's war was basically a struggle of the poor against the oligarchy and its main supporter, the occupying forces of the United States. This was well manifested in the social background of the guerrillas (overwhelmingly, landless peasants), and their enemies (wealthy landowners, both Liberal and Conservative).

The Liberal reforms of the late nineteenth and early twentieth century had created a class of landless peasants by breaking up indigenous communal villages and by developing coffee plantations at the expense of the small landholders. By the end of the 1920s, although large tracks of public land could be purchased very cheaply, the cost to clear and plant the land was very high. For example, coffee land obtainable at $5 per acre could cost as much as $40 or $50 per acre to cultivate.[38]

In addition to this new desperate landless agricultural class, there was a small proletariat formed by the influx of foreign capital and the "modernization" policies of the government. The new labor force, concentrated in the foreign-owned banana, lumber, and mining camps, was susceptible to the new ideas aimed at breaking down the oppressive social structure. Indeed, the first of Sandino's groups was formed in the American-owned San Albino gold mine. Although most of the guerrillas who formed the bulk of Sandino's army were landless peasants, many were also workers.

However, regardless of the composition of Sandino's army, it could not be branded as a vanguard army of the working class. The social reality of Nicaragua had imposed severe limitations on class struggle at this time. Although there were small clusters of worker concentrations in foreign-owned banana, lumber, and mining camps, they were not a significant part of the Nicaraguan economy. Lack of vast plantations and mines meant lack of large concentrations of laborers, which made the task of organizing workers very difficult. Even in the cities, the lack of a proletarian class was obvious. The urban workers were mostly artisans, construction laborers, carpenters, tailors, and shoemakers.

Therefore, Sandino's struggle, although manifesting signs of an embryonic class awareness, cannot be defined as the struggle of the working-class vanguard; nor can his demands be defined as the expression of the interests of a workers' organization.

Although aware of the class content of the struggle, Sandino himself believed that the main direction of the war should be nationalist and anti-imperialist.

In regard to land reform, although Sandino advocated heavy taxation of the rich, he did not believe their properties should be confiscated. He argued that there was no need for the class struggle in Nicaragua because (as he was quoted):

> Here the worker lives well; he struggles only against the American intervention, the rich as well as the poor should back the struggle, some with their money and others with their services. . . .[39]

The Catholic Church and Sandino

The Catholic Church hierarchy's consent to the United States' invasion meant the absence of the Church in the liberation struggle led by Augusto César Sandino. When the struggle intensified, the hierarchy openly opposed Sandino, and called on the Nicaraguan people to put down arms and surrender to the occupying army.

In early 1930, the North American director of the National Guard, Elias Beadle, met with Archbishop José Antonio Lezcano y Ortega to discuss the Catholic Church's role in supporting the National Guard and the American marines against the resistance movement. Following this meeting, Archbishop Lezcano wrote a letter to all ecclesiastical authorities of the country asking them to collaborate with the *Guardia* and the marines and to use Church influence all over the country, particularly in the war zones, for the "pacification" of Nicaragua. In this letter the archbishop informed his priests of Elias Beadle's attitude.

> If the prelates consider the reality of the positive benefits that the *guardia* would bring for the Nicaraguan citizens, and relate this reality to their followers, the National Guard will certainly be more successful in meeting the goals it was created to achieve. . . . Señor Beadle requested that all prelates welcome the National Guard officials in all cities and towns and extend to them their total moral support. . . .[40]

The archbishop then expressed his enthusiasm about the meeting with Beadle and told his clergy how well Beadle's ideas were received in his office. He asked the prelates to establish "cordial" and "reciprocal" relations with the National Guard officials in their regions.

On October 26, 1930, the archbishop of Managua, Lezcano y Ortega, and the bishops of León, Matagalpa, and Granada issued a pastoral letter addressing the people of Las Segovias, the stronghold of the Sandinista army.

> Let Christ, our Lord, in his infinite goodness extinguish the destructive fire, reconcile the hearts and extend the banner of peace over our dear children of Las Segovias. The orphans, the widows, and the disabled ask for clemency. Paternally, we exhort our children to abandon the sterile armed struggle. . . .[41]

In May 1931, the clergy in the León diocese initiated a religious campaign with a political message in Las Segovias. The objective of this campaign was to discredit the armed resistance movement. This campaign was denounced by Sandino. On May 12, 1931, he wrote, "At present the clergy is allied with the Yankee bankers. . . . Priests have come to Las Segovias preaching to the people passivity and acceptance of the humiliation brought by Yankee bankers."[42]

The Liberal Government

In November 1932, the Liberals, led by Juan Bautista Sacasa, won the national election, and in January 1933, following President Sacasa's inauguration, the last marines left Nicaragua. However, prior to withdrawl, the Americans created and trained the National Guard, which proved to be the most ruthless defender of American interests in Nicaragua and in the region for the next forty-five years.

Following his election to the presidency, Sacasa was faced with the pressure of the American Minister to Nicaragua, Matthew E. Hanna, to appoint General Anastasio Somoza as *Jefe Director* of the National Guard. On January 1, 1933, General Mathews, the last American commander of the National Guard, turned over command of the *Guardia* to Somoza, and left Nicaragua with the other U.S. marines.

A few weeks after the departure of the marines, Sandino agreed to negotiate a peaceful settlement with the government. The agreement reached by Sandino and the Nicaraguan authorities called for an immediate termination of all the hostilities, a general amnesty for all Sandinistas, and a grant of land in the Coco Valley to the Sandinistas for an agricultural colony. Sandino was allowed to maintain a small armed force of one hundred men to protect the colony.

The Nicaraguan people and the leading newspapers of both parties praised the agreement. However, Somoza, while publicly embracing Sandino as a gesture of the new friendship, was not happy with the agreement, and believed that Sandino's forces should be eliminated. In the following year, the hostility between the two men sharpened when Somoza asked Sandino to give up the rest of his arms. Sandino replied with an open statement condemning the National Guard as an unconstitutional organization, and asked President Sacasa to let his men protect the president against the National Guard. Sacasa invited Sandino to come to Managua to discuss the situation.

On the night of February 21, 1934, while President Sacasa was giving a formal dinner for Sandino and his aids in the Presidential Palace, Somoza and some other officers of the National Guard decided to assassinate Sandino. Leaving Sacasa's dinner party, Sandino and his aids were arrested and taken to a National Guard post, where they were executed and buried.

The next day, the National Guard attacked the Sandinista cooperative in Wiwili, and massacred many peasants. Without Sandino, the movement was crushed in a matter of weeks. After the elimination of Sandino and his armed forces, the next step for Somoza was to gain the presidency. He began to consolidate his power by removing officers of the National Guard who were loyal to Sacasa, and replacing them with his own men. Finally, under political and military pressure, President Sacasa resigned on June 6,

1936. Following a short term of an interim president, Somoza won the presidency in an "election."

Although the United States did not intervene in the final stages of Somoza's power drive, it was held responsible by many Nicaraguans for the creation of the dynasty.

The Catholic Church and Liberal Governments

Following the U.S.-sponsored Tipitapa Pact in 1927, and the first U.S.-supervised election, which in 1928 brought in a puppet Liberal government, the Catholic Church and its political allies, the Conservatives, accepted the results of the election and declared allegiance to the new government. The Conservatives had recognized the fact that they could not stop the rise of liberalism, the ideological arm of capitalism in Nicaragua. Therefore, they compromised their traditional political supremacy and halted their long war against the Liberals in return for a minor, but guaranteed, share in the political power and a secured place in the economic development of the country. The Catholic hierarchy went through a similar process. Reaching the conclusion that maintaining all of the old privileges was impossible in the absence of a Conservative-dominated government, the hierarchy overcame its long-time hostility toward the Liberals, and entered a new era of friendship with them, hoping to minimize the traditional anticlerical policies of the Liberals. On January 3, 1931, at the conclusion of a national conference of the Catholic Church (Primer Congreso Eucarístico), the hierarchy accepted an invitation to meet with the Liberal president, General José María Moncada, and his cabinet. In this meeting, Archbishop Lezcano offered the commemorative medallion of the conference to Moncada.

The Church's friendly gestures soon paid off in an obvious relaxation of the traditional anticlerical policies of the Nicaraguan Liberals. In 1939, a new constitution was drafted, which declared, in its Article 6, "The state does not have an official religion." However, other articles of the constitution guaranteed the rights of the Church. Article 73 exempted religious institutions from contributing to the government, and Article 74 reaffirmed the prohibition of protection or restriction of any given religion.

The next three decades of the Nicaraguan political history were marked by the almost total power of the Somoza family over the politics of the country. In the economic field, the country went through tremendous changes. A cash crop economy, which had started in Nicaragua in the late nineteenth century, was completed in the 1950s with the development of cotton production for export. In the cities, a fast industrialization under the umbrella of the Central American Common Market brought rapid changes in lifestyle and sociopolitical alliances in the 1960s. All these changes resulted in profound transformations in the social and economic structure and class formation in the country.

The Catholic Church, with its strong ties to local social groups and its traditional involvement in political affairs, could not escape the results of social changes and political pressures. To understand the profound transformation of some sectors of the Church in 1960s and 1970s, we have to study sociopolitical developments in the country.

However, the Nicaraguan Catholic Church as an integral part of the global Catholic structure was also profoundly affected by the theological and structural innovations of Vatican II (1962–65), and their reflections at the Second Conference of Latin American Bishops at Medellín, Colombia, in 1968. Liberation theology, born out of the process of applying the social teachings of the global Catholic Church to the realities of Latin America, also deeply influenced the developments in the Nicaraguan Church.

In the next two chapters, the socioeconomic and political developments of Nicaragua, and theological changes in the European and Latin American Churches will be discussed to set the stage for understanding the transformation of the Catholic Church in the sociopolitical context of Nicaraguan history.

CHAPTER 2

Economic Formation and Sociopolitical Conflict

Agriculture

Traditionally, agriculture has been an important sector of the Nicaraguan economy. By 1960, 25% of the Gross Domestic Product (GDP) was produced by different branches of the rural economy (agriculture, livestock, forestry, fishing, and hunting).

Although the agricultural sector has continued to grow since 1960, its share in the Gross Domestic Product, fell to 23.7% in 1974.[1] However, due to the labor intensive nature of the agricultural activities, this sector has always employed a higher proportion of workers than its corresponding share in the GDP. In 1974, for instance, it absorbed 299,900 laborers, or 45.6% of the total employment.[2]

The falling share of agriculture in the GDP continued in Nicaragua. The government estimates for 1979 accounted for 21.9% of the total Gross Domestic Product to be contributed by this sector, while it employed 319,400 persons, or 41.3% of the total labor force.[3]

The present agricultural system of Nicaragua is mainly export oriented. However, during the colonial time and a part of the national period, until late nineteenth century, the Nicaraguan economy was not unified around one "stable" export crop. The most important aspects of the economy were the production of meat (not for export) and, for most Nicaraguans, land-based subsistence. The

Table 1
Structure of the Production
(Percentage)[4]

	1965	1975	1979
Gross Domestic Product	100.0	100.0	100.0
Primary Activities	25.1	22.3	21.9
Agriculture	18.8	12.7	12.9
Livestock	5.7	8.3	7.9
Forestry	0.4	0.5	0.5
Hunting and Fishing	0.3	0.8	0.6
Secondary Activities	22.1	26.9	27.8
Industry	17.7	21.3	22.1
Construction	3.2	5.0	5.2
Mining	1.2	0.6	0.5
Tertiary Activities	52.7	50.8	50.3
Commerce	21.0	21.3	20.5
General Government	6.4	6.3	6.9
Transport & Communication	5.3	5.4	5.2
Banks, Insurance and others	2.5	3.1	3.3
Electric Energy & Water	1.5	1.6	1.9
Housing	6.7	4.4	4.4
Other Services	9.2	8.7	8.1

only export agricultural product was indigo, which never played an important role in the national economy.

In the second half of the nineteenth century, the spread of coffee cultivation all over Central America brought profound changes to the economic and political life of Nicaragua. The introduction of coffee, and its rapid development as an export crop, in the late nineteenth and early twentieth centuries marks the emergence of capitalism as the dominant mode of production in Nicaragua. It also marks the integration of the weak Nicaraguan economy into the world capitalist market. Since the beginning of the twentieth century, the Nicaraguan economy became dependent on the quotas, prices, and oscillation of the international market.

On the political scene, the Liberals, mainly identified with the artisans of León and the coffee producers of the country, took over political power from the Conservatives, representatives of the mer-

chants and cattle-raising interests of Granada. The Liberals, under
the leadership of President José Santos Zelaya (1893–1909), tried
to modernize the economic system and the colonial structure of
the country.

As in the rest of Latin America, one of the results of the Liberal
reforms in Nicaragua was an accelerated rate of land expropriation
in indigenous villages, and its redistribution among private landowners. In 1906, the government abolished title to all communal
lands, and villages were ordered to divide the land among their
members and outside purchasers.

These new reforms expanded the latifundia system in Nicaragua, and with it, the economic power, prestige, and social position
of the coffee producers. The agricultural bourgeoisie, oriented
toward world commerce, with coffee production as their base, initiated an era of capitalist modernization in the Nicaraguan economy.

In short, the period of development of coffee production
(1880–1950) was the transitional period in Nicaragua, from an
economy based on the closed ranching haciendas of the eighteenth
and the nineteenth centuries, to a modern capitalist plantation
economy. Primitive technology in production, paternalistic structure, employment of a servile labor force, and nonmonetary
remuneration was replaced by production for market, limited
mechanization, control of cost and quality, dynamic relations with
other sectors of the economy, development of an infrastructure, and
domination of the capitalist mode of production.

Development of a highly export-oriented system was
demonstrated in the growing proportion of the export sector to the
whole of the agricultural production. Nicaragua's Planning Office
estimated the value of export at 39% of the total value of agricultural
production in 1950, and 49% in 1962.[5] However, coffee as the
leading agricultural export declined sharply in the 1950s owing to
several factors, including inefficient technology in production.

But while coffee production declined, the United States'
demand for cotton created a new incentive for Nicaragua. In a few
years, cotton bypassed coffee as the nation's primary cash crop and
agricultural export.

In contrast to coffee, cotton production, from soil preparation
to cultivation, was highly mechanized. Large profits brought more
and more land under cultivation, and increased production and

export rapidly. According to one account, in 1949 cotton export increased from $212,000 to $5.5 million the following year.[6] The area devoted to cotton cultivation also increased rapidly from 1,100 Hectares in 1949, to 17,000 in 1951, 88,550 in 1955, 150,000 in 1960, and 282,000 in 1976. In a few years, cotton occupied 85% of the total farmlands of the Pacific Coast.[7]

Committing agricultural resources for export encouraged the concentration of land ownership in a few hands. According to a widely accepted estimate, the minimum size of a landholding necessary to feed a Nicaraguan family is ten manzanas (17.4 acres). However, according to a 1963 census, over 50% of the Nicaraguan farms were below ten manzanas. The same census shows that 51% of farms covered only 6.6% of the farm land, while the top 1.5% of the farms occupied 41.2% of all farm land.[8]

According to a detailed study published by the *Comisión Económico Para America Latina* (CEPAL) in 1973, 31.36% of the rural population had no land, while 34.9% had less than ten manzanas each. The same study showed that 66.2% of the total rural population controlled only 3.5% of the total farm land, while 1% of the rural population owned 41.2% of the land.[9]

Concentration of land was more noticeable on the Pacific Coast, which was the main site of cotton production. Many small farmers were converted to plantation workers, and many more were forced to leave the land altogether because of the new technology used in cotton production. The destination of the migrants was mainly the large cities of the Pacific Coast, in particular, León and Managua. This overloaded the urban employment market, and put more pressure on the already weak public service sector.

The population of Managua increased from 98,000 in 1950, to 234,000 in 1960, and to 434,000 in 1975. In Chinandega, the number of inhabitants increased from 12,000 in 1950, to 22,000 in 1960, and to 38,000 in 1975. And finally, León grew from a city with 30,000 residents in 1950, to one with 45,000 in 1960, and to one with 73,000 in 1975.[10]

The tremendous sociological imbalances created in the process are commonly known as "marginalization." On the outskirts of the Nicaraguan large cities, as in most of the other major Latin American urban centers, the marginal population, mostly jobless and not integrated into the mainstream of social life, lives in slum areas and shantytowns.

Industrial System

A British economic survey in the mid-twentieth century characterized Nicaraguan industry as "very under-developed." According to this survey, "practically the whole of its requirements of manufactured goods are imported."[11]

This totally undeveloped industrial sector changed rapidly in the 1960s, and the share of the industrial production in the Gross National Product increased from 12.5% in 1960 to 20.4% in 1970.[12]

Development of the industrial system in the second half of the present century was responsible for a relatively rapid economic expansion in the 1950s and the 1960s. The average annual rate of growth of production was 5.6% for the 1950s and 6.7% for the 1960s, the highest among the Central American countries.[13]

There were two important factors responsible for the economic expansion in this period: The developing of an agro-export sector based on cotton production in the 1950s, and the formation of the Central American Common Market in 1960.

The expansion of cotton production and the growth of the urban population, as a result of the mass immigration from rural areas, affected the development of craftwork and industry in the country. From 1950 to 1962, manufacturing production grew 7.8% annually. This development was basically in traditional industries.[14]

The formation of the Central American Common Market in the early 1960s created an expanded market for Nicaraguan exports. In the context of the specialization of the Common Market, Nicaragua concentrated on production of powdered milk, chemical production, and metallic goods. Between 1960 and 1973, the value of exports increased from $63 million to $188 million.[15] However, since the benefits of the economic expansion were distributed on an extremely unequal basis among the population, the upper class, the main beneficiary of the economic growth, developed a pattern of high consumption, very similar to that of more privileged countries. Consequently, the importation of goods, mainly for immediate consumption, increased rapidly, and prevented Nicaragua from developing a favorable financial situation compatible with the economic expansion of the country.

The high volume of imports resulted in a constant deficit in the balance of trade. The negative balance of trade increased from $8 million in 1960, to $20 million in 1970, and to $142 million in 1975.

At the same time, to maintain economic growth, the government had to increase investment in the public sector, and maintain and develop the physical infrastructure. The public investment increased from $56 million in 1960, to $165 million in 1970, and to $877 million in 1975. To cover the increasing public expenditure, the government mainly relied on foreign loans, which increased from $22 million in 1960, to $165 million in 1970, and to $637 million in 1975. By the end of Somozas' regime in 1979, the country's total foreign debt amounted to $1,504 million.[17]

Table 2
Nicaragua: Balance of Trade, 1960–1977
(1,000 dollars)[16]

Year	Export FOB	Import CIF	Balance
1960	62,871	71,712	– 8,841
1961	68,357	74,354	– 5,997
1962	90,170	98,226	– 8,056
1963	106,767	110,787	– 4,020
1964	125,185	137,031	– 11,846
1965	148,946	160,288	– 39,715
1967	151,682	203,910	– 52,228
1968	162,301	184,646	– 22,345
1969	158,748	176,989	– 18,241
1970	178,623	198,748	– 20,125
1971	187,242	210,441	– 23,199
1972	249,439	218,486	30,953
1973	277,885	326,982	– 49,097
1974	380,921	561,679	– 180,758
1975	375,172	516,864	– 141,692
1976	541,901	532,136	9,765
1977	636,805	761,927	– 125,122

Another result of industrialization under the guidance of the Common Market was a trend toward monopolization of the economy by large firms, many of them foreign owned. George Black later observed that

> of the 600 industrial plants employing five or more workers, 136 generated 72% of total production, and 28 alone (principally in chemicals, plastics and food stuff) accounted for 35% of industrial output in 1971. A mere 5% of the country's industrial output came from 13,000 small enterprises whose owners derived no benefit from Somocismo and who turned overwhelmingly against the system.[18]

Although historically, foreign investment in Nicaragua was low, it was still high enough on the Nicaraguan scale. Since the beginning of the twentieth century, the government had encouraged foreign investments by passing favorable laws, which allowed foreign capital, including profits and reinvested earnings, to leave the country without restriction. One such law, approved on February 26, 1955, by the Nicaraguan National Congress, spelled out this policy. According to Article 1 of this law, "Foreign capital may come into and leave the country without restriction. . . ."[19]

A report by the United States Department of Commerce in 1962 estimated that foreign investment in Nicaragua accounted for 80% of the total in mining; 90% in lumbering; 80% in commercial fishing; 50% in commerce; and 33% in manufacturing.[20] Although the book value of direct foreign investment in Nicaragua remained low (9.4% of the total investment in the 1970s), the most dynamic sectors of the industrial system — principally petrochemical and metallic industries — were established directly by transnational companies, most of them based in the United States.[21] There is no exact figure for the North American investments in Nicaragua. As Roberto Incer, President of *Banco Central*, once said, "We don't have the exact figure. We don't impose restrictions on foreign capital by keeping records of it."[22] Secrecy of operation was very advantageous to foreign investors. They were granted exemption from foreign exchange purchase restrictions, fiscal incentives, unlimited rights of transfer of capital and profits, free importation of machinery, and export of finished products.

The major part of foreign investments belonged to North Americans. By the end of Somoza's regime sixty three American transnational companies and seventy subsidiaries were operating in Nicaragua — 76% of all foreign-controlled enterprises. The most powerful were Exxon (an oil refinery), Hercules and Pennwalt (chemicals), United Brands (a plastic subsidiary), Nabisco and General Mills (food processing), Sears Roebuck and Co. (department stores), and U.S. Steel, which operated the METASA plant jointly with Somoza.[23]

Even intermediate and traditional industries which were originally founded by native capitalists were later infiltrated by foreign capital during the process of modernization in the framework of the Central American Common Market. However, a more important factor in making the Nicaraguan economy dependent on outside forces was the pattern of importation of industrial inputs. In the period 1951–58, the imported industrial input was between 17% and 28% of the total input. Following the formation of the Common Market, and division of labor and production among the member countries, the imported material for the industrial input increased to 30% in the 1960s. For the 1970s it increased to 47% in footwear and clothing, 35% in leather and leather products, and 36% in the wood and cork industry (these are the sectors which could use primary materials generated in the country). In other sectors, like petrochemical and pharmaceutical products, the import input was 100% and 96%, respectively.[24]

Another important weakness of the Nicaraguan industrial system was its incapacity to employ a significant portion of the labor force in relation to its share in the Gross Domestic Product. In the initial phase of industrial development, 1950–62, although the manufacturing production grew 7.8% annually, the number of workers in this sector increased from 38,000 in 1950 to 50,000 in 1962.[25] In other words, the developing industrial sector was absorbing only about 1,000 new workers each year, less than 2.3% of the industrial labor force. In the later phase of industrial development, the situation did not improve. For example, although the share of industrial production in the Gross Domestic Product jumped from 10.2% in 1950 to 22.9% in 1974, the percentage of the workers employed in this sector increased only from 11.4% to 12.2% of total employment.[26]

In short, the Nicaraguan industrial system, which developed in the framework of the Central American Common Market, proved to be incapable of absorbing the large number of dispossessed peasants immigrating to the cities in search of jobs. The developmentalist approach, which was the main theoretical force behind the economic programs of the Alliance for Progress, including the formation of the Central American Common Market, has been unable to explain the total failure of the Nicaraguan industrial system in solving the problem of the impoverished Nicaraguan masses and the growing size of the marginal population in the cities. The extreme poverty and hopelessness of this segment of the population was one of the important factors in the final destruction of the Somoza regime and the impetus for a total break with the political, social, and economic system of the past.

The Nicaraguan economic crisis of the 1970s prepared the ground for the revolutionary explosion, and by exposing the structural weakness of the system, caused the popular movement to aim not only for the overthrow of the political regime but, more importantly, the destruction of its economic basis. The crisis of the 1970s was not peculiar to Nicaragua. It was a global crisis, which, naturally, hit harder at the weakest links in the international economy. The declining prices for Nicaraguan exports, and the rising prices of imports, especially petroleum, put the Nicaraguan economy in a critical situation.

During this period — except for 1976, in which the exceptionally high price of coffee helped the balance of payments — the deficit was about 10% of the Gross Domestic Product.[27] The economic crisis resulted in an increase in unemployment. The official data for 1970 reported 12% unemployment in urban areas, and an estimated 22% in the rural areas.[28] According to official figures, unemployment reached 28% of the economically active population in 1979 (231,000 persons).[29] Unofficial estimates put the unemployment rate for 1979 above 50%.

At the same time, real wages were dropping. According to a study by Pedro Belli, a Nicaraguan economist, the average real wage remained at the same level between 1961 and 1970.[30] Between 1971 and 1975, the legal minimum wage increased from 1.35 cordobas per hour to 1.50 cordobas. However, in the same period, the index for the prices of consumer goods jumped from 98.77 to 143.9.[31] According to Belli, the real wages dropped 14% in this period.[32]

In 1978, the economic crisis reached its peak. Investment, which had shown a negative growth rate in 1975 and 1976, increased briefly in 1977, but dropped again in 1979.[33] The government, unable to pay external debt servicing, which had grown to 22% of the value of Nicaraguan exports in 1979, tried to increase taxes, an act which intensified the opposition of the bourgeoisie to the government. The intensification of the revolutionary war added to the regime's problems. On the one hand, the government had to increase its military expenditure, and on the other hand, political instability contributed to an unprecedented flight of capital, which amounted to $220 million in 1978.[34] The overall economic and political crisis which resulted in a drop of the Gross Domestic Product by 7% in 1978,[35] revealed the structural weakness of the regime, and made it impossible for Somoza to continue his rule, despite his increased use of repressive measures.

Sociopolitical Conflict

Anastasio Somoza García consolidated his political power in the early 1930s following his appointment to the directorship of the National Guard in 1933, the assassination of Sandino in 1934, the coup against President Sacasa in 1936, and a fraudulent presidential election in 1937.

The first few months of Somoza's formal rule were very troublesome. The effect of the world depression on the Nicaraguan economy was too pervasive to be eliminated rapidly. Somoza had to devaluate the cordoba, an action which resulted in higher prices and unrest among the workers and even among some of his own National Guardsmen. To eliminate the opposition, Somoza turned to force. The first clash came when the National Guard attacked a Conservative gathering, arresting fifty-six of those present. The next step was censorship of the press. Somoza also created an intelligence service and a network of informers to spy on the opposition. Although these harsh measures virtually destroyed overt opposition, anti-Somoza sentiment remained high.

Somoza continued to consolidate his power. In 1937, he arranged an election to form a constituent assembly to change the constitution. Since the Conservatives boycotted the election, the result was an assembly totally subordinate to Somoza. According to the new constitution, the term of the presidency increased to six years with no reelection. However, the assembly exempted the incumbent president from this restriction. The new constitution also recognized the National Guard as "the sole armed force of the republic," and gave its leadership to the president. Moreover, the Assembly became the legislative body, replacing the Congress until May 1, 1947. The new "Congress" then chose Somoza as president for the period 1939–47.

In spite of all the undemocratic and unconstitutional practices of Somoza, the United States government remained a firm supporter of Nicaragua's regime. In 1939, President Roosevelt sent a special mission to Nicaragua, and invited Somoza to make an official visit to Washington.

World War II drew Washington even closer to Somoza. Nicaragua was strategically important to the United States as a military base to safeguard the Panama Canal. During the war, an American naval base was constructed at Corinto. Somoza took advantage of the situation to build up the National Guard even more. Nicaragua's tiny navy received several small patrol boats from the United States, and the Air Force also received numerous new aircraft under the Lend-Lease Agreement. Somoza further increased his political power by declaring a state of siege and suspending all constitutional guarantees.

By the end of World War II, the general democratic movement in Central America that had toppled the Guatemalan dictator, General Jorge Ubico, and created problems for the Salvadoran dictatorship, was also felt in Nicaragua. These developments encouraged the opposition to demand a general election in that country. The Nicaraguan Conservative Party played a major role in mobilizing anti-Somoza groups between 1944 and 1948, and put forward an opposition candidate, Dr. Enoc Agüado, for the upcoming election.

Frightened by the prospect of an alliance between the labor movement organized by the Nicaraguan Socialist Party (PSN — the newly formed Moscow-line Communist Party) and the Conservative opposition, Somoza tried to separate the two groups by a temporary alliance with the PSN. The general policy of the Communist International during WWII, reflected in the anti-fascist United Front promoted by Moscow, allowed Somoza to easily gain the support of the PSN against his Conservative opposition. The International ordered all member parties to cooperate with any existing government, as long as that government's policy was anti-German. Somoza weakened the opposition by isolating it from the labor movement, and after a short period of repression, he resorted to political negotiation with his opponents. In 1948, he signed a political pact with the Conservative leader, Carlos Cuadra Pasos, and another one in 1950 with General Emiliano Chamorro, buying their cooperation in return for a constitutional amendment granting judicial appointments and one-third of the seats in the National Assembly to the Conservatives.

During all these turbulent events Somoza enjoyed the strong support of the Catholic Church. The hierarchy justified its support of the government by stating that "all the authorities come from God." This idea was confirmed by all the bishops of Nicaragua in a 1950 pastoral letter.

> For all Catholics there is a certain exalted doctrine: all authority comes from God. God is the author of whatever exists, and from the author comes the authority. . . . When Catholics obey the government, they do not degrade themselves, but their act fundamentally constitutes compliance with God.[36]

The hierarchy's preaching of submission to the political authority was well received and publicized by the Somoza regime. To emphasize its loyalty to the Somoza family, the Church hierarchy in 1942 reduced Managua's cathedral to a circus ground to celebrate the coronation of Lilliam Somoza, Tacho's daughter, as the Queen of the Army. Archbishop Lezcano y Ortega led the ceremony and used the gold crown of the Virgin of Candelaria to coronate Tacho's daughter.

In the 1950s, the Nicaraguan economy developed the characteristics of peripheral Capitalism. On the one hand, there was swift economic growth and diversification of the agricultural and industrial sectors reflected in the rapid growth of exports; but on the other hand, the benefit of economic expansion was unevenly distributed among different social sectors. While the number of unemployed workers, landless peasants, and marginal elements was increasing, a small sector of the Nicaraguan population, a group of large landowners and wealthy capitalists, benefited tremendously from the economic growth which amounted to 6.1% annually between 1950 and 1960.

The Somoza family, ruling the country with an iron fist, enjoyed the support of the agricultural and industrial capitalists, who needed a strong government to check the inevitable social unrest resulting from a rapid and massive economic dislocation of a major sector of the population, the peasantry. However, the traditional political factionalism among the ruling class, and the ever-growing economic power of the Somoza family, which threatened other sectors of the bourgeoisie, encouraged the Conservative leaders to try to seize political power several times. As the only major political opposition in the country, the Conservative Party could mobilize all anti-Somoza elements, Conservative or otherwise. However, the leadership, predominantly members of a few old upper-class families (Chamorro, Cuadra, Zavala, Solórzano, and Pasos), used their social support as leverage in wresting economic and political favors from Somoza for their own clan.

Another social ally for Somoza was the increasing number of public workers employed by the state bureaucracy to build the necessary physical infrastructure, and to formulate the implement regulations imperative for mobilization of human and material resources for the new economic growth. The number of state employees increased from nine thousand in 1950 to twenty thousand in 1960.[37] The urban middle class was the main beneficiary of the growth of the state bureaucracy, and provided the bulk of the public employees and a new social base for the dynasty. However, the middle-class support for Somoza proved to be fragile. Close contact with the misery of the new urban poor and the mushrooming marginal lifestyle in the major cities resulted in development of a profound awareness of social problems among the middle-class intellectuals. Since the dictatorial regime had closed all legal avenues for public expression of social frustrations, many Nicaraguans, especially the young university students, resorted to clandestine organizations and activities to find a solution to increasing social problems.

In 1956, a young Nicaraguan poet and a member of *Frente Juvenil Democrático* (FJD), Rigoberto López Pérez, reached the conclusion that elimination of the dictator would open the way for social reforms.[38] He shot Somoza García, hoping for a change in the political system which would pave the way for more profound changes in the society. However, the social base of the dictatorship among the upper classes was strong enough to cope with the political crisis following the assassination of the dictator. While Somoza García was struggling for survival in a hospital in the Panama Canal Zone, the National Congress appointed his older son, Luis Somoza Debayle, as the new president of the country, while his younger son, Anastasio Somoza Debayle (Tachito), maintained the family grip on the armed forces as the Chief Director of the National Guard. The strong alliance of the Somoza family and the rest of the bourgeoisie, mainly cotton and coffee producers, had guaranteed continuity in a political system beneficial to both.

Another important part of the alliance was the Catholic Church. The warm relationship between the bourgeoisie and the Catholic hierarchy in the 1950s could be attributed to the common cause they both were fighting for: preservation of the existing sociopolitical and cultural structures in Nicaragua against an emerging enemy, that is, a revolutionary movement with strong leftist inclinations. The global conflict of the 1950s, which was crystalized in the Cold War exchanges between the two dominant international sociopolitical camps, provided a favorable ground for strong anticommunist sentiments in Central America. The Church became heavily involved in the conflict and shared the anticommunist offensive launched by Somoza. The Church's role in the campaign was to support and justify government actions in suppressing all opposition under the banner of a war against communism. The hierarchy was present in every official ceremony, in every presidential inauguration following every fraudulent election, and in every religious celebration, to pray for the health and success of the dictator and his family. Finally, when the dictator was assassinated in 1956, an official benediction and statement of condolences was sent by Pope Pius XII, and by Cardinal Spellman, archbishop of New York. Archbishop González y Robleto of Managua called the dictator "the Prince of the Church," and offered two hundred days of indulgence to the Catholics who would participate in his funeral.

The anticommunist sentiment of the Church was manifested in a meeting of the Episcopal Conference of Central America and Panama, held in San José, Costa Rica, in 1956. The conclusions of the meeting were published in May 1956 in the First Pastoral Letter of the Episcopal Conference of Central America and Panama. In accordance with the atmosphere of the Cold War, this Pastoral Letter indicated a militant anticommunism. For Central American bishops, communism was "the greatest political and religious enemy." They considered Marxism a threat to the ideological structure of their societies.[39]

This Pastoral Letter also marked a profound change in the content of Catholic teachings in Central America. The Central American Church always had a strong tendency to reduce the ecclesiastical mission to spiritual confines. Therefore, the idea that "joys of eternal life compensate for the suffering on earth," was predominant among Catholics. This religious teaching was very much in accordance with the interests of the rich and oppressors. In contrast to this tradition, in the 1956 letter, the hierarchy felt obliged to discuss the Catholic social doctrines at length, an obvious attempt to show that the Church's social teachings were superior to communism. The bishops affirmed: "The Church has always condemned the usury and avarice, inequality and injustice resulting from the harnessing of wealth, insufficient salaries for minimum necessities of life and the hated latifundia and monopolies."[40] The bishops insisted on social justice, equitable distribution of land, and effective protection of workers in Central America.

This letter manifested the concerns of the Central American bishops about growing revolutionary movements promising to solve the socioeconomic problems of the region. Realizing the susceptibility of the poor masses to the leftist sociopolitical programs, the Catholic hierarchy indeed began to compete with Marxists to take up social slogans in an attempt to win over the hearts and minds of the lower classes.

However, the sincerity of the bishops' sudden concern for social justice, workers' rights, and equitable land distribution in Central America was questionable if viewed against the background and the political activities of some of the delegates participating in the Conference, among them the Guatemalan Catholic hierarchy headed by Archbishop Mariano Rossell Arellano. Archbishop Rossell was well known in Central America because of the role he played in condemning the democratic regime of Jacobo Arbenz in Guatemala, his collaboration with the C.I.A. in the 1954 coup, and his statements in support of the United States' intervention in Guatemala to protect "anti-communists and Christians."[41] When Castillo Armas came to power following the coup, and reversed the land reform program in order to give back 1.5 million acres of land to the United Fruit Company and the latifundia owners, the Archbishop called him a "legitimate saint," and sent him and his companions a telegram to assure them of the Church's blessing: "May our Lord God guide you and your heroic companions in your liberating campaign against atheistic communism. You all have my pastoral benediction."[42]

The ultraconservative and anticommunist political line of the Nicaraguan bishops was well developed through the Catholic educational system. As they were in many other Latin American countries, the Catholic private schools in Nicaragua were chiefly supported by the wealthy minority devoted to the preservation of the social structure, and the reproduction and nourishment of its value system. The common interest of the Church and the wealthy in fighting against any changes endangering their traditional privileged status was reflected in the text books and the classroom instruction. For instance, a history text, used in the Catholic high schools as late as the 1960s and 1970s, listed the following institutions and ideologies as the major enemies of Catholicism throughout history: the synagogue, the Roman Empire, the barbarians, the Protestants, the French Revolution and its offsprings, the Masonry, and atheistic communism.[43]

The class alliance between the Nicaraguan bourgeoisie and the Somoza family became even stronger in the 1960s. Formation of the Central American Common Market in the early 1960s gave Nicaragua an opportunity to establish an industrial sector to meet a regional demand.

One of the consequences of the economic expansion, shared

largely with the foreign capital, was a sharp increase in the economic and political power of those Nicaraguan businessmen and politicians who were in close contact with foreign investors. The trend was toward concentration of economic power in fewer hands.

Political Opposition

In 1967, following ten years of relative relaxation in the political atmosphere under the presidency of Luis Somoza Debayle and René Schick (a hand-picked candidate of the Somoza family), Anastasio Somoza Debayle (Tachito) tried to revive the iron-fist government of his father. The announcement of Tachito's presidential candidacy was followed by the most serious opposition to the family's rule. The big bourgeoisie, frightened by the prospect of an even larger share of the economic pie for the Somoza family under another dictatorship based on the control of the National Guard by Tachito, joined forces with smaller capitalists who were dissatisfied with the monopoly tendency in the economic structure under Somocismo. They formed *Unión Nacional Opositora* (UNO — National Union of Opposition) to support the candidacy of Dr. Fernando Agüero from the Conservative Party. The Socialist Party's support of UNO added the force of small organized labor to the opposition block.

A massive demonstration of UNO in January 22, 1967, was crushed by the National Guard. The official figures put the number killed at 201, but National Guard sources privately admitted at least 600 casualties in the massacre.[44]

The memory of this mass demonstration shadowed Tachito's attempt for presidential reelection in 1971. This time Tachito chose to control the mounting opposition by a political pact with the Conservatives, similar to those signed by his father, Anastasio Somoza García, and his brother, Luis Somoza Debayle. The leadership of the Conservative Party, in spite of the opposition of some of its members, accepted the political compromise offered by Somoza in 1971. According to the new agreement between Somoza and Fernando Agüero (the presidential candidate of the opposition in the 1967 election), the Conservatives' participation in the Congress was raised to 40% of the seats, and a Constituent Assembly was formed to rewrite the constitution to prepare the way for the election of

Tachito Somoza in 1974. Somoza agreed to hand over executive power to a triumvirate to govern from May 1972 to December 1974. Fernando Agüero was given a seat in the triumvirate, with the other two members being Somoza's appointees. The dictator himself maintained his control over the country as the director of the National Guard.

Agüero's decision to collaborate with Somoza alienated many anti-Somoza elements in the Conservative Party and caused several splits in the group. There was heavy desertion to different small political groups, such as the Social Christian Party, the Conservative National Action (Acción Nacional Conservadora) formed by Pedro Joaquín Chamorro, the Authentic Conservative Party (Partido Conservador Auténtico), and the Democratic Conservative Party (Partido Conservador Democrático). More radical elements, especially among the young members of traditional Conservative families, abandoned conservatism totally and opted for a radically different way of struggle — that of armed resistance. Having chosen armed struggle as a necessary alternative to peaceful methods for bringing down the dynasty, most of these young members of the traditional opposition joined the *Frente Sandinista de Liberación Nacional* (FSLN), which had been fighting against the Somozas since its formation in 1961–62.

Although the Conservative Party continued to have a nominal presence, the 1971 pact with Somoza was the end of the party as an effective political institution in Nicaragua.

The massive earthquake of Managua in December 1972 cut short the life of the new triumvirate, and put absolute executive power back into the hands of the dictator.

CHAPTER 3

The Response of Latin American Catholics to Socioeconomic Problems[1]

This chapter explores the historical and social roots, and the basic components, of a process of renovation in Catholic theological teachings known as liberation theology. I will focus primarily on liberation theology's social and political rather than religious aspects.

The triumph of the Cuban Revolution in 1959 shocked Latin America. Oppression and social injustice, the seeds of the revolution, could be found in most Latin American countries. The new alternative presented by the Cuban Revolution found a large and receptive audience among the Latin Americans, in particular the young middle-class intellectuals.

The response to the revolution varied among different sectors of the elite. Some resorted to military control, hoping to curtail revolutionary sentiments in countries such as Brazil, Argentina, and Bolivia. Others agreed to the relatively flexible reform program of the Alliance for Progress, aiming at redress of social ills, the underlying cause of the revolution. This reformist trend echoed the position of the Christian Democratic movements, which promised an alternative to radical changes by revolution on the one hand, and the maintenance of the status quo by military force on the other hand.

The Catholic Church, shaken by the flight of 70% of the Cuban clergy following the revolution, was also searching for an alternative of its own to prevent the spread of communism on the continent.

The poor and laboring classes, victims of poverty and social injustice, and sectors of the middle classes, sensitive to the social ills, no longer found sufficient recompense in eternal salvation. They now rallied to earthly alternatives, including socialism and communism.

Long before the Catholic Church began to address social problems in Latin America, the European Church had begun to slowly respond to social and economic changes. By the turn of the century, the Industrial Revolution had already taken place. Shattering traditional community and family ties, and judging individuals on the basis of their economic achievements, modern capitalism sharply undermined traditional and religious values. The foundation of Catholicism and its nearly exclusive emphasis on spiritual values, in contrast to worldly economic concerns, came under heavy criticism. However, for a long time the Catholic Church strongly resisted the pressure to change its focus from eternal to temporal matters. In 1891, in his encyclical *Rerum Novarum*, Pope Leo XIII emphasized this fact.

> It is only when we have left this life that we shall begin to live; this truth . . . is a Christian dogma on which rests as its basic foundation the entire structure of religion. Indeed, God did not create us for fragile and decaying ends but rather for celestial and eternal ones.[2]

Nevertheless, the historical forces were so strong and the social unrest among the poor so pronounced that, in the same encyclical, Pope Leo XIII felt obliged to address the temporal life. He complained about social conflicts, and appealed to different classes to avoid class struggle (see below).

The turbulent history of the first half of the twentieth century, including two world wars which left millions of Europeans dead and many more displaced and homeless, further forced the Catholic Church to reconsider its traditional, almost exclusive focus on eternal life, and to develop a doctrine which addressed temporal concerns as well. The culmination of decades of gradual changes in the Catholic Church was the ideological and structural innovations introduced by Pope John XXIII in the early 1960s. In his encyclical *Mater et Magistra* of 1961, John XXIII asserted that although Holy Church has the special task of sanctifying souls and of making them shares of heavenly blessing, she is also solicitous for the requirements of men in their daily lives, not merely those relating to food and sustenance, but also to their comfort and advancement in various kinds of goods and in varying circumstances of time.[3]

The Second Vatican Ecumenical Council (1962–65) tried to elaborate on John XXIII's teachings. As Daniel Levine, a scholar of Latin American politics, observed, Vatican II

marked a major attempt to rethink the nature of the Church, the world, and the proper relation between the two. Alongside the traditional model of the Church as an institution, which had stressed eternal, unchanging aspects of belief, structure, and hierarchy, the Council elaborated a vision of the Church as a "pilgrim people of God" — a living, changing community of the faithful making its way through history.[4]

When Catholics began to view the Church as a "pilgrim people of God" and emphasized the historical changes in the community, the first institution to come under attack as rigid, ahistorical, and static was the Church itself. Vatican II attempted to begin a process of change in the internal structure of the Church from a rigidly stratified pyramid, with a clear chain of command, to a community of equals, whether they be laity, priest, or bishop.

The Latin American bishops did not participate actively in writing the Vatican II documents, and most of the innovations of the Second Vatican Ecumenical Council came to them as a surprise. However, the Latin American Church, which was still dealing with the shock of the Cuban Revolution, rapidly responded to the Vatican II. For many clerics who were attempting to find ways to neutralize the seeds of violent revolution, Vatican II was a green light for social involvement.

Significantly for Latin America, Vatican II described the Church in service to the world, but the *world* of Latin America was different from that of Europe. It was a world of underdevelopment, poverty, and oppression. The different sociopolitical realities in Europe and Latin America were ignored in the documents of

Vatican II, for there was no reference to political conditions that would shape the framework in which the social reforms, recommended by the Church, were to be achieved. The Council did not anticipate political problems in Western Europe, where liberal democracy with mild socialist inclinations would not challenge the Church's participation in social and political spheres.

For the Latin America of the late 1960s, however, the immediate period following Vatican II was a time for change toward stronger military regimes in many countries. Military coups in Brazil and Bolivia overthrew the populist democracies of these countries in 1964. In Argentina, a military coup occurred in 1966. And in most of Central America, military regimes were already in power. The first phase of the Alliance for Progress, a short period of political opening and economic liberalization, was already over, and the majority of the Latin American repressive dictatorships were enjoying massive economic and military assistance from the United States. The U.S. advisors and trainers in Latin America were launching a strong anticommunist campaign, which helped the totalitarian regimes to suppress all forms of opposition to the existing sociopolitical structures.[5] The anticommunist sentiments, prevailing in the United States in the 1950s, now had found the target close to home. The fear that Cuba would become a base for the Soviet Union and for spreading communism in the hemisphere deeply influenced the U.S. Latin American policies. The military assistance and training for the Latin American governments intensified and took aim at the elimination of any potential support for another Cuban-style revolution in the continent. The U.S. military training programs focused on internal security and policing the "law and order" in Latin America. Between 1961 and 1969, the United States spent $8.2 million on police assistance to Central America.[6]

The training was not confined to military and police tactics, it also had an elaborated ideological dimension. Injecting a well-developed ideological intolerance into already ultraconservative Latin American military structures did not help the advancement of democracy in the continent. As Don Etchison, a Latin American specialist, observed:

> Such an effort . . . to politically indoctrinate Central and South American soldiers about the "evils" of Communism has

probably helped increase their fear of political groups that advocate reforms. The emphasis on anti-communist propaganda in the Canal Zone training courses during the 1960s served only to reinforce and to promote conservatism while instilling a vehement mistrust of reformism and liberalism. The propaganda aspect of the Southern Command's training of Central American soldiers also seems to have augmented the tendency of the Central American military officers to justify the use of military repression under the pretext of retarding communism.[7]

One of the Central American countries on the top of the U.S. list for military assistance and training was Somoza's Nicaragua. Between 1950 and 1976, the United States trained 5,167 members of the Somoza's army.[8] As Etchison observed:

> In fact U.S. military training [was] so instilled in the minds of General Anastasio Somoza, Jr., a West Point graduate and the President of the country, and other high-ranking Nicaraguan military officials that the cadets of the Nicaraguan Military Academy [spent] the fourth year of their education at the School of the Americas under the supervision of the Southern Command in the Canal Zone.[9]

The repression imposed on the country by Somoza and his army, and the brutality of the National Guard in suppressing any legitimate demand for change in Nicaragua, later became a source of embarrassment for the supporters of U.S. military training programs in Latin America. In the early 1960s, when the United States government began its vigorous campaign against the alternative presented to Latin America by the Cuban Revolution, the military training of Latin American army officers was held out as a feasible road to introduction of "reformist military regimes," who would be strong enough to prevent a communist revolution, and at the same time, were exposed to the democratic ideas of the U.S. society and institutions as a future model for the management of their own countries. However, when in 1977, a list of the National Guard officers involved in torture and murder of Nicaraguan peasants was presented to a congressional hearing, twenty-four out of twenty-six officers charged had extensive training background in the U.S.-run military schools.[10]

Intensive violence against any collective attempt, including those organized by religious groups, for the betterment of the quality of life in the countries ruled by the military regimes, radicalized individuals and organizations involved.

The Second Conference of Latin American Bishops at Medellín, Colombia, in 1968 was the culmination of the process of radicalization in the Latin American Church. The theme of the conference was "The Church in the Present-Day Transformation of Latin America in the Light of the Council." To analyze the situation in Latin America, the working document of Medellín[11] used statistics extensively to show the poverty of the majority of Latin Americans.

The Medellín conference coincided with an era in which the shortcomings of developmentalism were becoming evident. The foreign capital and technology which flooded Latin America, supposedly to promote industrialization and to strengthen the national bourgeoisie, had created a dependent, deformed industrial system incapable of national accumulation of capital, and had reduced a major part of the Latin American bourgeoisie to mere local agents of multinational corporations. Problems of land concentration, unemployment, marginalization, and mass poverty were intensified in the 1950s and the 1960s.

Medellín addressed the question of poverty at length. Traditional Catholicism views poverty as an individual failure; hence, charity and job training are stressed. In contrast to this, Medellín examined poverty in a social context, and related it to socioeconomic structure. Therefore, the solution was not only individual charity but a profound change in the social structure.

Liberation Theology

The theological response of the Latin American Catholics to poverty and repression is known as "liberation theology." Segundo Galilea, a prominent Latin American liberation theologian, explains it as follows:

> The theology of liberation starts out with three presuppositions that, for a Christian, sum up the contemporary Latin

American scene: the condition of underdevelopment and unjust dependence in which the masses are languishing; a Christian interpretation of that fact as a "situation of sin" and the consequent pressure on the consciences of Christians — and on the Church's pastoral planning — to commit themselves to remedying that situation.[12]

Based on these three presuppositions, liberation theology develops its key themes. It points to biblical passages revealing God's will to liberate humankind. Putting the biblical themes in the context of Latin American history, liberation theology derives pastoral guidelines for action in the present-day situation.

The Church and Politics

The opponents of liberation theology criticize it as a justification for political action by the clergy, and a profound diversion of the traditional spiritual role of the Church. Liberation theologians respond to these charges by pointing out that history and biblical text proves that Christianty has always been involved in political action. Gustavo Gutiérrez argues that

the liberation of Israel is a political action. It is the breaking away from a situation of despoliation and misery and the beginning of the construction of a just and fraternal society.[13]

However, biblical texts differ from each other in historical context as well as in the sociopolitical messages they bear. In contrast to Exodus and some other books of the Old Testament, where the spiritual leaders feel free to harshly criticize and confront the governments, the New Testament deals with political authority in a much more conservative manner, and even recognizes a divine status for it.

Historical Jesus did not regard it his mission to liberate the Jews from the political domination of the Roman Empire. There is no passage in the New Testament that calls on the people to revolt against the occupying army or to overthrow the sociopolitical order. Jesus confronted not the Empire but the power of the Temple and the priestly class, which played the role of the local ruling circle in occupied Palestine. Since the Temple's rule was based on its spiritual rather than political or militaristic power, Jesus' opposition was also spiritual and apolitical in form and content.[14]

The political conservatism of the early Christians increased after the death of Jesus. To spread their spiritual message and to break the religious power of the Temple, early Christians avoided any confrontation with the political domination of the Roman Empire. The conservatism of the movement was underlined in Paul's "Letter to the Romans," where he asserted:

> Every person must submit to the supreme authorities. There is no authority but by act of God, and the existing authorities are instituted by him; consequently anyone who rebels against authority is resisting a divine institution. . . .[15]

Following the conversion of Emperor Constantine, by early fourth century A.D., the justification of political authority by the Church resulted in a deep involvement of the Church hierarchy in politics. The history of the Church's political activities in medieval Europe does not need to be reviewed here.

Latin America has also witnessed the Catholic Church's political involvement for many centuries. The critics who try to undermine the sociopolitical activities of the new radical Catholic movement by emphasizing the apolitical nature of the Church ignore that the Church has always taken sides with the rich and powerful in the political arena. The innovative aspect of the Medellín conference was not a demand that Catholics take sides for the first time; rather, it was a call for them to change sides, and stand with the poor and powerless.

Although Medellín strongly demands the participation of the Church in the process of liberation of the oppressed and poor, it does not give the clergy a leading role in the process. The emphasis is on liberation through mass participation. The poor and the oppressed are to liberate themselves by a conscious involvement in the social and political struggle to change the structure of oppression. The Church's role lies in awakening the poor, and convincing them of the necessity of sharing in the process of liberation. The document on "Justice" makes this clear.

> The lack of political consciousness in our countries make the educational activity of the Church absolutely essential, for the purpose of bringing Christians to consider their participation in the political life of the nation as a matter of conscience and as the practice of charity in its most noble and meaningful sense for the life of the community.[16]

When Medellín's teachings affirmed that "it is indispensable to form a social conscience and a realistic perception of the problems of the community and of social structures,"[17] Latin American priests and nuns established thousands of Christian Base Communities (Comunidades Eclesiales de Base — CEB) and began an intense process of consciousness-raising, particularly in poor urban barrios and remote villages all over the continent.

The method of popular education was already developed by Paulo Freire, a highly respected Brazilian educator. According to Freire, the most important step in liberation is liberating the poor from an internalized oppressor, the value system instilled in individuals by the structure of oppression.[18] Using the same methods in demythologizing religious matters and practices, and freeing them of their ties with the established order, the poor can relate abstract religious values to their own lives and surroundings. For example, they can identify easily with the struggle of the enslaved Israelites against an oppressive order. Planted in the context of people's experiences, religious values assume tremendous power in the psychological and cultural liberation of Christian Latin Americans.

Catholicism and Class Struggle

A fundamental challenge for Catholicism in modern societies has been the often violent opposition of social classes to each other. Traditionally, the Catholic Church has always emphasized unity in the Christian community, and has tried to preach the gospel among the faithful regardless of their social status and socioeconomic functions.

However, by the end of the nineteenth century, the Church had begun to rethink this traditional view. In 1891, Pope Leo XIII, in his encyclical *Rerum Novarum*, recognized the historical forces which had changed what the Church viewed as the cooperative nature of medieval communities to the unequal distribution of wealth in industrial societies, which created a rich minority and poor majority. In response to this, he preached two fundamental Christian principles. The first principle was that social inequalities were natural and necessary. It was in accordance with natural law that there be rich and poor, capitalist and worker, ruler and ruled, landlord and peasant. According to the Church's teachings, social inequality profits all, society as well as the individual, for social life requires a very diverse organism and quite diversified functions. Leo preached that "man must patiently accept his condition; it is not possible in secular society that everybody be on the same level." To advocate equality through revolution and to make the poor and workers believe that the situation could be changed is a deception.[19]

The second principle preached by Leo XIII, in a society divided among classes, was class collaboration.

> Just as in the human body, the members in spite of diversity, adapt marvelously to each other, forming a perfectly proportioned whole, which might be called symmetric, so in society the two classes are destined by nature to harmoniously and mutually to maintain themselves in a perfect equilibrium.[20]

Leo's conservative view was based on biblical texts, in particular Paul's "Letter to the Romans," where we read:

> For just as in a single human body there are many limbs and organs, all with different functions, so all of us, united with Christ, form one body, serving individually as limbs and organs to one another. The gifts we possess differ as they are allotted to us by God's grace, and must be exercised accordingly. . . .[21]

In the twentieth century, the social teachings of the Church evolved markedly toward a more radical analysis of society, and the Catholic hierarchy put a strong emphasis on the right of the workers to a better life and better working conditions, and, above all, the right to organize in unions; however, the basic concept of class collaboration remained intact. In 1961, in *Mater et Magistra*, Pope John XXIII declared that workers and employers should regulate their mutual relations in a spirit of human solidarity and in accordance with the bond of Christian brotherhood. For the unregulated competition which so-called *liberals* espouse, or the class struggle in the *Marxist sense*, are utterly opposed to Christian teachings and also to the very nature of man.[22]

The Latin American Church and Class Struggle

Although the Latin American bishops in Medellín did not address the question of class struggle from a classical Marxist viewpoint, by accepting the just struggle of the oppressed against the oppressor the conference profoundly changed the fundamental principle of Christian unity and class collaboration.

According to Marxism, class struggle is the result of a mode of production which divides the members of a society into different classes in accordance with their role in the process of production. In accordance with its stage of economic development, in each society there is one major class which is the main producer (slave, serf, wage laborer), and another one which enjoys a major part of the production without working directly to produce it (slaveowner, feudal lord, capitalist). The class struggle arises from the contradiction between the fundamental interests of the two opposing classes of each society. However, because of the diversity of economic activities in each society, other classes and social sectors exist which cannot fit directly into either of the two opposing camps. These middle sectors and de-classed elements are involved in the process of production and distribution on different levels. They exploit the others' labor force, or are themselves exploited in a complex chain of socioeconomic relations.

In a society caught in an intensified class struggle, the middle sectors and de-classed elements join different poles of the social conflict because of their socioeconomic interests. However, the leadership of each camp belongs to one of the two main opposing classes (i.e., proletariat and bourgeoisie, in a capitalist society).

Following a detailed study of the laws of soocioeconomic development of class societies in general, and of advanced capitalist countries in particular, Marx concluded that in a society divided among classes, the class struggle is inevitable; moreover, it is the main drive of the historical development of mankind toward a higher stage of production.

Without reference to the class struggle as an inevitable phenomenon of class societies. Medellín began with a concrete analysis of the existing situation in Latin America. According to the working document of the conference, oppression was widespread throughout the continent. The proposed working document explicitly defined the "Latin American reality" as one of institutionalized violence, a state of "tyranny" maintained from within by national oligarchies and from without by "imperialism." In the absence of peaceful change, the working document confirmed that violent revolution is inevitable if the "sinful" situation is to be changed.

However, the working document, prepared by the Latin American Episcopal Council (Consejo Episcopal Latinoamericano — CELAM), was not the official view of the Vatican. Pope Paul VI had a different perspective on class struggle and violence. During his trip to Colombia for the inauguration of the Medellín conference in 1968, although acknowledging the poverty and repression in Latin America and identifying with the popular cause, Pope Paul VI used religious gatherings to condemn class struggle and revolutionary alternatives as solutions. For instance, in a meeting with the representatives of the Colombian peasants in Bogota, he warned the audience:

> Let us exhort you not to place your confidence in violence nor in revolution; such an attitude is contrary to the Christian spirit and can also retard the social betterment to which you legitimately aspire.[23]

On another occasion, addressing the youth and the workers in Bogota, the Pope underscored his earlier assertion.

> Many, especially among the young, insist upon the necessity of urgently changing the social structure. . . . Some conclude that the essential problem in Latin America cannot be resolved except through violence . . . we must reaffirm that violence is not evangelical nor Christian. . . .[24]

Rejecting class struggle and violent revolution, the Pope urged a response very much in accordance with the traditional principle of class collaboration. He pleaded with the "legitimate governments," "responsible authorities," and "upper classes" to "initiate the necessary reforms." Addressing the Latin American peasants, the Pope promised:

> We will exhort all of the ruling and upper classes to continue to initiate with broad and courageous vision the necessary reforms that guarantee a more just and efficient social order, with progressive advantages for the classes that are today less favored and with a more equitable allocation of taxes to the moid [sic] classes.[25]

All of these speeches were clearly opposed to the principles of the working document of Medellín. The Pope was promising a change for the better through the good will of the ruling classes. But the working document of Medellín, referring to the long history of the insensitivity of the Latin American rich toward the suffering of the poor, asserted that the change will only come if the lower classes demand it forcefully.

Although in Colombia the Pope repeatedly argued against the concepts of class struggle and violence used in the working document of Medellín, some of the final conclusions of the Medellín conference borrowed the language of the working document and totally disregarded the Pope's remarks. However, the final documents of the conference were written by different groups of bishops, so that they reflected diverse, if not contradictory, ideas. In the document on Justice, the reference to class struggle and violence is vague, and the appeal is merely for elite-initiated changes. The bishops, who prepared the document on Justice, appealed to economic and political leaders.

> On behalf of Latin America, we make an urgent appeal to the businessmen, to their organizations and to the political authorities, so that they might radically modify the evaluation, the attitudes and the means regarding the goal, organization and functioning of business.[26]

The language of the document on Peace[27] was much different. Referring to the existing tensions in Latin America, the document proclaimed that the unjust situation was created by oppression and by the "insensitivity of the privileged sectors to the misery of the marginated sectors."[28] It blamed the dominant sectors for resorting "to the use of force to repress drastically any attempt at opposition."

The subject of class struggle and violence has become a major concern of the liberation theologians. In *A Theology of Liberation*, published in 1971, Gustavo Gutiérrez, a prominent Latin American liberation theologian, used more precise sociological definitions in describing social classes. Writing about "the division of humanity into oppressors and oppressed," he equated the oppressors with the "owners of the means of production," and the "oppressed" with "those dispossessed of the fruit of their work."[29] Confirming the existence of "antagonism" among these social classes, Gutiérrez reached the same conclusion that Marx had reached more than one hundred years before him by studying the laws of development in capitalist societies. However, in contrast to Marx, whose work was sociological and scientific and not restricted by moral or religious concerns, Gutiérrez felt obliged to fit his sociological findings into a religious framework. He tried to reconcile the concepts of class struggle and consequent violence with the Christian maxim of universal charity and love. Challenging the abstract notion of universal love, Gutiérrez placed this doctrine in its sociohistorical context, and applied it to the real world with all its divisions, conflicts, and confrontations. He argued that in accepting the existence of class struggle, Christians have to take sides with one class or another. However, taking sides with the oppressed does not mean the lack of love for the oppressor: "Universal love is that which in solidarity with the oppressed seeks also to liberate the oppressors from their own power, from their ambition, and from their selfishness."[30] Therefore, for Gutiérrez and other liberation theologians, solidarity with the oppressed in fighting against the oppressor is a simultaneous process of liberation for both the poor and the rich. This is the only form of authentic Christian love, which by rejecting the structure of oppression, eliminates the "sinful situation" of "institutionalized violence," and by creating a classless society, constructs a genuine basis for Christian unity.

To participate in class struggle not only is not opposed to universal love; this commitment is today the necessary and inescapable means of making this love concrete. For this participation is what leads to a classless society without owners and dispossessed, without oppressors and oppressed.[31]

Although all liberation theologians accept the necessity of participation in the class struggle, the accompanying violence is still a theological challenge treated differently in accordance with the social conditions in which each individual lives, and the stage of the actual struggle in that society. Father Camilo Torres in Colombia and Father Gaspar García Laviana in Nicaragua both died as guerrilla fighters in the battle against the political regimes in power. On the other hand, Dom Helder Câmara, former bishop of Recife, while recognizing the legitimacy of violent reaction of the people to the "institutionalized violence" of the Latin American structures, is still preaching nonviolent resistance in Brazil.

The working document of the Medellín conference distinguished between two different kinds of violence. The first one was equated with oppression by unequal and unjust social and political structures. The document called this "institutionalized violence," and since it would prevent people from fulfilling a moral and decent life, it was sinful. Therefore, to believe in religious liberation meant to attempt to change the sinful social and political structure, and to liberate humanity from sin.

In contrast to the "institutionalized violence," the defensive violence was recognized by the conference as legitimate "in the case of evident and prolonged tyranny." For the first time in any official Church document, the bishops proclaimed that tyranny is not merely dictatorship but, more important, is an oppressive structure which "seriously works against the fundamental rights of man, and which damages the common good of the country."[32] Therefore, a revolutionary insurrection aimed at the destruction of the existing structure could be legitimate; and the negative consequences of violence were to be blamed not on the revolutionaries but on the ones who had created the ground for violence (i.e., the ruling classes). Referring to the "institutionalized violence" initiated by the upper classes, the bishops explained:

This situation demands all embracing courageous, urgent and profoundly renovating transformations. We should not be surprised therefore, that the "temptation to violence" is surfacing in Latin America. One should not abuse the patience of a people that for years has borne a situation that would not be acceptable to any one with any degree of awareness of human rights.[33]

Even prior to the publication of the Medellín documents, the subject of revolutionary violence was widely discussed among Latin American theologians. In 1968, Monsignor Fragoso, bishop of Crateus, Brazil, wrote:

At times violence is the only possible way of liberating man from an established, permanent and grievous violence. We have to recognize that the mature conscience of the citizens has the right to opt for violence.[34]

The long discussion of violence in theological writings is rooted in biblical texts. In contrast to the Old Testament, with its harsh language against oppressive sociopolitical orders, the New Testament can be read as a guide for a totally pacifist movement. Jesus taught his followers to love their enemies and to refrain from any violent action, even in the face of the worst repression.

The overwhelmingly nonviolent and pacifist language of the New Testament has led many theologians to take the nonviolence of Jesus as a universal ethical norm. Recently, however, the universality of nonviolence in the gospels has been challenged by historians of biblical society. They argue that rather than being an absolute maxim, nonviolence was a tactic of Jesus. According to this reading of history, Jesus' goal was to break the power of the Jerusalem's Temple, not to overthrow the political domination of Rome over Palestine. Jesus chose nonviolence as his tactic to avoid any military confrontation with the Romans while he attacked the local ruling and priestly classes centered in the Temple, who were exploiting the people through a religious network and their strong spiritual influence.[35]

Regardless of different readings of biblical history and theological interpretations of nonviolence, the history of Christianity is a lively account of the rejection of nonviolence as a universal ethical norm. As early as A.D. 314, at the Council of Arles, the Church recognized the right of the state to go to war. Later, the Church theologians developed the Doctrine of Just War. This doctrinal innovation, however, was not extended to the revolutionary struggle of the people against their oppressive governments, because, according to the Church's teachings, the government was eminently a servant of God, and any revolt against it was an act of opposition to God's will.

Later on, the Crusades and Holy War added another chapter to the violent history of Christianity, and made it very difficult to take seriously any attempt to revive the nonviolence of the gospels as a universal maxim, and to brand any violent action as anti-Christian. The new emphasis of the Catholic hierarchy and the Vatican on nonviolence, especially since the late 1960s and the development of revolutionary movements in Latin America, may be seen more as a political attempt to weaken the revolutionary struggle against the repressive regimes and unfair social structures than as an honest attempt to purify religious doctrine.

The Catholic Church and Socialism

Another important issue challenging the twentieth-century Catholic Church is the triumph of a new socioeconomic system — socialism. The Church's response to a socialist alternative has been diverse and highly controversial. Although early Christianity criticized the social gap between the rich and the poor, it stopped short of putting forward any alternative to the existing socioeconomic system. To show the Catholic concern for the poor, the theologians usually use the Church Fathers' statements on the subject. For instance, Juan Luis Segundo, a prominent liberation theologian, quotes St. Ambrose addressing the rich.

> You are not making a gift of your possessions to the poor. You are handing over to them what is theirs. For what has been given in common for the use of all, you have arrogated to yourself. The world is given to all, and not only to the rich.[36]

Segundo also quotes St. Clement of Rome: "All things in the world should be for the common use of men; but one man calls this thing his, another calls another thing his, and thus began the division among mortals." However, sharing wealth in biblical context was a voluntary act of charity and not an obligation for the faithful. Although there are examples of "communism of consumption, sharing the goods that they had acquired by private means" among some early Christians, it was not a general practice and not called for by the majority of the leaders.[37] As Robert M. Grant observed, "Private property remains private, though the Christian authors urge its owners to use it to express their love of their neighbor."[38]

Regardless of the social idealism of some early Christians, Catholicism developed historically in a strong alliance with the rich, and the Church itself became a rich and powerful institution.

The most serious attempt to challenge the economic foundation of social systems based on class divisions appeared in the nineteenth century in Marxist literature. Rejecting the division of society in classes as a natural state of being, Marx searched for the roots of this division in the historical development of productive forces. Studying the laws of socioeconomic development in nineteenth-century capitalist countries, Marx projected a future trend toward a socialist alternative. However, Marx believed that the socialist stage of development would not materialize without the active participation of the workers. In their daily struggle to secure their socioeconomic rights against aggressive capitalism, which tried to expand by accumulating more and more capital at the workers' expense, Marx predicted that the proletariat would organize and become aware of the fundamental contradictions of the capitalist system, and finally, as a conscious agent of history, would opt for destruction of the capitalist structure and construction of a socialist system in which the ownership of the means of production, as well as the process of production, would be socialized.

One important factor in Marx's projection was the cultural element, which could either facilitate or obstruct the process of achieving consciousness by the workers in order to fulfill their historical role. This is the root of Marx's strong criticism of religion. According to Marx, the exploiting group in capitalist society always finds a strong ally in religion. Since religious salvation promises an eternal life, it diverts attention from temporal suffering. As an individual process, it makes the believers take comfort in the Christian egoism of salvation, and concerns them with the well-being of their own souls rather than with the struggle to change the social conditions causing their own misery and that of others.[39]

Although Marx developed the theory of scientific socialism and its critique of capitalism and religion, the ideas which were the foundations of his theory did not begin with him. Long before the publication of Marx's books and articles, socialist and communist ideas existed in European workers' movements, and had already been in sharp conflict with the established political orders and their ideological arms, including the Church. As early as 1846, Pius IX condemned communism as an atheistic ideology, and declared: "Communism contravenes the natural law about as much as anything can." In 1878, in his encyclical, *Quod Apostolici Muneris*, Pope Leo XIII called communism "a moral plague."[40]

However, less than half a century after Marx's initial attacks on social injustices under capitalism, the Church also felt obliged to voice its opposition to these same social ills. In 1891, in the encyclical *Rerum Novarum*, Pope Leo XIII strongly criticized the misery of the masses under capitalism. In contrast to Marx, whose criticism of capitalism was followed by a workable plan for construction of an alternative socialist socioeconomic system, the Pope's reflection was limited to moral suggestions to remedy some of the social ills within the framework of the capitalist system.

As industrialization progressed, and the gap between the workers and the rich capitalists widened, the Church continued to speak out against the inequality. In 1931, Pope Pius XI, in his encyclical *Quadragesimo Anno*, declared that

> the immense number of proletarians on the one hand, and the enormous wealth of the very rich on the other, are an unanswerable argument that the material goods so abundantly produced in this age of industrialism are far from rightly distributed and equitably shared among the various classes of men.[41]

The strongest criticism from the Church was voiced by Pope Pius XII in 1942.

> The Church cannot shut her eyes to the fact that the worker
> in his effort to improve his condition, comes up against a whole
> system which, far from being in accord with his nature, is in con-
> tradiction to the order of God, and his purpose for the fruits of
> the earth.[42]

Nevertheless, even Pius XII, critical of capitalism, did not propose an alternative system. Instead, he emphasized the traditional teachings of the Church on the necessity of solidarity among the different classes. In 1945, he stressed, "This solidarity should extend to all branches of production and become the basis of a better economic order."[43]

It took the Church another twenty years to recognize the ineffectiveness of its moral mandates in correcting the social injustices of capitalism. In the 1960s, many Catholics, mostly in Third World countries, began to combine their opposition to the existing social order with a search for an alternative more compatible with Christian doctrines. Studying the structure of capitalism, some theologians found it in sharp contradiction to Christian principles. For instance, in an article published in 1970, González Ruiz argued that

> capitalism must be considered by Christian morality as something
> that is intrinsically perverse in its structure. . . . Christian morality
> is a morality of loving one's neighbor, whereas capitalism arises
> structurally from the search for a profit. . . . This is a society that
> is wholly in a state of sin, structurally invaded as it is by egoism
> as the supreme driving force of its dynamics of expansion.[44]

Although some liberation theologians criticize capitalism harshly, they are cautious in their critique of private property. The reason for caution lies in the fundamental principles of Christianity, which accept private ownership as a basic human right. Even Pope John XXIII, who revolutionized some aspects of the Church's structure and teachings, confirmed the right to private property in his encyclical *Mater et Magistra*: "Private property, including that of productive goods, is a natural right possessed by all, which the state may by no means suppress."[45] Addressing the doubt expressed by some clergy about the private ownership of the means of production,

John XXIII maintained, "Such a doubt has no foundation. For the right of private property, including that pertaining to goods devoted to productive enterprises, is permanently valid."[46]

Dealing with the Church's teaching on private property, liberation theologians accept private property as a natural right if it is necessary "for realization of one's human condition."[47] However, Dussel argues

> Private property is a *secondary* natural right. . . . I have a *natural* right to those means and resources which are necessary if I am to achieve my end or goal. The end of man is happiness, and he has a right to those means which will enable him to attain that end: i.e., to food, clothing, shelter, education and so forth. But what about those means that are not necessary? What about the second car, the second house, and so forth? I do not have a natural right to those things, because I do not need them to attain my end. . . . My power over secondary, non-necessary means is merely a positive right; it is not a natural right.[48]

Liberation theologians believe that their argument does not require an innovation in the Christian doctrine; rather, it simply applies the principles of early Christianity (regarded by them as egalitarian and socialist in nature) to the present situation. Dussel maintains, "In theory there is no reason why we cannot contemplate the implementation of socialism."[49] Segundo confirms socialism as "a political regime in which the ownership of the means of production is removed from individuals and handed over to higher institutions whose concern is the common good."[50]

Although the basic principles of a socialist system are similar for both Marxists and Catholic socialists, these two groups have accepted the necessity of socialism from two different points of view. For the Marxists, socialism is an inevitable phase following capitalism in the process of development of the forces of production. It is a direct product of the fundamental contradictions of the capitalist system. For the Catholics, however, socialism is a preferable alternative to the injustices created by the private ownership of the means of production.

Conclusion

As have all religions, Christianity has been used and abused to support or to oppose different sociopolitical structures and ideologies. Historically, the most dogmatic religious principles have been molded in the hands of political and spiritual leaders to facilitate the acceptance of existing orders or the need for change. Different theologians have offered understandings of the Bible that accord with the sociopolitical forces of their times. There is no single way of reading the Bible, and no single correct theology interpreting its message. Any biblical reading and theological understanding bears the weight of sociohistorical conditioning of the reader and the theologian.

The Bible itself embraces different and often contradictory messages; the most conservative and the most radical statements could be extracted from it. For instance, from Exodus we can conclude that it is necessary to defy unjust sociopolitical orders; on the other hand, Romans clearly tells us that, because all authorities are ordained by God, any defiance, even against the most repressive and unjust government, is a defiance against God's will. Reducing the ongoing debate between the traditional Church and the liberation theologians to the question of who is right according to the Bible is posing the wrong question from the wrong angle. To understand the debate we have to place it in its sociohistorical context. The progressive group, opting for the poor and the laboring classes, has found biblical justification for its participation in the ongoing struggle against the oppressive and exploitative capitalist regimes in Latin America. The traditional Church and the Vatican, for centuries allied with the ruling classes, feel uneasy about revolutionary movements attacking the existing sociopolitical orders in the Third World countries. The Catholic hierarchy, with its long history of leading or supporting violence in medieval Europe and colonial Latin America and Africa, now seeks to defend the international capitalist order and its fundamental pillar, private property, against the upheaval of the dispossessed by citing passages of the Bible that teach nonviolence.

The division in the Catholic Church over liberation theology has its roots in the ongoing class struggle in the Third World countries. The question is centered not on the doctrinal purity of the factions but on their sociopolitical alliances.

CHAPTER 4

Implementation of Liberation Theology in Nicaragua, 1968–72

A Conservative Hierarchy

By the late 1960s, the Nicaraguan Catholic Church, as an institution, was still alienated from the new radical Catholic movement in Latin America. The hierarchy was close to the ruling circle, and many clergymen were on the payroll of the government, serving as ambassadors and public employees.[1] Archbishop González y Robleto was himself extremely friendly with the Somoza family. He was always present at official ceremonies, and celebrated numerous masses for the Somozas on different occasions. The auxiliary bishop of Managua, Monsignor Borge y Castrillo, devoted a good part of his last years to business activities, and Monsignor Chávez Núñez, the youngest bishop at the time, was known to have close relations with the government.

Radical Clergy

In contrast to the right-wing hierarchy and the conservative policies of the official Church, a new movement was growing in different parishes among younger clergy, who were influenced by the new Catholic social doctrine developed in Europe. For them, the innovations of Vatican II transcended the liturgical sphere, and persuaded them to participate in the life of their communities.

The first group of clergy involved in renovation of the Church included Uriel Molina and Ernesto Cardenal among others. These priests did not deal with sociopolitical issues at first. The main emphasis was on the creation of a communal spirit, suppression of machismo in the Church, family integration, and liturgical renovation.[2]

The embryonic progressive movement in the Nicaraguan Catholic Church was still highly disorganized in the second half of the 1960s, and was chiefly manifested in individual acts by priests and nuns who had begun community work in different areas with no systematic connection to each other. A few Christian Base Communities were formed in both rural and urban sectors. This was the beginning of a much larger grassroots Christian movement which gained importance in the 1970s, and organized around three hundred communities by the end of the decade.

The first important Christian community in Nicaragua was Solentiname, which was established in 1966 by the Nicaraguan poet and writer Father Ernesto Cardenal. Father Cardenal believed in restoring the values of early Christianity, including living in communal form and sharing material goods and spiritual activities among the people. Recording the experience of the community he later wrote:

> In Solentiname, a remote archipelago on Lake Nicaragua with a population of campesinos, instead of a sermon each Sunday on the Gospel reading, we have a dialogue. The commentaries of the campesinos are usually of greater profundity than those of many theologians, but of a simplicity like that of the Gospel itself.[3]

With a deep appreciation for the campesinos' culture and their ability to understand and to interpret the Gospels, Cardenal created a classic case of consciousness-raising in Solentiname, an experience which was later documented in detail, and became a valuable case study for other Christian Base Communities in Nicaragua and throughout Latin America.

The basic dynamic of the discussion of Solentiname, and any other Christian Base Community, is the constant dialectical relation between the pastoral agent (priest, nun, or lay leader), who brings a knowledge of the Scriptures, and the community members, who bring their life experiences. The discussion results in a process of learning from one another for both the pastoral agent and the people. When developed, the discussion goes beyond the labor division between the pastoral agent, with the knowledge of the Scriptures, and the members, with life experience. The people develop an ability to think and express themselves, and to find new elements in the Scriptures which relate to their life. In a Christian Base Community, as Phillip Berryman, a former pastoral worker in Central America, observed:

> Both members and leaders acquire a "key" to the Scriptures, a basic approach that helps them to understand fundamental concepts and to make connection between the Scriptures and their lives. Underlying it all seems to be a basic change in attitude from one of accepting the world as it is to one aiming at transforming it — becoming active agents or subjects in history.[4]

This process of change is well documented in Cardenal's book, *The Gospel in Solentiname*, which recorded the community discussions in the period of 1971-76. On almost every page, the parallels are drawn between the passages and the characters of the Gospel and the sociopolitical realities of Nicaragua: the Herods are compared with the Somozas, Jesus before the Sanhedrin is like the Sandinista leaders being tried for defending the people, and the death of Jesus is comparable to the murder of Sandino.

In a few years, Solentiname became an internationally known example of Christian Base Communities. Cardenal's background as a poet and artist, and his devotion to the promotion of a full human life in the community, resulted in a rapid development of folk arts and popular poetry in Solentiname. A Venezuelan visitor to the community once commented that

> Solentiname is something so Godlike and so much of this world that it is a place where poetry, painting and the harvest do not divide people into poets and farmers, but constitute the wholeness of life.[5]

In Solentiname the people not only developed their community and changed the direction of their daily lives toward achieving a higher level of human dignity and progress, but they also developed a deep understanding of the national reality, and became actively involved in a rigorous attempt to change it. The later development of Solentiname and the revolutionary activities of its members in the 1970s will be discussed in later chapters.

Another priest who established a Christian Base Community of another type in the mid-1960s was Father José de la Jara, a Spaniard. Instead of selecting an isolated setting, such as Solentiname, Father de la Jara, accompanied by a team devoted to consciousness-raising methods of education, began working with the poor families in San Pablo parish of Managua in 1966.

In the beginning, biblical courses were organized and a cooperative was formed. After two years of basic community work, in 1968, the pastoral team began dealing with themes such as human dignity, the Christian position on political reality, and the encouragement of participation in popular political actions. Accompanying Father de la Jara in his patient work were the nuns from the Asunción and Maryknoll orders. In September 1968, two new Spanish priests joined the group: Mariano Velazquez and Félix Jiménez. In late 1968, the San Pablo community organized a meeting of a group of clergy working in other poor barrios of Managua and also in Waspan (Atlantic Coast), to share the experience of the community. Another achievement of the community was the development of the first Nicaraguan Popular Mass. The Catholic hierarchy swiftly condemned the Mass because it included the sentence "I believe in Jesus Christ who was born of our people." The hierarchy replied: that is "impossible. He was born of Virgin Mary."[6]

Although Father de la Jara returned to Spain in July 1969, the community work in San Pablo continued, and in the 1970s San Pablo was an active member of Managua's Christian Base Communities and was integrated into the anti-Somoza movement.

However, as mentioned earlier, the activities of progressive priests and nuns were individual acts and isolated cases with little connection to each other. The first group expression of the new ideas came in May 1968, when a group of seven progressive priests, influenced by the social teachings of Vatican II, issued a statement calling for, "a ministry of service and human development on the part of the Church, and demanding that the government halt repression and torture and free political prisoners."[7]

First National Pastoral Meeting

The impact of Vatican Council II, and the Second Conference of Latin American Bishops at Medellín in 1968, on the Nicaraguan Church was manifested in the First Pastoral Congress in Managua in January–February of 1969. Two hundred fifty-eight people participated in this meeting, among them bishops, secular and regular clergy, nuns, and lay persons. They studied the human and religious realities of Nicaragua, the responsibilities of the local Church in Nicaragua and elsewhere in Latin America, the reality of social transformation and the pastoral work necessary to lead the change, the teaching of the faith, and the plan for future pastoral work.

At this meeting the differences between the conservative hierarchy and the radical priests came into the open, and for the first time the bishops were sharply criticized by the progressive sectors. For instance, Father Noel García, a Jesuit priest from the Instituto Social Juan XXIII de la Universidad Centroamericana, characterized the hierarchy as "advancing only in age . . . conservative . . . apathetic . . . negative . . . disunited . . . non-accessible to the people . . . and incapable of effective and constructive leadership for the dioceses, or on the national level."[8]

Another important presentation of the conference was delivered by Dr. Ernesto Castillo, a professor at the Catholic University of Central America at Managua. He started with a historical analysis of the Nicaraguan situation, and the role played by the Catholic Church during the colonial period, in alliance with the Spanish colonists. He also criticized the Church for its collaboration with the post-independence regimes which were mainly oligarchic and oppressive.

In his analysis of the Nicaraguan reality in the late 1960s, Castillo pointed out the social injustices manifested in the prevailing poverty of the people, the lack of adequate health care, concentration of land ownership in a few hands, the miserable conditions of the majority of the Nicaraguan peasants, and massive illiteracy. Dr. Castillo's presentation reflected the widespread disillusionment among Latin American intellectuals, by the late 1960s, regarding the results of the developmentalist approach to the problems of the continent. Analyzing the Nicaraguan reality, Castillo reached the same conclusion that the bishops had reached at Medellín, where they studied the general situation in Latin America. His approach to the nature of the upcoming revolution was also similar to other Latin American religious intellectuals at this point of history.

> The question is not whether there will be a revolution or not; but rather, a peaceful revolution or a violent one. As Christians, we cannot but desire for a peaceful alternative. Christ came to bring us peace, and man by nature wants peace for himself and others. However, the revolution could be peaceful only if the ones maintaining the system let the necessary changes happen peacefully, and only if they recognize the rights of the poor masses. But if the ones in power oppose change, the people will have to use force and more drastic measures to take over and to implement the much needed changes.[9]

Dr. Castillo's conclusions proved to be too difficult for the conservative Nicaraguan Church hierarchy to digest. The hierarchy was not even prepared to criticize the existing unjust social system, let alone propose a revolutionary alternative. To disassociate themselves from Dr. Castillo's remarks, the members of the hierarcy were prompt in commenting on his presentation. Pablo Antonio Vega, prelate of Juigalpa, stressed that Dr. Castillo's "points of view, his judgments, and his proposed options are his own. They are all his responsibility as a layman, and not as a priest." Vega also declared that Castillo's presentation at the meeting, "is not a doctrinal exposure or a pastoral assumption. It is simply a presentation of the human situation in its global and concrete forms."

> It is not a priestly function to predetermine the political options of a layman. Supporting or separating from a political group are the inalienable rights of citizens. We, as priests and pastors, are obliged to help the layman with their basic spirituality, and not lead them politically. . . .[10]

Regardless of the conservative approach of the hierarchy, the Congress opened several important issues for discussion and future action, including the necessity of deepening the study of the social teachings of the Church and the documents of Medellín. It also discussed the importance of a dialogue between the Church and various contemporary ideological currents. The Congress also called on the clergy to emphasize their responsibilities, not only as the members of the Church but as the members of the community, and to denounce in word and action, social, economic, and political injustices. One of the suggestions of the Congress was the creation of a new organization to plan for an integrated pastoral project of evangelization, liturgy, and human promotion. The Congress suggested also the development of the Instituto Social Juan XXIII de la UCA into an official organs of socioreligious research at the service of the Nicaraguan Church. Another suggestion was the promotion of the organ of the Church's public outreach, such as the newspaper *el Observador*, and Catholic Radio.

Public Expression of New Ideas

In January 1969, about the time the First Pastoral Congress met, a new periodical, *Testimonio*, was published by a number of progressive religious individuals at the University of Central America at Managua. It was edited by Dr. Castillo, who had given a controversial presentation in the meeting, and Manuel Morales Peralta, one of the main leaders of the Social Christian Party. Eighteen issues of *Testimonio* were published in 1969–70. The first issue, printed by late January 1969, characterized the publishers as authentic Christians, standing with the poor and the oppressed.[11]

Testimonio opened a forum where progressive Church groups could express their ideas, criticize the existing sociopolitical order, and challenge the old traditional values of the Catholic hierarchy and its friendly attitude toward the government. Father Uriel Molina, one of the first priests trying to implement the Medellín teachings in Nicaragua, wrote several articles in *Testimonio* on liberation theology. One of the articles, discussing the position of Catholics on capitalism and socialism, concluded that the latter is a scientifically correct and morally valid solution for the underdeveloped societies.

In early June 1969, the progressive Church sectors held a seminar in the auditorium of the Central Bank in Managua to study the Agrarian Reform Law of the country, and *Testimonio* published detailed reports about the seminar. According to the paper, the discussion sessions of the seminar turned into a sharp criticism of government policies in the rural areas, concluding that the existing Agrarian Reform Law would not eliminate the structural obstacles to the development of the Nicaraguan peasants. Recognizing the unjust situation, the participants of the seminar expressed their concern for "the majority of the people" who had marginal access to "the necessary materials for their subsistence" and, therefore, were deprived of "any possibility of promotion." The seminar called the conditions "a situation of institutionalized violence," and called on Christians to join the ongoing efforts to change the situation.

Another subject discussed extensively in several issues of *Testimonio* was North American policies in Latin America, particularly in Nicaragua. The paper always expressed a strong criticism of United States policies, and blamed them for the major economic and political problems of Latin American countries. For instance, the following statement appeared in a discussion of the subject of "underdevelopment":

> The United States of America has been the one who, through imperialism, has established in Latin America the structures for an imposed peace based on the great imbalances which exist between the poverty of the many peoples [Latin Americans] and the riches of only one [the United States]. That is why they invented the humiliating cliche of "developing" in order to refer to those peoples [Latin Americans]. Thus we have stopped being people and human in order to be underdeveloped. But at present, an underdeveloped country is the one which is oppressed by a dictatorial government (usually military) supported, directly or indirectly, by the North American imperialism based upon political alliances which are nothing more than economic blackmail.[12]

The intensified criticism by the progressive sector of the Catholic Church aimed at the government and its North American supporters increasingly politicized religious activists, and raised their awareness of the sociopolitical realities of the country. On the other hand, the Church hierarchy, alienated from the new social movement among Catholics, continued its traditional attitude, and limited its horizon to religious detail. For instance, in April 1969 the Episcopal Conference issued a statement calling on all the priests and nuns to comply with the traditional dress codes. The bishops complained about some priests who appeared in public without their traditional cassocks. To cite an example, the bishops named San Pablo parish, which was one of the first parishes to form Christian Base Communities and to implement Medellín teachings. This indirect attack on the progressive Church sector angered many priests and Catholic intellectuals. One of them, Father Pallais, the rector of the university, wrote an article published in *Testimonio* (no. 5).

> It is lamentable that, after long mediation and consideration, the Episcopal Conference has found out that the only problem in Nicaragua is the priests who go around with no black or white cassock. . . . It is also depressing that, in their criticism [the bishops] refer to San Pablo parish, an example of dialogue and progress in the country and the rest of Central America, where God's word is taught to the faithful.[13]

Another incident provoking bitter debate and sharp disagreement among the two sectors of the Church was a physical assault on Father Francisco Mejía by the National Guard. In January 1970, a unit of the Guard attacked a Sandinista safe house in barrio El Eden of Managua. Father Mejía was accused of attempting to rescue the guerrillas, and was arrested and beaten up by the soldiers. The assault infuriated some priests and lay people, who bitterly complained about government repression and the brutality of the Guard. They called on the bishops to excommunicate all soldiers involved. However, Monsignor Chávez Núñez, the auxiliary bishop of Managua, vindicated the National Guard, and blamed the mistake on the fact that Father Mejía was not wearing priestly garb. This position aggravated the problem, and angry statements by the progressive sector continued. Even some of the bishops joined the group criticizing the government and the National Guard. Monsignor Calderón y Padilla, bishop of Matagalpa, and Monsignor Obando y Bravo, auxiliary bishop of Matagalpa, declared: "If the established power tries to solve national problems with violence, it will increase unrest, and will produce more violence."[14]

A group of clergy from León took advantage of the situation to condemn the military repression, and in an extended document analyzed the "profound crisis of broken values in the society,

which results in major disturbances." The document confirmed the
following:

> There are many expressions of dissatisfaction erupting every day
> in our society, strikes repressed by violence, theatrical forms of
> protest, student demonstrations . . . arbitrary detentions, substan-
> tially proven facts about repeated torture of political prisoners . . .
> and for the first time in Nicaragua, the physical and moral insult-
> ing of a priest, Father Francisco Mejía.[15]

However, the conservative sector of the Church went out of its
way to show its support for the Somoza regime. For instance, during
the same crisis Father Noel Buitrago of León welcomed Anastasio
Somoza Debayle in one of his reelection campaign trips to the town
of Malpaisillo, and asserted, "There has been three years of your
government, and we have felt the progressive hand of your administration." He praised Somoza for "his efforts to maintain peace."[16]

Another important event of 1970 that intensified the Church's
involvement in politics was the student demonstrations in the
University of Central America (la UCA). The conflict began over a
study done by the Student Center about the problems of the university. The students asked for a meeting with the university authorities
to discuss their findings. The university administration refused a
dialogue with the students. The conflict intensified when the
students took over the administration office, with the help of several
priests and lay workers of the *Testimonio*.

The next action was the occupation of Managua Cathedral by
the students, who added political demands to their requests. Several
progressive priests joined the students in the cathedral and condemned the unjust socioeconomic and political system. They protested against the violation of human rights and demanded an end
to the torture of political prisoners, and freedom for arrested
students and members of the FSLN. Following this action, which
forced Somoza to give in to some of the students' demands, the
strategy of occupying churches as a form of political protest was used
by the opposition repeatedly.

One of the clergy actively supporting the students and participating in the occupation of the cathedral was a Jesuit, Fernando

Cardenal. At the time, Father Cardenal was the vice-rector of the university. He later described the event as follows:

> Three priests accompanied about one hundred students to la UCA in the occupation of the cathedral. We also participated in a hunger strike in the cathedral demanding safety of life of the students who had been arrested in previous days. Another demand was the permission to talk to them [arrested students], and that, as the Nicaraguan laws specified, they be released in ten days or appear before courts with correct charges.
>
> The normal practice in Nicaragua was that the political prisoners would go through weeks of torture in the Office of National Security. The occupation of the cathedral caused a national upheaval. The army surrounded the building. We rang the bells every fifteen minutes, day and night, and announced that will keep doing it until they accept justice and respect the law. Large groups from principal parishes of Managua came to sit in the plaza [in front of the cathedral] to show their support. Thousands and thousands of people came in buses and their cars to salute us. . . . In three days and a half we forced the dictator to give in. . . .[17]

In a few days the Episcopal Conference published a pastoral letter condemning the action. In response, thousands of progressive Christians signed another letter criticizing the bishops and voicing their support for the students, their action, and their demands.

While the controversy among different sectors of the Church became increasingly public, quiet but gradual community work was continued by progressive priests and nuns throughout the country. The Capuchin Fathers' training programs for community leaders in the Atlantic zone grew in importance, with a more clear political direction, in the early 1970s. In Managua, the community work of barrio Riguero, started by Father Uriel Molina in the late 1960s, was gaining a leading role in the process of integration of the Christian Base Communities into the ongoing political struggle. The rural Christian Base Communities formed by the Capuchin Fathers and other religious groups and individuals will be discussed in later chapters. What follows is a brief review of the early stages of development of the community work in Riguero, which later attracted attention as a focal point for the mobilization of a broad Christian revolutionary movement.

Taking theological courses in Rome in the early 1960s, Father Molina, a Franciscan priest, came into close contact with and was heavily influenced by the discussions of Vatican II. When he returned to Nicaragua in the late 1960s, he was faced with a powerful Catholic hierarchy that was "lethargic, lifeless and married to the Somoza regime."[18]

Father Molina was sent to work in the parish of Riguero, a poor neighborhood of Managua. In his new parish, Molina began organizing the people, particularly the youth. In the early 1970s, a group of university students met with Father Molina, and asked him to organize a community of university students working with the poor residents of barrio Riguero. In the first meeting of the new community, each of the students expressed his own hopes and expectations of the community work. The long discussion clarified the goals of the group: (1) achieving a fuller personal realization of the members, (2) reaching a definite position regarding political problems, and (3) living the faith in a historical process in search of a political project.[19]

The initial members of the group included, among others, Joaquín Cuadra, Roberto Gutiérrez, Salvador Mayorga, Alvaro Baltodano, and Luis Carrión. After the triumph of the revolution they all served in leadership positions in the Sandinista government, both in the military and the civilian sectors. In the beginning of their community work in Riguero, all of the members considered themselves Christians, and none of them belonged to the FSLN.

The daily schedule of the group included morning gospel-reading sessions, and evening group discussions analyzing the sociopolitical reality of Nicaragua. For their analysis, they used Marxist methodology.

In the early 1970s, the cattle-raising ranchers increased the price of milk. The youth of Riguero, some of them members of the Christian Base Community, took the case to the parish council and the religious organizations in the area. When no results were achieved, they decided to boycott milk, and to paralyze the transportation of milk on trucks by spreading nails on the roads. The reaction to this first protest action was varied. The parents of the university students were appalled. They could not tolerate the fact that their sons had exchanged their comfortable houses and expensive clothes for impoverished slums and peasant shirts, and that they had rejected the values of their bourgeois class to adopt a new consciousness in solidarity with the marginal sectors. However, the parents of some of the youths living in the poor barrio were more positive. Although they were concerned about their children's involvement in a group with a radical option for the poor, some of them tried to understand the process, and a few even joined their children in the new experience.

Soon after, the base community decided to organize the whole barrio. They began open discussions once a month for the people from different sectors, and with various backgrounds. They also succeeded in starting a Bible school in which the university students taught the Bible in relation to present-day social problems. Their base of support broadened rapidly.

Some of the members of the FSLN often came to the community to talk to the youth. Interested in uniting the Christian experience with that of the Sandinista struggle, Father Molina encouraged conversation between the two ideologies in spite of the pressure from his superiors and the Church hierarchy.

However, Father Molina had some reservations. He later wrote:

> I did not feel capable of accepting armed struggle as an objective reality inherent in the same process which we were experiencing in the light of faith. I did not feel prepared to propagate a form of struggle which I myself couldn't initiate as an example. . . .
> In our [religious] formation, we had not developed the capacity to incorporate danger and struggle. The *Frente Sandinista* proposed to the youth something that I couldn't give them, the risk and the struggle until death for a cause.[20]

Father Molina was also concerned about theological inefficiencies in his orientation. He believed that theological principles developed in Europe were not sufficient to analyze the Nicaraguan situation. Thus, in 1972 he welcomed the chance to participate in the first conference of Christians for Socialism in Chile. He later wrote about this experience.

> In Chile, I could observe closely the liberation theologians and listen to their statements. I could taste the protest songs in the *Peña*, and closely watch the enthusiasm of the popular masses for Salvador Allende in the march toward constructing a new society.[21]

Since Molina had gone to the conference in spite of the prohibition by the hierarchy, he was faced with his superiors' reproach upon his return to Nicaragua. He also found that in his absence the relationship between his base community and the *Frente* had become firmly established.

Father Molina's patient community work, and the close contact of Riguero with the FSLN, culminated in the formation of the Christian Revolutionary Movement in the mid-1970s, which played an important role in the integration of Nicaraguan Christians in the revolutionary process. We will examine the experience in Riguero community and its later development in detail in later chapters.

New Leadership in the Catholic Church

Another important event in the beginning of the 1970s was the appointment of the auxiliary bishop of Matagalpa, Monsignor Obando y Bravo, as the archbishop of Nicaragua in April 1970. Prior to his nomination as archbishop, Obando had participated in a conference of Central American bishops at Antigua, Guatemala, and had signed the document of the conference condemning torture and the violation of human rights.

Obando's appointment created high expectations among the progressive sector of the Church, who hoped that the new archbishop would implement Medellín teachings in the country.

Archbishop Obando's first major pastoral statement was issued at the end of 1970. Denouncing social injustices, Obando promised Christians a peaceful transformation toward the liberation of the people; and, adhering to the Christian doctrine of nonviolence, he offered a reformist solution to social problems. The archbishop cited *Populorum Progressio* (an encyclical written by Pope Paul VI in 1967) as an implicit legitimization of revolutionary insurrection in the case of an evident violation of fundamental rights and the common good. At the same time, using excerpts from Pope Paul VI's speech in his trip to Colombia for the inauguration of Medellín Conference, 1968, he negated the armed revolution as an option to remedy social ills. Obando's vacillation between legitimizing the use of violence by the people to bring down the structure based on *institutionalized violence* and condemning any kind of violent revolution continued throughout his pastoral letters and public statements.

Obando's antidictatorial attitude was the beginning of a shift toward political liberalism in the Church hierarchy. In contrast to the traditional opposition of the bishops to any kind of political statement by the Church, the new episcopal documents increasingly began to deal with sociopolitical issues in the country. For instance in a Pastoral Letter, issued by the Nicaraguan Episcopal Conference on March 19, 1972, the bishops encouraged the participation of lay people in sociopolitical affairs, and also recognized the rights of priests to participate in political activities. Referring to a statement from the Roman Synod of 1971, *Priestly Ministry*, they asserted:

> In certain circumstances, bishops and priests may find themselves well-advised to refrain from intervening in party politics, but never when it is a question of struggle for a just order. When a number of political, social or economic options are offered, priests have the right to choose like anyone else.[22]

The bishops themselves did not hesitate to exercise their rights to voice their disagreement with the situation in the country. They wrote:

> Any observer of national scene will immediately see that, despite a semblance of political and social stability, Nicaragua is racked with tensions — which are all the more real and dangerous because they have no outlets for expression.[23]

Referring to popular unrest in the country, the bishops maintained that

> all these outbursts are only the anguished cry of a people that is at long last waking up to its plight and seeking to rend asunder the shackles that constrain it. People want a completely new social order.

This direct call for change created a lot of excitement in opposition to the Somoza-Agüero Political Pact of 1971.[24] The opponents of the regime interpreted the Pastoral Letter as a clear sign of the new position of the hierarchy which "after 40 years finally spoke out in favor of the people."[25]

A prominent leader of the opposition, Pedro Joaquín Chamorro, praised the Pastoral Letter as an important document which could serve as a "common ground for all opposition groups to act upon."[26]

However, a close examination of the Pastoral Letter reveals a conservative bias. Although the bishops quoted the Medellín documents to the effect that "changes are needed" and "sweeping reforms are indispensable," they themselves confessed that "the terminology is vague." And in their attempt to clarify the language and to put forward some concrete suggestions about the areas which needed immediate change, they emphasized the political structures: "If we look at what our country is today and how it is faring, we must admit that its political structures are inadequate to the demands of the day."[27] And they called on the layman "to work for his country's political progress."[28]

Focusing on changes in the political scene, the Pastoral Letter ignored the socioeconomic structure of the country as the basis for political oppression. In this way, although the bishops referred to Medellín documents several times, they left out the fundamental theme of the documents, which blamed the socioeconomic structures in Latin America for the existing situation of "institutionalized violence."

Another important difference between the radical line of the Latin American bishops at the Medellín conference and the Nicaraguan bishops in the Pastoral Letter of March 19, 1972, was the way they dealt with the options of lay people in the course of bringing about structural changes demanded by the Church. The Letter was clear in its pacifist approach. The bishops wrote, "everyone wants these changes to come about in peaceful way."

The ambiguity of the political position of this Pastoral Letter resulted in different interpretations among diverse sectors. While the opposition groups took it as a clear sign of the Church's position against Somoza and the newly signed political pact between him and Agüero, the supporters of the Political Pact read the Letter as a pro-

Pact statement. For instance, in an article published in the April 1972 issue of *El Pensamiento* . . ., Julio Icaza Tijerino, a deputy in the newly formed Constituent Assembly and a member of the Agüero faction of the Conservative Party, attempted to show the common content of the Somoza-Agüero Political Pact and the March 19 Pastoral Letter. He argued that the bishops' demand for "the change in the structures" was dealt with by the text of the Political Pact addressing the inevitable necessity of

> bringing about the indispensable socio-economic and political changes, by peaceful evolution, for the integral development of the nation [and] to overcome all kinds of obstacles to democratic, social, economic and cultural progress of the Nicaraguan people.[29]

Referring to the lack of concern about the necessary changes in the socioeconomic structure of the country and the limited demands for only political reforms in the Pastoral Letter, Icaza Tijerino called the bishops' position "timid" in comparison to the Political Pact. He suggested that the bishops could advance their position by at least demanding an agrarian reform, as the Political Pact had done.

Icaza Tijerino also pointed out the similarity between the March 19 Pastoral Letter and the text of the Political Pact in addressing the necessity of peaceful methods to achieve change, and rejecting revolutionary violence. Therefore, Icaza Tijerino concluded that the opposition was wrong in referring to the Pastoral Letter as a Church statement against the Political Pact; in fact, it was very much in conformity with the content of the Pact.[30]

Although both conservative, the texts of the Pastoral Letter and the Political Pact differed from one another in an important political point. The Pact was based on the division of political power between the two traditional parties of the country, Somoza's Nationalist Liberal Party and Agüero's Conservative Party. According to the Pact, 40% of all the legislative seats and judicial appointments would go to the minority, the Conservative Party, and the rest to the majority Liberal Party, and there was no possibility for other political groups to participate in the political structure. Therefore, the Pact was opposed by the Social Christian Party (PSCN), Independent Liberal Party (PLI), and newly formed anti-Somoza groups emerging as a result of the split in the Conservative Party over the issue of collaboration with Somoza. In contrast to the Pact, the Pastoral Letter did not recognize the exclusive rights of the two traditional parties in the government, and clearly took sides with the political opposition in calling for a broader base for the government: "Citizens have the right to freely organize political parties . . . and ultimately the law should guarantee that every legitimate party has a real chance of access to the government. . . . "

In sum, the Pastoral Letter of 1972 was a political statement against monopolization of power by Somoza's Nationalist Liberal Party and Agüero's faction of the Conservative Party, and a demand for recognition of the rights of other political groups in the power structure. However, by limiting their statement to the political framework, and avoiding any criticism of the socioeconomic structure of the country, the bishops drew a clear line between themselves and the more radical opposition.

However, even the conservative text of the Pastoral Letter was opposed by a sector of the hierarchy. For instance, the bishop of Granada, Monsignor Marco Antonio García y Suárez, did not sign the Letter. Although the rest of the bishops added a brief note to attribute the lack of García's signature to his poor health, some Nicaraguan Church historians have referred to García's close relation with the regime as the true reason for his abstention.[31]

Although the Church hierarchy was trying to hide the political differences among the bishops and to emphasize Church unity, statements by individual members of the hierarchy indicated sharp political disagreement among them. As Tommie Sue Montgomery has pointed out, none of the Nicaraguan bishops could be categorized as radical.[32] The main difference among them was their view of Somoza's regime. A small group in the hierarchy, most represented by Monsignor García, was overtly pro-Somoza; while on the other end of the spectrum stood Archbishop Obando y Bravo, an outspoken anti-Somoza figure. However, as will be discussed in later chapters, Obando always kept his distance from the radical opposition led by the FSLN. The rest of the bishops, although not outspoken, differed significantly from one another in their attitude and pastoral work. For example, Monsignor Salvador Schlaefer of Bluefields (Department of Zelaya) permitted and even encouraged his clergy to implement the new social doctrine of the Church as taught by the Second Vatican Council and the Medellín conference.

On the other hand, Monsignor Pablo Antonio Vega, prelate of Juigalpa, expressed his pro-Somoza sentiments in a strong campaign against progressive priests, including Father Ernesto Cardenal. In an article published by *La Prensa* on July 18, 1971, Pablo Vega accused Cardenal of "campaigning against the Church authorities" and being "devoted to the Castro regime," an instrument of propaganda for a "socio-collectivist" regime, which was "materialist," "totalitarian," "atheist," and in "open contradiction with Christian principles."[33]

In contrast to Vega's sharp attack on the progressive sector of the Church, some of Obando's statements were favorable to this sector and closely resembled the documents of the Medellín conference. For instance, in July 1972, Obando gave a formal speech at the National Autonomous University in Managua on the subject of violence. In his opening statement, Obando sharply criticized the unjust socioeconomic structures of Latin America.

> All through Latin America, the masses, who have always been poor and exploited without realizing it too clearly, are beginning to wake up. This is true not only in the industrializing countries, but also in those that are almost exclusively agricultural. Even the peasants are becoming aware of their undeserved misery. They are keenly conscious, too, of the scandalous disparities in access to goods — and to power. While an oligarchy lives off the fat of the land, the rest of the people, impoverished and fragmented, drag along with almost no chance of personal initiative and responsibility, indeed often languishing under working and living conditions quite unworthy of the human person.[34]

Obando identified the existing unjust socioeconomic structures with "the basic, institutionalized violence" which often masqueraded as "law and order" and is the source of the "violence of the oppressed," which is "a reaction to the institutionalized violence" and is directed towards the destruction of social injustices.

After clearly distinguishing between the institutionalized violence and the violence of the oppressed, Obando attempted to answer the basic question occupying the minds of many Nicaraguans: Is a structural revolution possible, without armed violence? Obando responded that in some cases the force of the truth, moral pressure, and organized solidarity could be enough. "In other cases," however, he added, "only through a revolutionary action, which may be bloody, can the violence of the system be halted."[35]

Elaborating on the subject, Obando reaffirmed that nonviolent struggle such as demonstrations, agitation, strikes, and acts of civil disobedience are valid instruments of social revolution. However, nonviolent revolution is only effective if the established regime maintains a minimum respect for human rights, and particularly, freedom of expression. Therefore, when all peaceful options are closed to the resistance movement, a resort to physical violence is justified.

> — When the state abuses its power in an exorbitant way, e.g., by violating essential freedoms, installing a regime of violence instead of law, of particular interest instead of the general good.

> — When all other peaceful means have been tried in vain.

> — One must be morally certain that the revolution will succeed, rather than simply worsen the situation.

> — Only as much violence may be used as is required to terminate the evil.[36]

One of the most popular sections of the Archbishop's speech came when he warned of the near inevitability of violent revolution.

> As a matter of fact, the widespread situation of violence in Latin America, and the violent repression unleashed against even the most pacific and legitimate protests, are breeding a psychological mood most propitious for violent revolution. Revolutions do not arise among satisfied, secured people; they explode among people who are frustrated and not listened to by their rulers. An authentic revolution is a surgical operation done to save a sick body and to build a new order.[37]

For many Nicaraguans the archbishop's analysis of violence was a green light for action. It was a clear sign of the support of the highest authority of the Catholic Church for armed revolution. However, during the social turmoil racking the country following the earthquake of December 1972, the archbishop, although maintaining and even intensifying his criticism of the Somoza regime, modified his position on social revolution significantly, and carefully kept his distance from radical revolutionary groups advocating armed struggle.

CHAPTER 5

The 1972 Earthquake and the Aftermath

On Saturday, December 23, 1972, a massive earthquake tore apart the center of Managua. The destruction was almost total in the downtown area. According to the Nicaraguan government, the estimated damage was as follows:

8,000–10,000	dead
20,000	injured
51,000	unemployed
101,700	displaced
50,000	houses destroyed and 24,000 damaged (cost: $103 million)
4	hospitals with 1,650 beds destroyed
340,000	square meters of public and private office buildings destroyed
400,000	square meters of commercial and storage buildings destroyed
95%	of small factories and workshops destroyed
162.1	million dollars lost in infrastructure
1,163.2	million dollars estimated total damage[1]

The destruction in Managua was accompanied by the rapid disintegration of almost all political and judicial institutions of the country. At 5:00 A.M. on December 23, a National State of Emergency was declared by the governing triumvirate, and martial law was imposed on the country, suspending all constitutional guarantees. The decree also announced the formation of a National Emergency Committee under the leadership of Anastasio Somoza Debayle, the director of the National Guard. The vice-president of the committee was the defense minister. The functions and the responsibilities of the National Emergency Committee were not defined by the decree which created it, a fact which contributed to the absolute power of the committee and its director.

In early 1973, other official bodies were established by decrees, all under the control of Somoza. Among them were the Civil Corps for Reconstruction, the Office of Program Coordination, and the Center for National Distribution of Food. Also on February 6, 1973, the National Assembly issued a decree to authorize the Ministry of Finance and Public Credit to represent the country jointly with the President of the National Emergency Committee in all contracts for loans for national reconstruction, whether foreign or domestic.[2]

During the twenty-three months of the State of National Emergency — December 23, 1972, to December 1, 1974 — the director of the National Guard exercised absolute power, while the Junta of the National Government (the Triumvirate) and the Constituent National Assembly both acted as rubber stamps for Somoza's decisions.

The total power of the National Guard and its director was especially felt in Managua, where freedom of movement was restricted and identification cards issued by the National Guard were required for everybody. The residents of Managua were not allowed to go back to their homes or workplaces to salvage the remnants of their belongings, and in the absence of the owners, many looters attacked the commercial zone and ransacked the shops under the noses of the Guardsmen. Many small and medium-size shops and some large establishments were destroyed by looting, and a profitable black market sprang up in stolen property and medical and food aid from abroad. The main looting and running of the black market were done by soldiers and officers of the National Guard.

Besides looting the residential and commercial districts of Managua, Somoza's clan and the National Guardsmen discovered other easy ways to build up their fortune in this period of national crisis. The abuse of international funds and materials became a common practice among the state officials. The government's refusal to publish an exact figure for the amount of international aid received by the country helped the authorities to continue their illegal financial activities. Lainez estimates that between December 23, 1972, and May 31, 1973, the total aid amounted to $31.5 million, of which $25.9 million came in the form of material goods, $2.6 million in cash, and $3 million in the form of temporary housing.[3] Later, the amount of the relief funds increased tremendously when the international organizations began granting low-interest loans and credits for the reconstruction of Managua. For instance, $78 million was granted by the Agency for International Development (AID) — $12.7 million in emergency grant assistance, and a further $65.3 million in reconstruction loans — and $54 million was granted by the Inter-American Development Bank (IDB).[4] Also, the International Development Association, a member of the World Bank Group, granted a $20 million credit for the reconstruction of Managua. Another $14.4 million loan came from the International Monetary Fund.[5]

Since Somoza and his Nationalist Liberal Party were the main channels for the distribution of the aid, and because there was no supervision by any civilian or voluntary association, many abuses occurred. For instance, the Nationalist Liberal Party's criteria for the distribution of relief funds and materials were often political. The victims who did not want to submit to the desires and arbitration of local political chiefs were deprived of any assistance. On the other hand, party members and associates were given aid even if they were not victims of the earthquake. A large part of the relief materials ended up in commercial establishments and was sold at high prices.

The total control of the mass media by the government officials, under the State of National Emergency and martial law, provided complete liberty for the authorities to continue the abuses of relief funds and materials in the absence of media exposure.

Another popular form of promoting individual wealth for the Somoza clan in this period was land speculation. The fear of another devastating earthquake had made the residents of Managua receptive to the idea of shifting the location of the city to a less dangerous site, preferably southeast of old Managua. Government officials and their family members and friends began buying the public land in that area at a very cheap price and selling it back into an inflated market. In one case, Cornelio Hueck, the president of the Constituent Assembly, bought up empty land earmarked for temporary housing for the homeless for $17,000. After a short time, he resold the land to the state housing bank for $1.2 million. The bank paid the price using the AID funds.[6] In another incident, Somoza's investment firm, NICARAAO, S.A., bought some land just outside Managua for $30,000. A few weeks later NICARAAO sold it to the National Housing Institute as a site for a housing relief project for $3 million, paid by a U.S. grant. The Housing Institute never built a house there.[7] This land speculation by the Somoza clan became publicly known, and irritated other sectors of the bourgeoisie which had to buy the land in the market, paying high prices.

When the government finally began some reconstruction projects, the investment was concentrated in the areas belonging to the Somoza circle. The construction materials were also bought from the factories owned by the ruling group. The new commercial centers were built in groups far away from each other. And then, to connect the new clusters mushrooming in remote suburbs, long highways and roads were built using cobble stones manufactured by the cement company belonging to Somoza.

International relief funds did little to reduce the suffering of Nicaraguans. In 1973, the government obtained a total of $240.4 million in the form of low-interest loans from governments and private banks abroad. However, in spite of the availability of the international relief funds and low-interest loans, the Somoza regime increased taxes, escalating the burden on the citizens, who had already lost most of their possessions to the earthquake. *Latin America 1973* reported that

> steps taken by the government to facilitate the Capital's reconstruction included extension of the work week from 48 to 60 hours, adoption of a 10% export duty and a two-year rent freeze, abolition of tax exemptions for two years, and a levy of one month's wages on public employees during 1973. . . .

Inflation, unemployment, housing problems, tremendous health hazards, and total insensitivity by the government toward the problems of the victims resulted in massive imigration out of

Managua. Many middle-class families who still could afford to travel to the other Central American countries left Nicaragua, while others, with limited resources, migrated to other Nicaraguan cities.

Growing Political Opposition

Somoza's growing greed and unrestricted abuse of the state apparatus for the economic benefit of his family soon surpassed the level of tolerance among different sectors of the society, including his main class ally, the big bourgeoisie (large landowners, wealthy industrialists, bankers, and large merchants).

In the 1960s, the economic upsurge and relative relaxation in the political atmosphere under the rule of Luis Somoza and René Schick had promoted class unity among the bourgeoisie. The three major economic groups, BANIC, BANAMERICA, and the Somozas, initiated some joint investments. Nicaraguan Corporation for Investment (Corporación Nicaragüense de Inversiones — CNI) was formed in 1964 with participation of all three economic groups, and was widely supported by the Alliance for Progress and AID. The three economic groups also invested jointly in higher education institutes such as the Central American Business Administration Institute (Instituto Centroamericano de Administración de Empresas — INCAE), which was affiliated with Harvard University; and Central American University (UCA), which was run by Jesuits. Both of these education institutions functioned as centers for training economic and technical cadres for the growing domestic capitalist market.

In the same period, a business organization, *Consejo Superior de la Iniciativa Privada* (COSIP — Superior Council of Private Initiative) was formed by different agricultural, industrial, commercial, and financial interests to coordinate the economic activities of the private sector. During this period, Somocismo seemed indispensable to the development of capitalism in Nicaragua. The government implemented basic policies to promote the economy, including (1) building a physical infrastructure and offering public services which reduced the cost of production and distribution for the capitalists; (2) maintaining a low wage level and controlling the working class through government unions and repressive measures, whenever necessary; and (3) facilitating the process of capital accumulation by channeling public credit to private capitalists through credit and banking institutions such as the National Bank. In addition, the generation of public employment and public expenditure through the purchase of goods and services by the government expanded the national market.

However, the general policies of the government to promote capitalistic development of the country, which resulted in the protection and promotion of the interests of the bourgeoisie as a class, also had a more specific goal: to advance the benefits of the Somoza clan as a distinctively advantageous sector of the class. Family members and friends were gaining from favorable terms in public bidding on state contracts for public works, buying from and selling to government agencies, fiscal and banking deals, tax exemptions, import or export quotas, and the licensing of new companies.[8]

The government effort to serve the interests of a small sector of the bourgeoisie resulted in complaints by the other sectors. For instance, in 1968, Pedro Joaquín Chamorro, a prominent member of the Conservative Party and the editor of *La Prensa*, reflected the dissatisfaction of the private sector in one of his editorials.

> Our economy is based on favoritism for a few, a case which was substantiated by the scandalous endorsement of certain private foreign loans by the government which put them in the same category as the national debt; also the 70 million cordobas in loans issued for the agricultural diversification and promotion of production, which went to three or four enterprises belonging to the members of the government circle, none of which had anything to do with agriculture.[9]

Listing several cases of corruption and favoritism, Chamorro called on the private sector to voice its dissatisfaction with the government policies.

> Spokespersons for the Nicaraguan Private Enterprise are obliged to consider all different angles of the problem and, above all, they should consider serious subjects such as mixing of the private interests of the government circle with the national interests. . . . It is precisely the role of the Private Sector to take up the

banner of separation of the "private" and "public" interests which is the way of achieving progress in a country.[10]

Another important complaint of the bourgeoisie against the Somoza dynasty concerned the role of the army as the protector of the interests of the members of the Somoza family and their close associates. In another *La Prensa* editorial on May 28, 1964, Chamorro addressed the problem and demanded the nationalization of the army and the creation of a military structure "which won't be subjugated to one person. . . . " He called for discipline and a hierarchical order for the army based on the laws of the country.

In spite of the complaints of the bourgeoisie and opposition from the middle class, the government policies of favoritism, and use of the army and other state apparatus for the private interests of the governing circle, continued and even intensified following the earthquake.

Collecting enormous sums of money from the black market, international relief funds, and land speculation, the Somoza clan began investing in demolition, earth moving, heavy equipment, construction materials, premixed concrete, paving, metal buildings, pipes and tubing, real estate development, land, and housing.[11]

The complaints of the bourgeoisie about the situation of "disloyal competition" created by Somoza's abuses of political power for personal gains were voiced even in the international news media. For instance, *Latin America 1973* reported:

> Local construction firms complained the government had awarded a contract to build a prefabricated children's home to the Miami Company, Panelfab, and its Nicaraguan affiliate, formed recently by a member of the ruling triumvirate, for about $1 million, although local firms had bid less than half that amount. Somoza reportedly took responsibility for awarding the contract. . . . Other firms claimed they were not given a chance to bid when a Brazilian government credit for heavy equipment was used to buy trucks from a company owned by Somoza. . . .[12]

Following the earthquake, private sector organizations such as COSIP and INDE (Instituto Nicaragüense de Desarrollo/Nicaraguan Institute for Development) became more critical of govern-

ment policies in handling the situation. To prepare the private sector
to confront the worsening conditions, COSIP and INDE sponsored
a convention of Nicaraguan businessmen in 1974. Their goal was to
create a government representative of all different sectors of the
bourgeoisie, instead of a small corrupt clan of members and friends
of Somoza family.

The Catholic Church and the Opposition

The earthquake and the accompanying intensification of
political and financial corruption also had a profound effect on the
Nicaraguan Church. Both the hierarchy and the bases of the Church
became politicized and radicalized, although on different levels and
to different degrees. The immediate period following the earthquake
witnessed a high degree of Church involvement in public services.
For a few weeks, Church organizations were instrumental in the
distribution of relief materials on which most of the residents of
Managua depended for their survival. However, when the Somoza
circle reestablished its power bases, the responsibility for distribution
of relief materials was given to the government agencies and local
offices of Somoza's Liberal Party.

The overt manipulation of a disastrous situation for personal
gain by the Somoza circle resulted in strong criticism by the Catholic
Church hierarchy as well as its membership. In February 1973, the
bishops issued a letter to ask for international solidarity, and called
for reconstruction of the country, not only in material forms but
more so in terms of a moral and social restructuring which would
give Nicaraguans more opportunity to participate in the life of the
country and to elevate their condition. The bishops rejected the kind
of assistance which would "strengthen the restrictions of human
development under the pretext of economic development," calling it
unjust and unacceptable.[13]

Although the above statement was another indication of the
intensified political activities on the part of the Catholic Church,
the patterns of involvement varied among different sectors of the
Church. While the priests and nuns working in the poor districts of
Managua became involved in mass mobilization against the govern-

ment, the hierarchy tried to restrict its criticism in a humanitarian and nonpartisan framework.

The year 1974 witnessed the intensification of opposition to Somoza, and also the heightening of the conflict between the Catholic Church hierarchy and the government. Using the state of emergency and martial law, Somoza increased repression in the country, particularly in the northern and eastern regions, the stronghold of the FSLN. Peasants accused of supporting the guerrillas were jailed, tortured, and killed. Many farmers were driven out of their farms and towns by the National Guard, and their lands were given to the Guard's officers and the local landlords. Meanwhile, the priests and nuns working in the rural areas came into close contact with local realities, and, in some cases, began recording and reporting the government atrocities (e.g., in Zelaya, Capuchin Fathers had an instrumental role in reporting government repression against the peasant population. Their activities will be discussed in detail in later chapters).

The involvement of the bases of the Church with the peasant movement, and their increasing activities to expose the repressive nature of the government, was too radical for the majority of the bishops who had been faithful allies of the Somoza government for decades. To explain the new situation and to legitimize the political involvement of the clergy against government repression, Archbishop Obando y Bravo issued a statement in April 1974. Justifying the new social concerns and political activities of the Church, he bitterly complained about capitalism, which for years

> had tried to give the Church an outlandish and absurd mission, regarding politics. The Church, it said, should stay in the sacristy, act on consciences, busy itself with private life. Its rightful mission, capitalism insisted, is to keep man from the dangers of this world, preach resignation and patience, focus exclusively on the after-life, and take care, charitably and mercifully, of those afflicted by drunkness, prostitution, desertion by their families, delinquency, etc. But it should stay well out of the social and economic area, acknowledge its incompetence in such affairs, and preach that established order, the classes as they exist, the prevailing structures and the political order in power reflect God's will for man.[14]

The archbishop held that such mentality was "old and outdated," and "no one with even a minimal knowledge of what the Church is can have such a mentality today." Archbishop Obando reminded his readers that "the Church has a clear idea of what man is, a precise image of his values, his dignity, his destiny. And this man is caught up in the political order." Since there are political orders which do not respect the dignity and destiny of man, "the Church can never be politically neutral."[15]

Under heavy pressure from local priests, nuns, and laymen, the bishops held an extraordinary meeting on May 27, 1974, and publicly denounced the abuses of human rights committed by government authorities in the countryside.[16] They concluded that these abuses would intensify the "demand for changes in the structure and the government authorities, demand for peace." The bishops called on the government to "prevent chaos and forceful repression which only adds to hatred and distances the road to peace."[17]

However, Somoza's response was the ratification of the new constitution,[18] and the announcement of his candidacy for the upcoming presidential election. To legitimize his presidential candidacy, Anastasio Somoza Debayle announced his resignation from active military duties, giving up the title of the Chief Director of the National Guard (Jefe Director de la Guardia Nacional). However, he retained his other position, the Supreme Chief of the Armed Forces (Jefe Supremo de las Fuerzas Armadas).

The announcement of Somoza's candidacy inflamed the bitterness of the private sector opposition to the dynasty. A group of twenty-seven prominent Nicaraguans, representing nine different political organizations and syndicates, issued a public statement proclaiming Somoza an unconstitutional candidate, and asking the people not to vote. Somoza immediately arrested all of them, charging them with boycotting the election. They were all convicted and lost their political rights.

The Church hierarchy reacted strongly to Somoza's heavy-handed policies, and the bishops issued a Pastoral Letter criticizing the political repression, announcing that, "No one is obligated to vote for any political group." Also on August 6, 1974, the Episcopal Conference denounced the fraudulent electoral procedures and declared that "the social order must not be a rigid, frozen mechanism, forbidding or restricting the exercise of human rights, nor should it make those rights the monopoly of any one faction."[19]

The strongest part of this Pastoral Letter was the section addressing the "right to dissent," which was a direct response to repressive measures taken by Somoza against his political opponents.

> As an answer to totalitarian regimes that seek to impose by law and police force a social order that runs contrary to the dictates of conscience, men assert, among their rights, the "right to dissent."
>
> This is the citizen's theoretical and practical title to object in the name of conscience against injustices and arbitrariness that infringe on his rights. It is no unreasoned insurrectional or armed protest, but a coherent, conscience-founded claim.[20]

To clarify the Church's direction in future political activities, the bishops declared, "The Church has a manifest duty to educate the people in their political obligations. The Church has no duty, however, automatically to approve everything that political authorities do."

The timing of this Pastoral Letter was important. It was published soon after the arrest of the twenty-seven political opponents of Somoza for boycotting the election. The theme of the Letter, "the right to dissent," was a clear indication of the Bishops' support for the group, and their right to protest against the dictatorship. Combining their ideological justification of the right to dissent with a clear statement of the Church's stand in relation to the government, that the Church has no obligation to give automatic approval to political authority, the bishops emphatically declared their rupture with the dynasty and their close association with the regime's opponents. However, the opposition itself was divided among reformists, who were preparing to form UDEL (Unión Democrática de Liberación/Democratic Union of Liberation), and radicals mobilized by the FSLN. Supporting the political opposition as "a coherent, conscience-founded claim" as opposed to "unreasoned, insurrectional or armed protest," the bishops drew a clear line between the political position of the Church hierarchy and the radical policies of the FSLN, a line which was also drawn by the private sector opposition by excluding the FSLN from their efforts to organize a broad coalition against Somoza.

Unión Democrática de Liberación (UDEL)

On December 15, 1974, the leaders of the opposition, including the twenty-seven arrested individuals, announced the formation of an opposition coalition, UDEL. This organization included most of the opposition groups of the center and the left, including the Confederación General del Trabjo-Independiente (CGT-I), and the Socialist Party of Nicaragua. Among the prominent members of UDEL were Pedro Joaquín Chamorro, the editor of *La Prensa*, and Ramiro Sacasa, a former Somocista and ex-member of Somoza's cabinet. The FSLN was not invited to participate in UDEL.

The political role played by UDEL in 1975–79 was chiefly determined by its social composition and the goals and strategies of different sociopolitical factions of the organization. The member groups and the individuals in UDEL had come from a diverse social spectrum, from the traditional oligarchies of Nicaragua (both Conservative and Liberal), to the working-class organizations (Socialist Party) and labor unions (Central de Trabajadores de Nicaragua [CTN], and Confederación General del Trabajo-Independiente [CGT-I]). UDEL's program was a reflection of the diversity of the groups and their strategic plans. An examination of these groups, the process of their formation, their sociopolitical compositions, and their ideological inclinations, will help to understand UDEL's role in later political developments.

Dissident Liberals

The main representative of Liberal opposition to Somoza was the Independent Liberal Party (PLI). It was formed in 1944 during a split in the Nationalist Liberal Party over the nomination of Somoza García as the presidential candidate for the upcoming election. As John Booth later observed, "the new party raised as its standard the democratic traditions of liberalism and advocated Keynesian economics, socialist economic reformism, and Jeffersonian democratic politics."[21] In the 1946 election, the PLI joined the

Conservative Party to support Dr. Aguado's candidacy for the presidency against the official candidate. In the 1950s, the PLI manifested a high capability for mass mobilization, especially among the youth. Its youth organization, the Democratic Youth Front (Frente Juvenil Democrático — FJD) played an active role in the northern areas of traditional liberal support. Its paper, *Vanguardia Juvenil*, published articles by radical members of the organization, among them Tomás Borge Martínez, who in the early 1960s, joined Carlos Fonseca Amador and Silvio Mayorga in the founding of the FSLN.

Another member of the FJD was Rigoberto López Pérez, who assassinated Anastasio Somoza García (Tacho) in 1956. Following the assassination of Somoza, the opposition groups, including the PLI, came under heavy attack by Anastasio Somoza Debayle (Tachito). Many members of the opposition were jailed and interrogated by the National Guard. Among the victims were old Dr. Enoc Agüado, from the Conservative Party and the presidential candidate in the 1946 election, and Tomás Borge Martínez, from PLI, a law student in Managua at the time. Despite constant harassment and repression, the PLI continued to oppose the dictatorship, and in 1974 joined UDEL.

Another dissident Liberal group in UDEL was *Partido Liberal Constitucionalista* (PLC — Constitutionalist Liberal Party) which was led by Ramiro Sacasa Guerrero, a former Somocista who had served in Somoza's cabinet several times and finally defected in the early 1970s and formed the new Liberal opposition to Somoza.

The Social Christian Party

Partido Socialcristiano Nicaragüense (PSCN — Nicaraguan Social Christian Party) was another major group in UDEL. The PSCN was formed in 1957 as a response to the inadequacy of the two traditional parties. In the introduction to a declaration of PSCN in 1961, the authors summed up the reasons for formation of a new party.

> The painful epoch during which our country has lived under the fruitless regime of the two parties, Liberal and Conservative, shows us that a total change in the Nicaraguan situation which

would bring justice and eliminate the exploitation of human being by another human being, and [maintain] respect for human rights, cannot be achieved through these parties.[22]

Therefore, a group of Nicaraguan intellectuals, who were chiefly the younger members of the wealthy middle-class families, formed a new party which was different from the two traditional ones both in the social function of the members and their ideologies. The Social Christians, mainly professionals, doctors, lawyers, and teachers, rejected both liberal capitalism and communism as their ideology. In the above-mentioned declaration, the PSCN declared that the Party "is not capitalist nor communist; [it] condemns private monopolies and also submission to the state." The declaration goes on to define the Christian democracy as "the government of the people, elected by the people, for the people, based on the Christian judgement of man."

Although the PSCN was formed around Christian ideas and values, it was, and still is, a secular organization. It has never had any organic relationship with the Church hierarchy. Indeed, the hierarchy at the time of the formation of the party was supporting Somoza's rule and had a hostile attitude toward the opposition, including the PSCN.

The main emphasis of the party in terms of a social system was a "communal society." It advocated "cooperatives, community development, Christian labor unions, reformist state intervention in the economy, and political reform, as keys to greater social justice."[23] The party tried to clarify this broad, somewhat idealistic, political program in its manifesto. The PSCN promised to work for "a democratic agrarian reform . . . which would attack the basis of latifundia, especially the unproductive ones, and would establish a rational system of land distribution to elevate the peasants."[24]

In comparison with the traditional parties, the PSCN had a radical concept of labor and laborer. The Party's manifesto promised to "vigorously struggle against the old and inhumane concept of work as merchandise." It declared that workers had inviolable rights which should be recognized by society: the right to obtain sufficient income for a dignified life for themselves and their families, and the right to enjoy different opportunities in their lives and to expand their horizons based on their legitimate aspirations. The PSCN's ideas about agrarian reform and a progressive labor code were later reflected in UDEL's program.

The Conservative Opposition

The traditional Conservative Party was badly damaged and splintered by the Somoza-Agüero Pact of 1971. Many alienated members of the party deserted and joined other opposition groups or formed new organizations; among them were Pedro Joaquín Chamorro's Conservative National Action (Acción Nacional Conservadora — ANC), the Authentic Conservative Party (Partido Conservador Auténtico), and the Democratic Conservative Party (Partido Conservador Democrático).

Chamorro's ANC was one of the founders and an active member of UDEL. Chamorro's leadership in UDEL was accompanied by the firm support of the only opposition paper in the country, *La Prensa*, which was owned by the Chamorro family, and had been constantly embarrassing the dictatorship by exposing the corruption and illegal activities of government officials.

The Socialists

The influence of socialist ideas had always been marginal in Nicaragua. The main explanation for this lay with the class structure of the country. A weak economy based on agriculture, and an almost total lack of heavy industry until the 1960s were the main obstacles to development of an organized labor movement as the breeding ground for socialist ideas. Even when, in July 1944, the Socialist Party of Nicaragua was born as a small link in the international chain of the traditional Communist parties all over the world, the lack of a working class was reflected in the party's leadership, which was mainly composed of artisans. A nonproletarian leadership and a low level of Marxist theory among the party's rank and file created a caricature of a workers' party which, instead of an authentic revolutionary opposition to the dictatorship, blindly obeyed Moscow's political line advocating an alliance with the bourgeois rulers, no matter how repressive they were, in the framework of an Anti-Fascist United Front during World War II. Therefore, the Socialist Party of Nicaragua (Partido Socialista Nicaragüense — PSN) was born in support of Somoza against the opposition in the mid-1940s.

Somoza García was pleased to find a new and unexpected ally, and used the party to separate the leftist opposition from the Conservatives who were demanding a general election. However, when Somoza finally came to an understanding with the leaders of the Conservative Party and signed a political pact with Carlos Cuadra Pasos in 1948, he turned against the PSN, and crushed the party in a repressive sweep. Somoza outlawed the PSN and its affiliates in the 1950 Constitution, and imprisoned or drove into exile most of the Socialist leaders.

As industrial development occurred in the late 1950s, and especially in the 1960s, the outlawed PSN began to organize among the growing number of urban workers and farm laborers. However, the formation of the FSLN in the early 1960s and the growing discussion of armed struggle among the rank and file of the party resulted in a split in 1967, and the younger, more militant members expelled the traditional leadership because of its intransigent opposition to armed struggle. Three years later, the expelled leaders of the PSN formed a small sectarian group called the Communist Party of Nicaragua (Partido Comunista de Nicaragua — PC de N.), claiming unconditional allegiance to Moscow. However, the Soviet Union continued to recognize and to have formal relationships with the PSN, which, while not hostile to it, continued to have reservations about the FSLN.

The PSN joined UDEL in 1974, and it was only after 1977 that the growing popularity and strength of the FSLN forced the party to change its attitude toward armed struggle and to look for a reapproachment with the Sandinistas.

Workers' Unions

In its heterogeneous composition, UDEL also embraced two trade unions: Central de Trabajadores de Nicaragua (CTN), and Confederación General Del Trabajo-Independiente (CGT-I).

The unbalanced Nicaraguan economic structure was reflected in the size and the formation of the working class. The early growth of the Nicaraguan working class was a result of the development of cotton production in the 1950s, and a massive expulsion of the peasants from the land. A great number of the landless peasants became plantation workers in coffee, cotton, sugar, and banana fields. Because of the high unemployment and underemployment in the countryside, the work force was highly divided and difficult to organize. Although the wages were low and the working conditions miserable, there were still many workers who would accept a lower wage and worse working conditions just to be able to work and barely provide for their families' survival. The low wages were usually spent in the landlord's store, which sold the basic foodstuff for high prices. By the end of the season the workers were even deeper in debt to the landowner and had to seek hard-to-find jobs in the cities for the rest of the year. The continuous mobility of the seasonal laborers and high competition for permanent jobs in the fields were the two main obstacles in organizing rural workers.

Until the 1960s, the only nonagricultural workers were the miners of the north. Although they were organized by Sandino to combat the occupying U.S. Army in the late 1920s and early 1930s, their combativeness and organization rapidly diminished following Sandino's murder by Somoza in 1934. Most of them were Miskito Indians with a totally different culture from the workers of the Pacific Coast. The racial and cultural differences were important obstacles to organizing the workers on a national scale.

The Nicaraguan urban proletariat originated during the industrial development in the 1960s, and was mainly concentrated in the major cities of the Pacific Coast, such as Managua, León, Chinandega, and Carazo. The first attempt to organize the urban working class was initiated by the Socialist Party in the period from 1944 to 1948. Although most of the workers organized by the PSN were closer to the artisan sector than the modern proletariat, the potential of an organized labor movement was frightening enough to compel Somoza to formulate a policy for neutralizing the movement. In 1945, he adopted an advanced Labor Code which strengthened the government alliance with the PSN and the labor leaders. However, when Somoza co-opted the Conservative opposition leaders by a political pact in 1948, and turned against the PSN, massive repression dismantled the embryonic labor movement, and many of the workers' leaders had to flee the country.

The next step in Somoza's labor policy was creation of a pro-government workers' organization, the General Confederation of Workers (Confederación General de Trabajo — CGT), in 1949. The main task of the CGT was to control the labor movement and protect government interests in workplaces.

In spite of intense repression and tight control of factories by Somoza agents, clandestine labor groups emerged and provided continuity in the movement. In the 1960s, the relative liberalization under the rule of Luis Somoza and René Schick created an opportunity for different political parties to influence the labor movement, and to establish their own workers' organizations. In 1962, the Social Christians, with the help of the international Christian labor organizations, established *Movimiento Sindical Autónoma de Nicaragua* (MOSAN), which in 1972 joined the broader Nicaraguan Workers Center (Central de Trabajadores de Nicaragua — CTN). In 1974, the CTN joined UDEL.

Another important development in the labor movement of the 1960s was the defection of some unions of the Somoza-controlled CGT. The dissident unions formed the Independent General Workers Confederation (Confederación General de Trabajadores-Independiente [CGT-I]), which had close ties to the PSN, and in 1974 joined UDEL.

The other two important labor unions were the Center for Union Action and Unity (Centro de Acción y Unidad Sindical — CAUS), established by the Communist Party of Nicaragua in the early 1970s, and the Council for Union Unity (Consejo de Unidad Sindical — CUS), which was sponsored by the United States government and the AFL-CIO (1968). The CUS policies were limited to job-related demands, and the organization remained apolitical in the period of intensification of the anti-Somoza movement in the 1970s.

UDEL's Program

UDEL's heterogeneous social composition was well reflected in the program of the organization. The only strong part of the program was the section addressing the basic point of unity among the member organizations, the overthrow of Somoza.

In an introduction to the program, the authors defined the organization as

> an alliance of the parties and trade union organizations which have reached the necessity of unity for eradication of the public power of the Somoza dynasty, as an indispensable stage for Nicaragua to be able to create the minimum conditions for formation of a more just society.[25]

It is clear, from the above passage, that the main goal of the coalition was to negate the individual dictatorship of Somoza. The authors of the program summed up the reasons for their decision to overthrow Somoza.

> Democracy and its institutions have become juridical fiction to perpetuate Somoza's power. The parliament, a heavy burden for the people, is only to enhance the benefit of Somoza. The Army has failed to fulfill its professional and institutional projects because it has been converted to the personal guard of Somoza.

Although UDEL's program was strong and explicit in rejecting Somoza's regime, it was weak and imprecise in dealing with the proposed socioeconomic alternatives. Indeed, when the program attempted to address concrete social and economic problems, the language became rhetorical and offered few alternatives to construct a future for Nicaragua.

In the introduction, the authors recognized three main focuses for the program: political democracy, socioeconomic justice, and independence. In the main text of the program, each of these three points was addressed separately. The first part of the text dealt with political democracy and promised:

> (a) A complete democratization of the country's political life with the participation of all ideological sectors.

> (b) To guarantee freedom of information, expression and publicizing ideas through the means of social communication and any other methods.

(c) The promulgation of a law of honesty to severely punish fiscal fraud and embezzlement, and to eradicate the duplication of functions and nepotism.

(d) The promulgation of an Electoral Law which, without discrimination, guarantees an effective and free suffrage.

(e) To guarantee the alteration in exercising public political power, and inviolability of the principle of no re-election.

(f) To institute a system of rights, based on respect for the Republic's Political Constitution.[26]

All these goals could well have been implemented in the existing socioeconomic structure of the country, and there was no need to propose any alternative. Indeed, the last clause explicitly stated that the reforms should be pursued in the framework of the "Political Constitution of the Republic." The only obstacle to the application of the above principles was the personal dictatorship of Somoza, which UDEL was formed to eradicate.

Strong political language was not present in the rest of the program addressing social structures. When dealing with the necessary changes in the socioeconomic framework, the UDEL program was a collection of different points borrowed from member organizations' plans and manifestos. For instance, to address agrarian reform, the program used statements identical with the PSCN 1961 declaration.

Realization of an integral agrarian reform, which radically transforms the situation in the countryside, elevates the level of life for the peasants, and guarantees that the land belongs to those who work it. To utilize the uncultivated latifundia, and also all properties which do not fulfill their social function. The agrarian reform will include education programs, rural credit, technical assistance, etc., for small and medium size producers. The small property holders shall enjoy the special protection of the government, which develops the infrastructure in the countryside, plans agricultural diversification, and promotes cooperativism.[27]

The presence of Socialist Party and trade union organizations was reflected in a clause of the program proposing a labor code

> which guarantees for the workers of both public and private sectors the unrestricted freedom to trade union organizations in the cities and the countryside, which assures the right to strike, which establishes and respects the unremoveability of the union leaders from their jobs; which guarantees the job stability and assures just salaries and wages for all the workers.

The clauses dealing with agrarian reform and the labor code, which were accepted by the bourgeois sectors under the pressure of the PSCN, the Socialist Party, and the trade unions in UDEL, later became points of disagreement and internal debate within the organization. The conflict over these clauses sharpened when the political and economic crisis of 1975–79 radicalized the working class and militant elements of the middle sectors, and pushed the frightened bourgeoisie to take more conservative positions.

Besides the sections addressing the aspirations of upper-class opposition (political reforms), and the needs of the lower classes (agrarian reform and the labor code), there were many other clauses in the program dealing with sociopolitical demands of the middle sectors, such as Article 6 of the section on National Development, which promised "to suppress monopolization and to establish equal opportunity in agricultural, commercial and industrial activities." Other sections promised judicial and educational reforms, eradication of illiteracy, and free elementary and secondary education.

Although the diverse groups of UDEL had finally agreed on one single program, the contradictory nature of these groups became a source of constant tension in the organization. The upper-class sector, whose maximum program was overthrowing Somoza with the fewest possible socioeconomic changes, was trying to use the popular bases of UDEL as a leverage in the power struggle against Somoza. It became clear in 1977–78 that they were ready to sacrifice the program of the organization in return for Somoza's resignation. However, the middle and lower classes, especially the Socialist Party and the trade unions, had joined UDEL to compensate for the numerical and organizational weakness of the working class. They believed the overthrow of Somoza was the first stage in a more comprehensive socioeconomic program for betterment of the plight of the lower classes. As the economic and political crisis intensified, each faction of UDEL was pushing more forcefully to pull the whole organization toward its own program. This constant conflict among different groups created a favorable ground for the maneuvering of prominent individuals who, although belonged to specific sectors, could rally support and temporarily patch up differences, thanks to their long anti-Somoza struggle and their social recognition as oppositionist intellectuals. Among these individuals was the outstanding personality of Pedro Joaquín Chamorro, who played an essential role in the initiation of UDEL, and later in keeping the organization together until his death at the hands of Somoza's men on January 10, 1978.

Chamorro, who belonged to one of the wealthiest families of the traditional Conservative oligarchy of Granada, had struggled against Somoza García and later against his two sons for most of his life. Starting his political life in the Conservative Party, and frustrated by political pacts between his party and Somoza, he took up arms in 1959 to overthrow the dynasty. The life of his armed uprising was cut short by a quick defeat in the hands of the National Guard. Serving time in Somoza's jails and in exile, he later joined the more militant faction of the Conservative Party to support the candidacy of Fernando Agüero in the 1967 election. When it became obvious that Tachito was going to arrange a fraudulent election, Chamorro joined the mass demonstration of January 1967, which was brutally suppressed by Somoza's National Guard. When in 1971 Agüero signed a political pact with Somoza, Chamorro finally split from the Conservative Party and formed Acción Nacional Conservadora (ANC — Conservative National Action). Chamorro was an important force behind the formation of UDEL in 1974, and was appointed as its first president. Long before the creation of UDEL, Chamorro had formulated the idea for a broad coalition in his editorials in *La Prensa*.

For Chamorro and many other Nicaraguan intellectuals, the prerequisite to developing the country was reconcilation of the interests of the workers and the capitalists. In an article written in the 1960s, and later reproduced in the 1970s, Chamorro wrote:

> We have always maintained that development of each country
> has to take two parallel paths, the path of labor and that of
> business. In other words, to resolve the socio-economic problems

of the people, it is imperative that the worker understands that society and himself need business, and the business also should understand that it needs the worker.[28]

Therefore, Chamorro believed that if an understanding could develop between the workers and the businessmen, they both would change their attitudes. The workers would feel responsible to "produce cooperation between the laborer and business," and the capitalist would decide "to establish a true social justice."

Chamorro maintained that this ideal picture was shattered because of the

> reactionary concept of people who consider business only as an instrument to create more money. The people who consider labor as a commodity which could be acquired in any market. . . . And on the other hand, the labor leaders who seek to unravel a war in enterprise; who demand more and more, without considering the limits of what is there to be effectively distributed. . . . The individuals who with reason or without, but generally with reason, resent a society because it doesn't give them equal opportunity to rise, or to subsist with dignity, and instead of searching for a harmony to bring a better subsistence, they seek a war of revenge with no limitations.[29]

Chamorro strongly invited his fellow countrymen "to struggle against these two extremes . . . ," and this was exactly what Chamorro had in mind when he helped in the formation of UDEL in 1974. He hoped the organization would become a vehicle for class reconciliation, a means to realize the bourgeois intellectuals' dream of a harmonious class society, in which both the exploiter and the exploited accept their status and collaborate with each other to prevent either class struggle or monopolization of the system by a few.

Chamorro's idea of a harmonious society and class collaboration was almost identical to the old social doctrines preached by the Catholic hierarchy since the late nineteenth century, and well developed in different encyclicals beginning with the *Rerum Novarum* of Pope Leo XIII in 1891.[30] This ideological resemblance between the bourgeois leadership of UDEL and the traditional Catholic theology provided a favorable ground for close ideological and political alignment between the two groups.

CHAPTER 6

The FSLN and the Progressive Church

The triumph of the *Frente Sandinista de Liberación Nacional* in July 1979 was the culmination of a long process of profound changes in the socioeconomic and political structures of Nicaragua. An important element in this long process was an alliance gradually formed between the Marxist and the Christian sectors of the opposition. The development of the FSLN from an isolated small guerrilla group operating in the mountains of northern Nicaragua to a major popular force by the end of the Somoza regime, governing the large cities, was accompanied by the evolution of a major sector of Nicaraguan Catholics from a politically ultraconservative, religiously superstitious, and fatalist group to a combative opposition force. This change resulted in the creation of a political opposition which was not dogmatically Marxist, nor sectarian Christian, but rather a democratic, humanistic alliance with diverse ideologies, all united in overthrowing a dictatorship and a suppressive, dehumanizing socioeconomic structure, and constructing a new society based on common values of both Marxism and Christianity. To understand the process, we have to study the formation and the development of both of the elements: the armed guerrillas who formed the FSLN, and the Christian Base Communities which integrated Christian Nicaraguans into the revolution.

Frente Sandinista de Liberación Nacional

The death of Augusto Cesar Sandino in 1934 was not only the end of the struggle by the original Sandinista army but also the end of a unique historical experience in Nicaragua: the struggle of a group sharply in contradiction with both ends of the mainstream political conflict between conservatism and liberalism.

Although basically a nationalist army, the Sandino's guerillas combined their anti-interventionist war with a blend of class struggle which was the direct result of their social background (mainly, landless peasants and mine workers), and that of their enemies (wealthy landlords, both Liberal and Conservative).

Following Sandino's death, this opposition was neutralized for at least two decades. The power struggle was again reduced to a conflict between the Liberals and the Conservatives. Even those organizations not representative of traditional parties in their social composition and declared sociopolitical goals (e.g., Socialist Party) in practice took sides with one of the two major groups and mobilized their membership and social base for the political advancement of one of the traditional political foes.

In the late 1950s, the political scene changed after the sharp social changes resulting from the development of cotton production and the massive dislocation of the Nicaraguan peasantry. The capitalist expansion of cotton changed life both in the countryside and the city. In the rural areas, the mass expulsion of the peasants from their lands and the rapid change of labor relations from a small family farming and *colono* labor force to seasonal day laborers intensified unemployment and underemployment, and worsened living conditions. In the cities, the pressure of a rapidly growing number of immigrant peasants seeking urban employment was felt on an already poor public service network and scarce housing. The result was intensified social unrest, which, in the absence of an organized opposition with programs for social change, manifested itself in scattered spontaneous protests among different social sectors against the increased cost of living, poor housing conditions, and lack of public services.

The basic demands of the workers' protests during this period were implementation of the labor code and establishment of social security. The urban middle sectors, such as university students, teachers, and employees of radio and newspapers, who were being politicized by close contact with the growing marginal lifestyle in the large cities, were forming political organizations. Some resorted to open demonstrations in the late 1950s; however, none of these movements had a clear political direction.

In the rural areas, especially in the northern part of the country, a few scattered peasant uprisings were led by veterans of Sandino's struggle. For example, in 1958 Ramón Raudales, a survivor of Sandino's original army, led a small group of peasants around Jalapa in a series of armed actions against the National Guard.[1]

The Student Movement and the FSLN

The peasant uprisings coincided with the student movement in the cities. From the beginning, the Somoza dynasty had to face constant opposition among university students, and occasionally, high school students. As early as 1939, Nicaraguan universities became the scene of political demonstrations and violent clashes with the National Guard. However, the student movement did not have a clear political direction, and was divided among the supporters of different political organizations. Both the Conservative Party and the Independent Liberal Party (PLI) were active in the universities. Indeed, most of the leaders of the 1970s opposition, both political reformists and radical FSLN fighters, had begun their political life as student activists.

Pedro Joaquín Chamorro, leader of the UDEL, was exiled to the Corn Islands in 1944 for his role in the student movement. Also, Tomás Borge Martínez, one of the founders of the FSLN, began his political orientation as a high school student active in the Youth Democratic Front (FJD), the student wing of the PLI.

The student movement of the 1940s intensified by the end of World War II as a result of a general movement for democracy and free election. In 1948, large student demonstrations occurred in the universities of Managua and in León and resulted in violent clashes with the National Guard. The repression which followed temporarily halted the movement. However, the political agreements signed by Somoza García and the Conservative Party in 1948 and 1950 were the basic reason for the movement losing its momentum. Somoza's policy of co-optation of the Conservative elements of the opposition effectively divided the movement as some of the Conservative student leaders opted for new opportunities in working with the government.

The Liberal faction of the student movement (the FJD of the PLI) continued its activities among the youth in the northern part of the country. It was a member of this group, Rigoberto López Pérez, who assassinated Somoza García in 1956. The repression which followed the assassination sent some of the student activists to jail and exile, including Tomás Borge and Pedro Joaquín Chamorro. However, repression did not prevent the spreading of Marxist ideas among some student activists, including Carlos Fonseca Amador and Silvio Mayorga, who had joined the outlawed Socialist Party and started a Marxist study group in Matagalpa in the late 1950s.

The Cuban Revolution in January 1959 inspired many Nicaraguan student leaders, and created hopes for change through radical means. A new student organization, Nicaraguan Patriotic Youth (Juventud Patriótica Nicaragüense — JPN), was formed by activists with diverse political backgrounds, all of whom had as a common goal the overthrow of the Somoza dynasty. Widespread student demonstrations in 1959 were met with repression, which on July 23, 1959, resulted in a massacre of the students by the National Guard.[2]

In contrast to the events of 1948, the repression in 1959 radicalized the movement and convinced many activists that the only hope for Nicaragua was to overthrow the regime in an armed confrontation. Indeed, some student leaders with very different political orientations (e.g., the Conservative Pedro Joaquín Chamorro and the Marxist Carlos Fonseca Amador) travelled to Cuba to learn from the new revolution. Upon their return to Nicaragua, both Chamorro and Fonseca, totally independent of one another, organized armed groups to fight against the dynasty. Both movements were rapidly defeated at the hands of the National Guard and the leaders were arrested and put in jail (Chamorro), or badly wounded (Fonseca). However, Fonseca, having full moral support and some material assistance from Cuba, did not lose his faith in armed struggle as an effective means of overthrowing the Somoza dynasty, and in 1961 he joined Tomás Borge Martínez and Silvio Mayorga in the formation of the *Frente Sandinista de Liberación Nacional*.

The Political Opposition and the Reforms of the 1960s

Although the student movement of the late 1950s endured repression, and channeled many of its radical elements toward the armed struggle, it could not survive the political reforms of the 1960s.

Following the Cuban Revolution, the U.S. government, under the Kennedy Administration, began a massive sociopolitical offensive in Latin America to curb some of the problems which had resulted in the triumph of Castro in Cuba. The Alliance for Progress was formed, and in many Latin American countries changes were implemented, even though some were only cosmetic.

In Nicaragua, the election of René Schick in February of 1963 was presented as the beginning of a democratic era, and temporary prosperity in the framework of the newly organized Central American Common Market was publicized as a starting point to terminate underdevelopment. The combination of the new internal and international politics created optimism in Nicaragua and forged a hope for the possibility of change through legal avenues. Reformism rapidly grew and effectively curbed the radicalism of the opposition, including the student movement.

In this period, the only opposition group maintaining its radical antiregime attitude was the FSLN. To publicize their analysis of the new political and economic changes under the administration of René Schick and the strong support of the Alliance for Progress for him, a group of Sandinista activists in March 1963 took over a radio station in Managua (Radio Mundial), and broadcast the FSLN statement condemning a meeting held in San José, Costa Rica, between John F. Kennedy and the presidents of Central American countries. The statement strongly opposed the farcical presidential election of February 1963 and the Alliance for Progress in Central America as an imperialistic program to increase the dependency of the region on the United States.[3]

In the northern part of the country, around Río Coco, the FSLN guerrillas began their efforts to mobilize the peasantry. On June 23, 1963, they took over the town of Raiti, and organized a meeting to explain the revolutionary goals to the campesinos.[4] They repeated this form of mobilization in other towns of the area. However, as Carlos Fonseca later pointed out, one of the basic

weaknesses of the movement in the early 1960s was "lack of an adequate revolutionary organization tied with large popular masses and
especially the campesinos."[5]

Lack of a firm support among the peasants resulted in a
military defeat for the FSLN in 1963. Following this failure, the
remaining cadres of the organization decided to concentrate on
intensive work among the masses, both in the cities and the
countryside.

In the early 1960s, the traditional left (Socialist Party) had tried
to organize the peasants in campesino syndicates, especially in the
northern region. These organizations were basically composed of
poor farmers and small landholders who were against Somoza.
However, these syndicates did not include plantation day laborers
who were the main victims of the economic expansion and who
formed the lowest level of the rural social structure. The demands of
the syndicates were basically economic, and they never went beyond
an antidictatorial line and never questioned the social structure.
When the FSLN began its organizational work among the rural
population, the basic goal was mobilization of the most exploited and
the most impoverished sector of the campesinos in the syndicates.
This was seen as the first step to prepare them to join the armed
struggle, and to establish an organic relationship between the
revolutionary organization and the peasant population.[6] Therefore,
although there were some similarities between the methods used
by the FSLN and the traditional left in organizational work in the
countryside, the goals were basically different. Later, when the
anti-Somoza struggle intensified, the campesino syndicates, organized by the PSN, chose a peaceful path in their political activities,
while the peasant organizations, linked with the FSLN, joined
the armed struggle and formed the basis of the guerrilla army in
the countryside.

In the cities, the FSLN was working with the traditional left
more closely in the formation of neighborhood committees. However, even in the cities there was a sharp difference between the mild
demands and pacifist slogans put forward by the PSN, and the agitation work of the FSLN.

During the 1960s the ideology of the FSLN was clearly Marxist.
Fonseca emphasized the need to see the socialist nature of the revolu-

tion, its objective being to "defeat North American imperialism and its local agents, the false opposition and the false revolutionaries."[7] Referring to the power of the bourgeois opposition parties, Fonseca warned the revolutionaries about the danger of the "reactionary capitalist" opposition. He felt they would use the revolutionary insurrection against Somoza as "a ladder to power." He asserted that the revolutionaries had a double goal: to destroy the criminal regime of Somoza, and, at the same time, to prevent the capitalist opposition from obtaining political control by taking advantage of the revolutionary situation.

FSLN and the Catholic Church

In the beginning, the FSLN was deeply suspicious of the Catholic Church. This suspicion was based on two important factors. As Marxists, accepting historical materialism, the founders of the organization could not reconcile their scientific world view with religious beliefs based on metaphysical assumptions. The FSLN approach to religion was still strongly influenced by the orthodox Marxist criticism of religion.

The history of the Catholic Church in Nicaragua was another important factor in forming the FSLN's negative relationship with the Church. The traditional conservatism of the Church hierarchy, its close alliance with the Somoza regime, its historical animosity toward any liberation movement in the region, and its strong anticommunist stand, had logically left it out of any sociopolitical alliance striving for change in the existing situation in Nicaragua.

The first positive contact by the Sandinistas with the religious community occurred about 1966, when Father Arias Caldera, the parish priest of a marginal barrio in Managua, extended his moral and material support to the guerrillas of the FSLN. This contact was of a personal nature, and did not develop into a political alliance.

Ernesto Cardenal was the first priest who attracted the Sandinistas' attention as a potential ally, because of his progressive work in Solentiname. The first contact was established in 1968 when Tomás Borge Martínez wrote a letter to Cardenal inviting him to a meeting to discuss the mutual interests of the FSLN and the progressive clergy. Cardenal accepted the invitation. The first meeting was long and fruitful. Borge questioned Cardenal about the Church hierarchy, and about conservative and reactionary bishops, and expressed his hope for a change in the Church's political stand. Cardenal talked about the struggle, his support for most of the FSLN ideas, and the limitations that his priesthood put on his participation in an armed struggle. Carlos Fonseca and Father Uriel Molina joined the next meeting, and the discussion between the two groups continued.[8]

In the beginning, the Sandinistas were interested in a tactical alliance with the progressive clergy in their antidictatorial activities. To fulfill this alliance, the Frente began a systematic effort to attract progressive Christians into revolutionary politics. For instance, in 1969, an FSLN communiqué used religious terminology and symbolism to reach an audience whose social consciousness was formed in a strong religious tradition.

> Two thousand years ago, there was a redeemer who described his brothers as the persons who did the will of one in heaven, from whom proceeded justice and truth. . . . Augusto César Sandino also called brothers the ones who accompanied him with their rifles in the resistance against yankee aggressors.[9]

The communiqué continued to describe the people who are addressed as brothers by the FSLN.

> The ones who have travelled the difficult path of the combatants sacrificing their life until death in the altar of liberation of the oppressed and exploited. . . . We do not have any brothers but the ones who share the martyrdom for building a new world, a just and free world.

Later, the work of other progressive clergy in poor barrios of Managua, and the positive impact of their work on community organization, particularly among the youth, created more interest in the FSLN for collaboration with the progressive sector of the Church.

Following the 1972 earthquake, which brought a sharp increase in the social involvement of Christian Base Communities, and also the rapid radicalization of a sector of religious community influenced by liberation theology, the Sandinista leadership were convinced that the Christian groups could be integrated into the revolutionary process. The contact between the two increased and took a more systematic form.

Military and Political Work

The social composition of the FSLN in 1966–67 was still basically urban middle class, especially student activists, with a few urban workers in leadership positions and as regular guerrilla fighters. The peasants, while supportive of the FSLN, held no leadership roles, but served as irregular combatants. The low level of social awareness among the peasants and their lack of revolutionary discipline contributed to their absence among the leadership of the organization. Not being prepared for the hardships of guerrilla warfare, the peasants had the tendency to become demoralized by the news of enemy troop movements, scarcity of food, and difficult long marches. Although the FSLN could count on the peasants as mountain guides, suppliers of food and other materials, and informers on National Guard activities, integrating them into the regular guerrilla columns created many problems and even some desertions.[10]

By the late 1960s, the FSLN was still firmly committed to armed struggle as the basic form of revolutionary activity. This commitment was manifested in planning the armed actions in Pancasán, thirty miles east of Matagalpa, in 1967.

The Pancasán campaign of 1967 resulted in military defeat for the FSLN, and the organization lost several of its leaders, including Silvio Mayorga. Politically, however, the FSLN gained from the publicity of the campaign, and the popular recognition of the organization among different social sectors. The campaign was especially important because it took place during a repressive period which followed the massacre of unarmed demonstrators in January 1967 by the National Guard, and an easy victory for Somoza in a farce presidential election. While Somoza was boasting about his absolute power in Nicaragua, the Pancasán battle broke the political tranquility, and loudly announced the continued existence of an armed opposition.

Taking advantage of a favorable popular response to the Pancasán campaign, the remaining leadership of the FSLN opted for political consolidation among the lower and middle classes, both in the cities and the countryside, by forming intermediate organizations which were connected to the FSLN but were not operating under its name. For example, in the urban poor and working-class neighborhoods, *Comités Cívicos Populares* (Popular Civic Committees) were formed to organize the lower classes, and to direct the political discontent among the people toward the FSLN political line. Also in the universities, the *Frente Estudiantil Revolucionario* (FER — Revolutionary Student Front) organized by the FSLN, became a major force after Pancasán, and caused many student activists to become more closely connected with the FSLN.

This new attention toward political work among the poor was a positive development in encouraging a more systematic collaboration with the progressive sector of the Church, which had already begun an organized community work in poor urban barrios, especially in Managua.

The FSLN in the 1970s

Although the FSLN had recognized the importance of political work in both the cities and the countryside, it was still emphasizing rural armed struggle as the focus of the revolutionary activities. Following the military defeat in Pancasán, the leaders of the organization began to study and to discuss the theories of "Prolonged Popular War," and the Chinese and Vietnamese revolutions.

The culmination of extensive political and organizational work among the peasants was the formation of a guerrilla column composed of peasants in Zinica, Matagalpa, in 1970. The Zinica guerrillas' harassment of the National Guard's positions left important government casualties, including the downing of a helicopter gunship. For the first time, Somoza's National Guard was unable to destroy a guerrilla column.

The Zinica campaign instilled self-confidence in the local peasants, and opened the way for a thorough class struggle against the regime in the countryside. Recognizing the improving ties between the FSLN and the peasant population in the area, the National Guard launched a systematic terror campaign against the campesinos, to intimidate the guerrilla supporters. However, the intensified repression backfired, and encouraged many more peasants to cooperate with the FSLN.

The beginning of the 1970s was also a period of economic crisis and political unrest in the cities. The disruption of the Central American Common Market in 1969 following the war between El Salvador and Honduras, and the maturation of inherent weaknesses in developmental policies based on an unstable regional market and a dependent industrial sector, shattered the promising picture of the 1960s. In the political arena, the repression of 1967 and the termination of the limited democracy of the 1960s ended hopes for reforms through legal avenues, and added to political discontent among different sectors of the population.

Although still invisible in the cities, the FSLN cadres, having established themselves in various student organizations, workers unions, and neighborhood committees, could organize a series of protest actions on behalf of political prisoners. The student movement, partly organized by the *Frente*, played a major role in this period. For instance, in May and June 1970, mothers of political prisoners, mobilized by university students, carried out a hunger strike demanding the release of political prisoners, and in September a massive national protest swept through all major cities. In January 1971, when the cost of transportation was raised in León, students and workers mobilized demonstrations. More hunger strikes followed in April, and peasant groups began a protest campaign against National Guard repression in the north. Angered by the wave of demonstrations in most of the cities of the Pacific Coast and the northern zone, Somoza sent helicopter gunships to suppress protests in Matagalpa in May. However, far from halting the movement, the government actions intensified the wave of political unrest, and throughout 1971 and 1972 more hunger strikes and protest marches demanding the release of political prisoners occurred, along with student and worker demonstrations against price hikes in the major cities.[11]

The earthquake of December 1972 further deepened the sociopolitical crisis and resulted in many spontaneous economic and political protests, especially in Managua. Job insecurity, a drop in real wages, and longer work days, combined with the general deterioration of living conditions and public services, stimulated workers activities in 1973–74.

In this period, organized labor, affiliated with different political parties, broadened its bases and added some political goals to its economic demands. The basic force among the labor unions following the earthquake was the Confederación General de Trabajo-Independiente (CGT-I) of the Socialist Party (PSN). The successful hospital and construction workers' strikes of 1973, organized by the CGT-I, increased the political influence of the PSN among the workers.

The Sandinistas, still mainly based in the northern mountains, could not directly lead the urban workers movement. Their main leverage among the workers was the strong backing which the Sandinista student organization (FER) gave to the strikes, and its attempt to put forward a more radical political line to encourage the workers to surpass the economic demands and slogans of the PSN. However, the increasing influence of the reformist political parties in the workers movement was manifested by the participation of the CGT-I and the CTN (Central de Trabajadores de Nicaragua) in UDEL (Unión Democrático de Liberación) in late 1974.

On December 27, 1974, a successful and well-publicized guerrilla action, launched by a FSLN commando unit, changed the general atmosphere and temporarily turned the political balance within the opposition in favor of the FSLN.

On the night of December 27, a group of Sandinista fighters attacked and seized the house of José María Castillo Quant, a close friend of Somoza and the ex-minister of agriculture. At the time of the attack, a Christmas party was taking place in the house, and members of the Somoza and other ruling families were taken hostage by the guerrillas, who demanded the release of eighteen imprisoned Sandinistas, a ransom fund, and public broadcasting of their message to the Nicaraguan people. The head of the guerrilla unit later explained the goals of the commandos.

> In addition to the concrete aim of the operation, which was the release of 18 imprisoned Sandinistas, the action had other goals; [to trigger] a destructive strike against Somoza dictatorship, and to communicate to the world the tragic situation of Nicaragua as a result of the government repression, administrative corruption, and other grave abuses. . . . [12]

Seeing the lives of some of his most important friends and advisors in danger, Somoza agreed to meet the demands of the FSLN guerrillas, including the broadcasting of the FSLN communiqué by the mass media. Analyzing the historical development of the dynasty and the opposition forces, the communiqué discussed the role of armed struggle as the only effective way to overthrow the dictatorship and to build a new independent Nicaragua.

The immediate success of the operation, in freeing the imprisoned guerrillas and gaining access to the mass media, had a tremendous impact on the people. They could see the vulnerability of the dictator when faced with a determined armed group of guerrillas. However, the positive results of the operation for the FSLN did not last very long. The repression which followed took a heavy toll on the organization. Somoza declared a state of siege, and used all the forces at his disposal to crush the organization.

The guerrillas, particularly in the cities, were repeatedly ambushed by the army, and many members and leaders were killed or arrested in 1975-76. Intensified repression forced the FSLN into extreme secrecy in its operations, and internal communication became more difficult. The result was the isolation of teams operating in different regions. The new communication difficulties and the old debate over the strategy of the organization (political work among the lower classes, especially in the cities, versus guerrilla operations based in the rural areas) gradually caused the formation of diverse political factions and finally a three way split in the organization.

The first faction, formed in 1975, was known as Proletarian Tendency. It emerged from urban guerrilla teams, with the leadership of intellectuals and academics. Their strategy was based on intensive political work among urban workers, preparing them for the upcoming revolution. This faction was criticized by the rest of the Sandinistas for its excessive emphasis on orthodox Marxism and political propaganda, as opposed to guerrilla operations.

The second faction believed in a Prolonged People's War (Guerra Popular Prolongada — GPP) and the implementation of the tactics of the Chinese and Vietnamese revolutions. It was chiefly composed of the remaining old leadership of the FSLN based in the northern mountains. Its cautious strategy of accumulating forces before engaging in a major confrontation with the regime was criticized by the other factions.

The *Terceristas* (third force) was formed in 1976–77. In contrast to the other two factions, both emphasizing Marxism as their ideology, the *Terceristas* relaxed the Marxist rigor of the original Sandinistas and opened their ranks to non-Marxist and bourgeois elements of the anti-Somoza opposition. Their main objective was to broaden the support base of the FSLN among different sectors of the society and to prepare the ground for a popular armed uprising. They were criticized for their excessive emphasis on urban guerrilla operations and a lack of ideological purity. All three factions continued their work under the name of FSLN until March 7, 1979, when they were all again united in one single organization.[13]

Radicalization of the Christian Base Communities in Managua

Although the process of consciousness-raising had started in some poor barrios of Managua by the end of the 1960s, and a few Christian Base Communities had been formed, the earthquake of December 1972 was an important factor in the radicalization of the Christian activists in Managua, especially the priests and nuns working in the poor barrios. Rampant government corruption and scandalous abuses of international relief funds and materials were most strongly felt in the lower-class neighborhoods of Managua, and in many cases shocked the priests and nuns who were working hard to help the people endure the disastrous situation. For many Church members, the earthquake was a turning point in their religious beliefs and their sociopolitical standing. Some of them had already begun questioning the structures which gave a major part of social benefits to a few, and left the majority in total misery and subhuman living conditions. During the weeks and months following the earthquake, close contact with government agencies, and personal experience with corruption, created a tremendous anger among these religious people, and added to their desire to find the roots of the problem and ways to deal with it.

The life of Maria Hartman, a North American nun of St. Agnes Congregation, working in Nicaragua since 1962, is a good illustration of the process of profound change in the religious beliefs and sociopolitical activities of many Church members during the 1970s in Nicaragua.

Maria came to Nicaragua to teach Nicaraguan children in Catholic schools. Like many other nuns, she was only in contact with the upper-class Nicaraguans who could send their children to private Catholic schools. Therefore, the initial experience of life in Managua for Maria was the tremendous wealth and the comfortable lifestyle of the upper class. In 1964, she went to Puerto Cabeza on the Atlantic Coast of Nicaragua, and then to Waspán, a small town on the Río Coco shore, which was the center of the Miskito Indian population.

The living conditions in Waspán were very different from those that Maria had experienced earlier in Managua. Many Miskito Indians working in the mines, owned by the North Americans and the Canadians, were sent to their villages when they became ill with tuberculosis. There was no protection for them or their communities, no medical care, no workman's compensation, no social benefits. They were sent home to die. For the first time, Maria began to question her work and that of the other members of the Church.

> Our work was not enough. We did help, but we didn't do anything to really alleviate that suffering. It was like saying, 'God loves you, you are poor but God loves you.' What they really needed was for us to find more food or to talk about why people have to live like that.[14]

Maria returned to Managua with many questions in her mind. She began to work in the parish of barrio Riguero of Managua. She joined the parish about the same time that Father Molina had come back to Managua after studying theology in Europe. In early 1970, a group of university students came to the barrio to live and work with the community and to deepen their own understanding of social realities by working with the poor and studying the roots of the existing social problems.

For Maria, the contact with liberation theology, through discussions with Father Molina, contact with the university students, and most importantly, her experience while living in Waspán, and now in Riguero, were basic forces which opened her eyes to the social realities.[15] Talking about the group discussions and Bible courses,

Maria later recalled:

> The course opened my eyes. I saw the Bible for the first time
> from the point of view of the situation we lived in. We studied the
> book of Exodus, where God say, 'I have seen the suffering of my
> people, and I am going to save them, free them.' And then we
> thought about the suffering of the people right around us, in the
> barrio. We listened to them, it was quite a testimony . . . what they
> lived, their problems and their faith that something could
> be done.[16]

Then came the earthquake. Maria and the other Church
members, through their contacts with international religious
organizations, knew that the relief materials and funds were pouring
into Nicaragua from other countries. Also through their daily experiences, they knew that the aid was not reaching the people. "You just
became angry and angry inside."[17] They did all they could do legally
to get the relief materials for the people. It was all in vain. A few
months later, Maria became seriously ill and had to go back to the
United States for medical treatment. In the United States, she met
the people and organizations who had sent aid to Nicaragua. When
she began to tell them that the aid never reached the people,
Somoza's friends and agents began a campaign of denouncing her as
a liar. Frightened by the possibility of not being allowed to go back
to Nicaragua, Maria kept her silence.

Returning to Nicaragua, Maria went back to Riguero. Most
of the university students had already gone underground in clandestine activities, but their persistent work of consciousness-raising
and their unselfish services to the community had left a group of
Christians with a more clear political vision and an active support
for the FSLN. This support was manifested in different ways, including demonstrations, occupation of churches, and demands for the
release of political prisoners. In response to the demonstrations
and church occupations, the National Guard increased its repressive activity.

Maria's anger about the situation and her enthusiasm to change
it were the basic reasons for her positive response to a call for help
from the FSLN. First, she was asked to take medicine to the jail for
prisoners, and then to the mountains for the fighters.[18] She was very

much impressed with the courage and unselfish work of the members of the FSLN.

> The people who were most active were the people who were willing to take risks. They had given up their comfortable life style. They were living clandestinely. The conditions were miserable, always with the risk of not knowing whether they were going to be alive for the victory or not. To me it was just an unselfish love.[19]

Maria helped the FSLN, believing that Nicaragua needed a profound change that "would bring the people, the poor and oppressed, a voice in the government. They would gain their dignity and necessary conditions to live a human life."[20] She was not concerned about the ideological differences between herself and some of the FSLN members, who did not believe in God. She was confident that every true Christian would participate in the revolution: "This is what God would have done and Christ would have done."[21]

Maria was not alone in the process of reaching a new dimension in her faith in the light of deplorable social reality. Many other nuns and priests went through a similar process, following their experience with the disastrous situation created by the earthquake and government corruption and repression. The Sisters of Assumption, in barrio San Juda, and the Maryknoll Sisters in barrio OPEN 3, are other examples of a gradual change from a quiet religious life to active participation in the social upheaval in the country.

The Process of Radicalization in Barrio Riguero, 1972–77

Meanwhile, the radicalization of the Christian Base Communities in barrio Riguero of Managua was continuing. Following the earthquake, the university students working with Father Molina came to the barrio to help the community clean up the neighborhood and repair the earthquake damage to houses and business centers. They also mobilized the barrio's youth into work brigades to provide different services for the people. Following a period of intensive work to help the Riguero community, some of the university students left the barrio to begin a clandestine life as fighters for the FSLN. However, their unselfish community work and their devotion to social programs left a long-lasting impression in the neighborhood and encouraged active support for the FSLN.

The pro-Sandinista Christian communities in barrio Riguero later joined the national campaign of occupying the churches as a form of political protest. This form of political action, which was initiated by the pro-Sandinista student organizations in early 1970, gained increasing importance following the earthquake, when it was adopted by the Christian Base Communities all over the country.

Following the earthquake, the residents of Riguero began gathering in the streets of the barrio every night, singing protest songs and reading biblical passages or poetry. Then they organized demonstration marches in the barrio calling on the people to join the struggle and to unite. At the beginning, the National Guard was indifferent to the gatherings, but after a few months, repressive measures were taken to stop the community mobilization. First the Guard used tear gas and, later, bullets. When it became impossible to mobilize in the streets, the people began to gather in the church for overnight vigils continuing until dawn. As the repression intensified, the church gatherings became more politically radical.

Following the earthquake, Father Fernando Cardenal, a Jesuit priest and a supporter of the FSLN,[22] joined the community and participated in the founding of the Revolutionary Christian Movement.

The movement was initially formed around the Riguero community and was independent from the FSLN. Most of the founders of the Movement were university students who had worked with Father Molina in the barrio since 1970. The experience of one of the original members of the Movement, Monica Baltodano, who later became an active member of the FSLN, is an example of a process most of these activists went through.

Monica began her activities as a member of a Christian group founded by progressive clergy, including Fernando Cardenal. As a Christian activist, she became aware of social realities and necessity of change, "not only an internal [individual] change, but a change in structure."[23] She later accepted the necessity of armed struggle, and joined the FSLN in 1973 and began her political work for the organization.

Another FSLN member, Dulce María Guillén, also began her political activities as a member of a Christian group.

> We were working in Christian groups. . . . We spent a lot of time in meetings of Christian youth, and in group reflections until 1972, when we faced the necessity of a more effective struggle for freedom of political prisoners.[24]

The Christian groups decided on a hunger strike in the cathedral. The hunger strike was cut short by the December earthquake. Following the earthquake, Dulce María and other members of the group became involved in intensive community work to help the victims. This social involvement raised their awareness of sociopolitical problems, and intensified their confrontation with the corrupt government. Dulce María and many other Christian youth joined the Revolutionary Christian Movement. The next step, joining the FSLN, came as a logical development in this process of political radicalization. As Dulce María later recalled:

> It was necessary. The FSLN was the vanguard of the anti-dictatorial struggle, and an isolated group [Revolutionary Christian Movement] could not play any relevant role [if not connected with the vanguard]. If we really wanted to do something and to participate in the revolutionary process we had to do it under the leadership of the FSLN, and as part of the political and military vanguard. First it was a matter of political identification. The leadership [of the Revolutionary Christian Movement] directly joined [the FSLN], and later, little by little, the rest of us joined. There were some compañeros who did not join. They did not have the clarity of the conditions. The cadres were chosen according to the guidelines [for membership] set up by the Frente at this time.[25]

The Movement later became an intermediate organization serving as a major pool for FSLN recruitment. Its basic task was to integrate "a large number of Christians in the revolutionary process."[26] In 1975, in a statement published by the *Gaceta Sandinista*, the

Movement declared:

> Being situated in the process of liberation of our people, the
> *Movimiento cristiano* identifies with the *Frente Sandinista de Liberación*
> *Nacional*-FSLN. . . . The Movement was born as a historical syn-
> thesis of the Latin American Christian movements emerging out
> of the necessity to respond to the authentic realities of the [Chris-
> tian] message of the Kingdom of God.[27]

The Movement clearly accepted and made use of class analysis,
and in the ongoing class struggle in Nicaragua took sides with the
lower classes, the oppressed, against the capitalist class, the oppressor. In the same statement published in *Gaceta Sandinista*, in 1975, the
Movement asserted:

> The struggle is for peace, for real order based on justice, and con-
> struction of a socio-economic system in which man lives as a
> human being. [However,] the construction requires struggle
> against injustice, hunger, misery and exploitation of the majority
> [of our people]. This struggle of popular sectors requires confront-
> ing the capitalist system, today in its highest stage of imperialism;
> and against its Nicaraguan intermediaries, criollo oligarchy, and in
> all forms of struggle: economic, political, ideological and military.[28]

To recruit others to the Movement, some of the members of the
Riguero community left to live in other poor barrios of Managua.
By the mid-1970s, the Movement had adherents in most of the lower-
class neighborhoods, including San Judas, Ducalu, Larreznaga, La
Fuenta, Catorce de Septiembre, and Nicarao.

One of the coordinators of the Revolutionary Christian Movement, Roberto Gutiérrez (later vice-minister in the Ministry of
Agriculture and Agrarian Reform), later explained the work in different barrios.

> We carried out a kind of investigation into the main problems
> of each barrio: water, electricity, transportation, health . . . and
> then started mobilizing people around these problems. We worked
> to reframe the religious ideas of each community, usually through
> the priest or other well-respected members. We promoted a more

political reading of the Bible and connected that to discussions about the problems in the community. The idea was to have the Christian base communities become community organizations which would begin to deal with the barrio's problems and would thus constitute a kind of leadership for the barrio. And that's exactly what happened in most cases.

The work in the barrio had a tremendous impact on the people and the political struggle in Nicaragua. It was not well known because most of the work had to be clandestine, even when the comrades didn't belong to the Front. The repressive conditions in Nicaragua forced us to work secretly, underground. We recruited many of those involved in the base communities to the Front and others became collaborators by lending their houses, etc. . . . We also started organizing Christian groups in high schools. . . . We recruited some people and organized them as leadership in the schools. We managed to mobilize the schools around their problems.[29]

Later, the collaboration of the Christian Base Communities in Riguero with the FSLN took a more concrete form. The Sandinistas were allowed to use the parish buildings for their meetings and some of the FSLN leaders, including Tomás Borge Martínez, had long conversations with the members of the communities and Uriel Molina in Riguero. Both sides agreed on the necessity of recruiting the Christian youth for the struggle.

The new recruits continued their consciousness-raising work among the Christians. They talked to the people about the situation in Nicaragua, saying that they "were not predestined to live this way, that it wasn't God who wanted it."[30] They pushed the people "to look for solutions to the problems."[31] They also initiated an intensive ideological campaign to show other Christians the necessity to join the struggle. In an article published by *La Gaceta Sandinista* in October 1975 in Managua, they stated:

Facing a situation of social sin and the class struggle in our country we, the Christians, have to clarify our role and to participate, in the most effective manner, in the ongoing struggle for the elimination of the structures which generate exploitation of man by man. . . .

The high-ranking clergy has not taken the role corresponding
to its position as the apostles of Christ. It has sided with the dominant classes by voicing only timid protests, or even worse, by justifying the actions against our people [by dominant classes].[32]

The decision to work closely with the Christian communities
and to recruit among the Christian youth had an ideological aspect.
The FSLN knew that the majority of Nicaraguans were Christian
and would not easily accept Marxism. But what was important at the
time was recruiting anti-Somoza elements who were ready to fight
against the dictatorship. According to the testimonies of many
Christians who joined the FSLN, the organization never put any
pressure on its members to reject their Christian beliefs. In many
cases, the FSLN members continued to be believers; and if they
rejected their religious ideas, it was an individual choice, not an
organization policy.

José David Chavarría Roca, another member of the Riguero
Christian Community who later joined the FSLN (and who is now
a member of the Sandinista Popular Army), never lost his faith in
God. Talking about his decision to join the FSLN, he later
explained: "I never felt far from the Church. I had rediscovered within
me a faith that was becoming more concrete, taking shape through
practice."[33] Before the triumph, he was arrested by the National
Guard for his connection with the FSLN. From jail he wrote to
Father Molina assuring him that his faith was alive and that he
would be following Christian teachings in all fields of struggle.[34]

For many people, both in religious circles and among the Marxists, the close collaboration between the Christians and the Marxists
in the FSLN is still an unanswered puzzle. But for the Christians
who joined the Marxists in the process of the revolution, the puzzle
did not exist. Alvaro Baltodano, a former member of the Riguero
Christian community (now head of the Office of Combat
Preparedness and the military training centers of the Sandinista
Popular Army), later explained it this way:

Whether there was a God or not, wasn't the concern. The concern was the practical politics we were involved in and how our
Christianity got expressed. For us to be Christian meant to work
with those who were poorest and at that time it meant working

with the Sandinista Front. That gave us the possibility of helping liberate the people and working towards a different world, the kind of world that the Bible talks about.[35]

For many Nicaraguan Christians, joining the FSLN in its fight against Somoza was a necessary step in proving their belief in the Bible, and in fulfilling their historical role and their religious commitment to the Kingdom of God. As Alvaro Baltodano later said:

> We read the Bible, studied liberation theology and discovered that if you really read the Bible with your eyes open you find that the history of the Hebrew people is a history of their fight for liberation. When you read about the life of Jesus Christ, you realize that whether he was or wasn't God, he was a man who was with the poor and who fought for the freedom of the poor.[36]

Reflecting the beliefs of the Christians in barrio Riguero, and of the members of other Christian Base Communities, the Revolutionary Christian Movement, in 1975, declared:

> To eliminate oppression and exploitation, Christianity joins with revolutionary forces as a united power which tries to return dignity to dehumanized man. We join the oppressed in their struggle which is the only way to liberate the exploited as well as the exploiter, because only breaking with the relations based on exploitation of man by man can we construct the new man and the new society.[37]

It was not only the Christians who reached the conclusion that they should work with the Marxists to overthrow the dictatorship and to build a new society; the Marxists, in their own analysis of the Nicaraguan reality, were aware of the indispensability of an alliance with the Christians in the revolutionary process. As *Comandante* Oscar Turcios, one of the top leaders of the FSLN, told Father Fernando Cardenal in the early 1970s:

> I don't care that you believe that there is another life after this one, or that you have other religious ideas. So it shouldn't matter to you that I believe that this life is all there is. What should matter to both of us is that we can work together to build a new nation.[38]

Tomás Borge Martínez also very much in favor of close collaboration with the Christians.

> I always held the view that over the long term it is possible in Nicaragua for progressive Christians and revolutionaries to live together. The participation of the Church seemed to me to be essential to avoid a situation where, after the fall of the tyranny, there might be a great bloodbath, a massacre. . . . Hatred had accumulated for so many years and I was afraid that an uncontrollable violence would be unleashed against the *Somocistas*, the Guard.[39]

The gradual alliance between the Marxists of the FSLN and the Christian Base Communities, which had started in the beginning of the 1970s, continued well into the second half of the decade. Many Christian activists who had joined the FSLN gained leadership positions in the organizations, and the FSLN gradually was converted to an organization of revolutionaries with different personal beliefs, all rallying together to overthrow an anti-Christian, anti-Marxist dictatorship and to build a new society based on common ideas of Christianity and Marxism.

The Christian Base Communities in Riguero and other poor neighborhoods of Managua were instrumental in the process of building the strategic alliance between the FSLN and the Nicaraguan Christians. As Luis Carrión, one of the members of the university student group working in barrio Riguero (and now commander of the revolution and a member of the national leadership of the FSLN) explained following the triumph:

> The communities played three important roles. They were recruiting grounds and places for propaganda. They were very important in that they served to break the myth about a conflict between Christianity and Sandinistas. The communities also spread a version of Christianity that favored the interests of the people.[40]

The close connection between Riguero Christian Base Communities and the FSLN, and the important role played by Father Molina in the barrio, made him an ideal target for government repression. He and other progressive priests were branded as "Communist priests," and government officials, including the chief of the Police of Managua, Roberto Cranshaw Guerra, publicly declared that "it is necessary to begin killing the Marxist priests in the country."[41] Cranshaw continued:

> We accuse and blame all the red-cassock priests for the violence and death of the youths. [They] directly or indirectly lead the youth toward armed struggle, and in this way offer their services to Castro and his guerrillas.[42]

Cranshaw went on to specify individual names, including, "Father Uriel Molina Oliu, Vincente Cauleli, Ernesto Cardenal, Fernando Cardenal, some Capuchin and Jesuit priests, and the nuns of *La Asunción* order," as being involved in "subversive activities and collaboration with the elements which work against the national peace."[43] In another part of his interview, Cranshaw announced the formation of an anticommunist organization, *Mano Blanca*, which was created by the elements from the army, civilians, and members of the private sector. According to Cranshaw, *Mano Blanca* had a list of "progressive elements who will be eliminated."[44] However, these accusations actually mobilized a large number of people and religious authorities in support of Molina and other progressive priests.

The Process of Radicalization in Barrio OPEN 3, 1972–77.

Another case of radicalization of Christian groups and their religious leaders in Managua in the 1970s was the example of the barrio OPEN 3, and the Maryknoll Sisters who worked in the area as missionaries since 1969.[45] OPEN 3 (now called Ciudad Sandino) was a small and extremely poor slum located west of downtown Managua prior to the earthquake.[46] It grew rapidly during 1973 with the influx of displaced persons from other barrios of Managua. The Christian Youth Club of the barrio, formed by the Maryknoll Sisters prior to the earthquake, played an important role in the distribution of the relief materials for a few weeks. Then the government took over the relief efforts, and the supplies into the barrio virtually ceased. This was a first-hand experience with government corruption both for the Maryknoll Sisters and the Christian youths.

The influx of the jobless, homeless people into OPEN 3 continued, and the barrio grew to a densely populated neighborhood with more than thirty thousand inhabitants. Located about twelve kilometers west of Managua's center, OPEN 3 was connected with the capital by dirt roads. Not even one paved road existed in the barrio. Most of the houses did not have electricity, and nobody had potable water. OPEN 3 was so poor that the inhabitants lacked even a cemetery to bury their dead. By the mid-1970s, more than 50% of the barrio's adult population was unemployed. Malnutrition and lack of health care resulted in a very high infant mortality rate, 330 per 1000.[47]

Barrio OPEN 3 was not the only one in Managua suffering from miserable living conditions. Many other neighborhoods shared OPEN 3's agony and first-hand experience with government corruption, which created a general atmosphere of anger and frustration among the residents of Managua, especially the marginal population. Popular anger against intolerable conditions was demonstrated in scattered protest actions and workers' strikes. However, severe repression and lack of leadership were basic obstacles to the formation of an organized active opposition among the lower classes.

In this atmosphere of public frustration, the guerrilla operation of December 27, 1974, acted as a strong catalyst to break the myth of the absolute power of the regime, and the passive nature of the popular opposition to Somoza.[48] The FSLN communiqué, which was broadcast by the mass media, had a profound effect on the people. The communiqué began with a general history of Nicaragua, the nature of the Somoza regime, and a descriptive analysis of the opposition groups and past actions of the FSLN. Defining the role of different sectors in the revolutionary process, the communiqué praised the role played by the progressive sector of the Catholic Church and condemned the government repression against the Church.

> An important sector of the Catholic Church and some elements of other Churches are persecuted by the repressive police as a consequence of their identification with the poor, wounded, and exploited sectors of our people.[49]

Referring to the revolutionary Christians, the FSLN declared:

> The Sandinista Front of National Liberation [FSLN]
> expresses its warmest sympathy for the revolutionary Christians
> who are salvaging the good name of the Nicaraguan Church and
> have identified themselves with the best messages of Christ.[50]

The FSLN's successful action of December 1974 created tremendous support among the Nicaraguan lower and middle classes. This well-publicized operation demonstrated to the people that the "dictator was vulnerable,"[51] and the myth of Somoza's omnipotence was broken. The action was welcomed among the members of the Christian Base Communities. In OPEN 3, the residents were "filled with jubilation" when the report came in over the radio; as one Maryknoll Sister said, "It was like hearing our own salvation history."[52] The people listened to the FSLN leaders review the preceding twenty years of Nicaraguan history, detailing injustices of the regime and the struggle of the opposition. As Dodson and Montgomery, two Latin American experts, observed:

> With this success, the Frente gained stature in barrios such
> as OPEN 3, Riguero, 14 de Septiembre, and San Judas, while
> Somoza lost face, and ordinary people had a glimpse of the possibil-
> ity that popular opposition could be effective against his regime.[53]

The residents of Managua manifested their joy and support for the FSLN by crowding the road to the airport to cheer the commando unit and the released FSLN members leaving the country for Cuba, accompanied by the Archbishop of Managua, Miguel Obando y Bravo, who had played an important role as a mediator in negotiations for the release of the hostages and the prisoners.

As previously discussed, following the FSLN operation in December, Somoza stepped up repression and declared a state of siege and martial law all over the country. However, intensified repression did not restrain the popular opposition's increasing radicalization.

The experience of the Maryknoll Sisters living and working in barrio OPEN 3 of Managua is a good illustration of the increasing involvement of the Christian groups and their religious leaders in the anti-Somoza struggle.

In its two-year formation program for preparing missionaries, the Maryknoll Order did not include any political courses or formal classes on liberation theology until the mid-1970s. The sisters would develop their own political understanding and social direction in the place of their missions in accordance with the sociopolitical environment and their own personal interests. In an interview conducted in Managua in September, 1981, one of the Maryknoll Sisters working in Nicaragua for several years explained: "I went to Nicaragua to help the people. I didn't have any definite political view at the time." But living with the people and experiencing the life of the poor taught many of the Maryknoll Sisters that they could not solve people's problems by giving them limited health care or education. The challenge was much greater than they expected or were prepared to deal with. Endless questions about the roots of the problems and possible solutions forced the sisters to study liberation theology, different socioeconomic systems, and the history and the political structure of the country. "Study was very helpful," one of the sisters explained, "but the main thing was living experience which would tell you something was wrong. The most basic needs of the people wouldn't be met, couldn't be met."[54]

One of the most pressing problems of the barrio was the lack of potable water. Finally, in June 1976, the water company decided to provide running water for OPEN 3.

> Everybody was happy. The hook up fees were small. But when the first bills came in, the whole barrio began to realize that they were paying three times as much that the people were paying in Managua.[55]

The people were outraged. There was a spontaneous movement in the barrio to struggle against the water company. Every day the people gathered in the streets of the barrio to protest the prices, and to ask other residents to refuse to pay the water bills. The neighborhood had never been organized before, and this was its first organized struggle, as it was for the Maryknoll Sisters. "For me it was a tremendous opportunity," one of the sisters reported.

> It was a lesson and a unique experience to watch a people having moved collectively, the way they organized, the risks they were willing to take in order to cut the prices, and how it gave them a sense of themselves.[56]

For the sisters it was "a concrete type of coming together of political thought, political action, organization, theological and gospel understanding."[57]

Evaluating the movement as just, and its demands as rightful, the nuns decided to stay with the people and accompany them in their struggle to cut the water prices. Although the sisters' decision resulted in some criticism by more conservative sectors, and condemnation by the government, it was in accordance with their religious beliefs and their organizational policies. The Maryknoll Constitution reads:

> As religious women called to participate in the mission of the Church, we see evangelization not only as proclaiming the Good News with truth, clarity and challenge, but also as witnessing brotherhood of all men in Christ, and to denounce that which deprives man of his legitimate claims for dignity, equality, sharing and friendship.[58]

Therefore, when the struggle began in OPEN 3, the sisters saw it as their religious duty to join the community.

The sisters were not the only group in the religious community of the barrio to participate in the people's struggle. The majority of the parish team, including the Jesuit Fathers of OPEN 3, agreed to join the movement. Parish buildings were used for the meetings and demonstrations, and parish authorities were present in the coordinating committee.[59] And when the government repression intensified to stop the struggle, the sisters and the priests suffered the consequences along with the other residents of the barrio, feeling the atmosphere of terror created by the government in the neighborhood.[60]

The demonstrations continued, and after three months the government and the water company backed down and the price of water was cut in half. But the greatest achievement of the water struggle was the people's realization of their power when acting collectively.

The struggle continued. Barrio residents now organized to gain a cemetery for the neighborhood.

> They had been promised [by the government] for years, to get a piece of [public] land for the cemetery but the lot was never handed over to the barrio. Therefore, the people occupied the land, cleared it and buried two dead children. After fifteen days, the Guard came and unburied the children, which was a terrible scandal in Nicaragua.[61]

The angry people continued to protest and to bury bodies on the same site, and finally they were successful in gaining for the barrio the legal title to the cemetery.

A few months later, in December 1977, the OPEN 3 residents organized again, this time to change the worsening conditions of public transportation in the area. The few buses that served the barrio were so crowded that the people had to hang from the doors. It took them two hours to get to Managua by bus, compared to fifteen minutes by car. The barrio residents had unsuccessfully petitioned the government authorities for six years to get more buses. And finally, when they organized a peaceful demonstration in Managua, the police attacked, beating up the demonstrators. Three of the Maryknoll Sisters were with the barrio residents at the time of attack. A few days later, the National Guard attacked OPEN 3 residents in front of the parish church. They also attacked a group of nuns and priests in front of the Maryknolls' house in the barrio, beating up a priest, two nuns, and a lay missioner, screaming, "You're the cause of all this disorder and subversion, you Communist priests."[62] Although shaken by the experience, the Maryknoll Sisters decided to continue their participation in the movement. In a letter addressing the Nicaraguan people, they wrote:

> We cannot sit with our arms crossed in our convents, as some have said we should. Our role is to be with the people in their struggle to achieve a life of dignity and justice. Our commitment urges us to accompany the growth of the Kingdom of God in the midst of our communities, always among the poor of Nicaragua.[63]

The process of politicization intensified when the OPEN 3 struggle gained the attention of and received help from the members of the Revolutionary Christian Movement, which was very active at the time. The influx of people from different barrios and different organizations opened up a tremendous atmosphere of discussion and learning for the residents of OPEN 3. Therefore, it was a combination of "practice, study, discussion, and praying with the Christian community," which deepened the religious beliefs and social practices of the Maryknoll Sisters in OPEN 3. They even began to study Marxism, finding Marxist analysis useful for understanding the ongoing struggle in the country. They were fully aware of the controversy of using an analysis apart from its philosophical framework. But as one of them explained later:

> When you are working in practice, it doesn't become a very big issue. It becomes an issue of you seeing in Marx and others as tools and aids to understand what is going on in the country.[64]

Radicalization in San Pablo Parish

In the early 1970s, the San Pablo parish organized youth movements and courses of *concientización*. The themes about social and political realities were emphasized, and outside speakers such as Pedro Joaquín Chamorro, Fernando Cardenal, and Uriel Molina were invited to lecture. In late 1972, for example, the *concientización* courses covered themes such as rights and responsibilities of man and his mission in the world, the mission of Christians in the existing situation in Latin America, the family, work and progress, Christians and politics, and peace and justice. Biblical texts and documents of Vatican II and the Medellín conference, pastoral letters, and papal encyclicals were used for discussions.

In addition to *concientización* courses, San Pablo communities participated in the antidictatorial movement and demonstrations against the hike in bus fare in 1971 and the increase of milk prices in 1972. These actions resulted in government repression which brought fear to the community. Some members, especially parents fearful of endangering their children, pulled out of the movement and discouraged their children's participation. According to Rosa

María Pochet, the Costa Rican sociologist who later studied the San Pablo community in detail, the membership dropped rapidly around 1973. However, the remaining members "deepened their social and political commitment."[65] Study of liberation theology intensified and members increased their involvement in antidictatorial activities.

At the time of the insurrection in 1978–79, San Pablo communities had already passed through years of active confrontation with the regime. The insurrection drew the whole community together. The youth built barricades and fought the National Guard, and their parents created a vast network of support for the fighters.

Following the triumph of the revolution on July 19, 1979, the communities' activities and social and political involvement continued and intensified, although they took a new form.

Rural Population and the Catholic Church

To understand the Church's activities in the countryside we have to study the local conditions and the roots of tremendous disparity between urban and rural conditions in Nicaragua.

Geographically, Nicaragua's 57,143 square miles (about the size of Michigan) is divided into three distinct zones: the Pacific one, consisting of the most populated provinces of Chinandega and León (in the north), Managua, Masaya, Granada, Carazo (in the center), and Rivas (in the south); the interior or Central Zone, with Nueva Segovia and Madriz provinces (in the north), Estelí, Jinotega, Matagalpa (in the center), and Boaco, Chontales, and a part of the Río San Juan province (in the south); and finally the Atlantic zone (Caribbean Coast), which consists of Zelaya and the Río San Juan provinces.[66]

According to government statistics of 1979, the majority of the 2,644,161 Nicaraguans lived in the Pacific zone, about 28% of them in the Department of Managua. Although the Atlantic zone consists of 56.2% of the total area, it had only 8.17% of the total population. According to the same statistics, the Pacific zone, with only 15.4% of the land, accounted for 62.5% of the population; and the Central zone, with 28.4% of land, had 29.3% of the population.

Table 3
Population, Area, and Density (1979)[67]

Zones	Population	% of population	Area in km²	% of area	Density in km²
Republic	2,644,161	100.0	118,404	100.0	22
Pacific	1,652,897	62.5	18,219	15.4	91
Central	775,053	29.3	33,597	28.4	23
Atlantic	216,211	8.2	66,588	56.2	3

As shown in table 3, the average population density of the country in 1979 was 22 persons per square kilometer, ranging from 91 persons per square kilometer in the Pacific zone to 3 in the Atlantic zone.

Since 1950, an important shift in the population distribution has been visible in Nicaragua. More and more people live in the Pacific zone in contrast to a very slow rate of population growth in other regions. Two major factors are responsible for the concentration of the population in the Pacific zone, especially Managua: first, the excellent agricultural soil of the region; and second, the government policy to modernize the West Coast, especially Managua, resulting in a concentration of urban services and the best communication system and road network in and around the capital. According to the 1979 statistics, 50% of the total roads of the country and 63% of all paved roads were located in the Pacific zone, while the Atlantic zone had only 8.9% of the total roads and 3.6% of the paved roads.[68]

Table 4
Roads of Nicaragua (1979)[69]

Zones	Total	Type of road (kilometers)			
		paved	coated	all year	dry season
Republic	18,238.5	1,612.1	2,585.1	4,663.8	9,377.5
Pacific	9,134.1	1,018.9	986.6	1,611.9	5,516.7
Central	7,469.8	535.0	1,429.2	2,251.9	2,983.7
Atlantic	1,634.6	58.2	169.3	530.0	877.1

Another important difference among the regions is the rate of urbanization. A *NACLA* research study in 1976 classified 51% of the Nicaraguans as rural, in contrast to 49% as urban.[70] In 1979 these figures shifted to 47% rural and 53% urban. However, a closer look at the statistics demonstrates a significant difference in the rate of urbanization in different regions of Nicaragua. In the Pacific zone, the rate of urbanization for 1979 was 68.3%, while in the Central and Atlantic zones this rate stood, respectively, at 28% and 27%.[71]

Table 5
Nicaraguan Population (1979)[72]

Zones	Total	Urban	% of total	Rural	% of total
Republic	2,644,161	1,404,444	53.0	1,239,717	46.9
Pacific	1,652,897	1,128,316	68.3	524,581	31.7
Central	775,053	217,832	28.1	557,221	71.9
Atlantic	216,211	58,269	27.0	157,915	73.0

The degree of urbanization becomes more important when the literacy rate is taken into consideration. In 1963, for example, while the literacy rate for the republic was measured at 50.5%, the rural areas; 29.6% literacy rate was far behind the urban areas' 79.6%.[73]

Statistics for 1978 offer further proof of a great discrepancy between different regions in terms of education. According to government figures, in 1978 there were 2,402 elementary schools in the republic, of which 1,207 (50.2%) were located in the Pacific zone, in contrast to 776 (32.3%) in the Central zone, and 419 (17.4%) in the Atlantic zone. The total number of high schools in 1978 was 279, of which 194 (69.5%) were situated in the Pacific zone and only 18 (6.5%) in the Atlantic zone. All of the 6 higher education institutes were located in the Pacific zone, in León and Managua.[74]

A brief review of health data further reveals the unevenness in quality of life in different regions. According to the 1979 statistics, Nicaragua had 42 hospitals with a total of 4,813 hospital beds. More than half of the hospitals, 22, and more than 70% of all hospital beds, 3,391, were located in the Pacific zone, while the Central zone had 11 hospitals (26.2%) with 976 beds (20.8%). Nine hospitals (21.4%) and 446 beds (9.2%) were allocated to the Atlantic zone.[75]

Additional revealing data is the number of physicians, dentists, and nurses working in different regions of Nicaragua. According to the statistics of 1973, there were 942 physicians in Nicaragua, of which 858 were practicing in the Pacific zone, 71 in the Central zone, and only 13 in the Atlantic zone. According to the same data, of a total of 71 dentists, 60 were working in the Pacific zone, 6 in the Central zone, and 5 in the Atlantic zone. In the same year, 330 nurses were divided among different zones: 299 in the Pacific, 22 in the Central, and 9 in the Atlantic.[76]

Racial composition also accounts for differences among the Nicaraguan population. The great majority of the present-day Nicaraguans are mestizo (a mixture of indigenous people and Europeans). However, until the late nineteenth century, the majority of the population was indigenous. Historically, since the conquest, Nicaraguans of European descent were mainly concentrated on the Pacific Coast. While the British influence on the Atlantic Coast added a large number of blacks to the native population, the interior of the country remained predominantly indigenous.[77] An estimate, in 1906, counted the indigenous inhabitants as 55% of the total population.[78]

By the beginning of the twentieth century, the effect of the new Liberal government's policies was felt on the composition of the Nicaraguan population. Although it has never been suggested that the indigenous Nicaraguans were exterminated, the sharp decline in their population is attributed to a destruction of the economic and cultural basis of their life. The new government's land policies, emphasizing private ownership of land, resulted in the destruction of the communal villages. The indigneous population, losing the basic means of their support, were forcefully integrated into a larger society as small landed farmers, landless peasants, or city workers.

There are some ethnic communities still living in Nicaragua, especially in the Atlantic zone. The population of the Atlantic zone is a rich diversity of ethnicities. According to the latest study by *Centro de Investigación y Documentación de Costa Atlántica* (CIDCA — Investigation and Documentation Center of the Atlantic Coast), there are 67,662 Miskitos living in Zelaya.[79] They occupy two major areas: the Coast itself, from Bluefields north to Cape Gracias a Dios, and around the Río Coco (from near its mouth to Bocay).[80] They are believed to be descendants of the Chibchas of Colombia. According to CIDCA, they compose 24% of the population of the Atlantic zone.

English-speaking blacks total 27,279 (10% of the population of the Atlantic zone).[81] Their origin can be traced back to various waves of immigration. Some of them came as escaped or shipwrecked slaves, and others came as slaves from Jamaica and other parts of the Caribbean, brought in by the British to work in the lumber camps and large plantations. The majority of the blacks or criollos (as they are known in the area) live on the south coast and in the Bluefields-Corn Islands area.

The Sumo Indians, still maintaining their own language and customs, have a population of 6,741, and live mostly in the northern mountainous areas of the Atlantic zone.[82] There are also a small number of Rama Indians in the southern part of the Atlantic Coast. Their language and culture is almost completely lost.

Another ethnic group in the Atlantic zone is the Chinese. Although very small in number, they are spread throughout the area. They are mostly involved in business, and most of the shops in the Atlantic zone are run by Chinese owners.

Because of frequent intermarriage, it is difficult to visually distinguish one group from another. Most of the time it is the culture in which one has grown up, rather that the percentage of a particular ethnicity, that determines a person's ethnic identification.

Even in the Atlantic zone, the majority of the population belongs to the Spanish-speaking mestizos, who are estimated at 172,000 (63% of the coastal population.[83] Many of them live in the agricultural "frontier" between the Pacific and the Atlantic zones, and also around the mining areas of Bonanza, Siuna, and Rosita.

Because of low population density, particularly in the northern and eastern regions, and the poor agricultural quality of the soil, especially in the east, the Nicaraguan farming communities are separated from one another by large areas of uncultivated and uninhabited land, such as the swamps and jungles of the Zelaya region. The lack of adequate communication and transportation systems has helped to create an extreme isolation for a great part of the rural population. The inaccessibility of remote villages and the traditional concentration of the churches in the major cities had resulted in a very limited Church presence in rural Nicaragua.

Following Vatican II, and particularly after the Second Conference of the Latin American Bishops at Medellín in 1968, some of the Church groups attempted to reach the people in the countryside.

The expansion of Church activities in the countryside was not a simple task. The tremendous differences between the conditions in the urban and rural areas shocked many clergy who went to the country to evangelize the peasants but found themselves caught in a sharp social and political conflict.

The Capuchin Fathers in Zelaya

In the new move toward the rural areas, North American Capuchin Fathers were instrumental, especially in the eastern zone of the country. In 1968 they began to organize rural communities in Zelaya with training courses for the *Delegados de la Palabra* (Delegates of the Word) in Rama.[84]

The work of the Delegates was to organize gatherings, to help the Christians in marriage ceremonies, to visit the sick, and to arrange burial services for the dead. The program gradually developed into training community leaders to teach health, agriculture, and literacy, and to establish rural schools. In each village, different committees were created to perform community services and to elect their coordinators to be sent to several training sessions in Zelaya. Almost all of the indigenous communities around the Río Coco participated.

Within three years, 1968–71, agricultural clubs were formed in fifty-seven villages. They were run cooperatively by Miskito leaders. They began agricultural programs in their communities and borrowed money from banks to introduce new varieties of rice and beans, the basic diet among the Nicaraguan rural population, into the community farming.

Beginning in 1971, the Capuchin Fathers began a consciousness-raising program for the peasants, which they believed would cause them

> to value their dignity as the children of God, and to realize their rights according to the Nicaraguan Political Constitution, to discover their capacity to form their destiny and above all, to work together.[85]

With the unity and increasing economic power of the agricultural clubs, came political influence and political pressure. Some of the government officials in the area, who had good relations with the clubs, were transferred under pressure from non-Miskito merchants, who felt threatened by the unity and political awareness of the Miskito Indians.[86]

Another area of emphasis in the Capuchin Fathers' program was training health leaders for rural communities. Each community would choose a health leader who would participate in a two-week training course for basic health. The leader then was sent back to the community with a small supply of medicine to treat minor health problems. The training renewed on a yearly basis.

Repression in Zelaya

To stop growing guerrilla activities in the country, the National Guard increased its presence in the peasant communities in 1974. The agricultural clubs were among the early victims of the repression. The Guard was suspicious of any organization it could not control, particularly the agricultural clubs. However, the work of consciousness-raising slowly and carefully continued, and in some cases, took a clandestine form. Many of the Delegates of the Word used the booklets published by the Capuchins and other progressive religious groups to educate the campesinos about basic human rights and the political constitution of Nicaragua. The Delegates found a very enthusiastic audience, the peasants of Zelaya, who eagerly began to study the constitution and the labor code.

Ironically, National Guard repression became a major factor in raising the consciousness of the peasants about the reality of their lives and the nature of the Somoza regime. The peasants, who, with the help of the Church, had begun the process of developing a critical knowledge about their human and political rights, were now experiencing a vivid example of violation of their rights by the brutality of the National Guard.

The repression also provided a favorable ground for the FSLN to launch a political campaign against the regime and to expose the Guard's intentions in driving the peasants out of their lands under the pretext of punishing the guerrilla supporters. The lands left behind by the terrorized campesinos, were then given to the Guard's officers or local pro-Somoza landlords. The Sandinistas loudly denounced the expulsion of four hundred local peasants from their farms, and called on the rest of the peasant communities in the area to condemn this campaign of terror. The response was very positive, and many communities declared their solidarity with the expelled campesinos. However, any manifestation of solidarity was regarded by the National Guard as a sign of support for the FSLN, and the repression was extended to many more peasant communities.

One of the priests working in the area later described the process of political conversion of the campesinos in simple terms.

> In Zelaya, they [National Guard] killed about 300 peasants and jailed many more. . . . However, most of the campesinos jailed with the activists of the FSLN became politicized, and later joined the organization.[87]

The politicized campesinos went back to their communities to educate the peasants about the situation and the FSLN. And as the repression heightened, the support for the Sandinistas increased among the peasants. Therefore, a combination of the process of consciousness-raising efforts by the Church, the repression of the National Guard, and the political work of the FSLN gradually converted passive peasant communities of Zelaya to strong anti-Somoza bases for revolutionary activities.

Repression in Other Rural Communities

A similar process was repeated in other sectors of the country. In the northwest, in Jalapa, the process of integration of Christians in the revolutionary process was slow but consistent. Until mid-1960s, Jalapa was mostly forgotten by the Church. There was no resident priests in the area, and the only contact with the Church officials were occasional visits by a priest, who would perform a series of sacramental functions and leave the area immediately.

A group of four North American Capuchin priests arrived in the area in 1965 and began their work in Jalapa, Jícaro, Wiwilí, Quilalí, and Santa Clara. One of their first actions was to organize married couples into groups called Family of God. They also organized youth clubs in the area. The Capuchin Fathers' work at the beginning was totally apolitical and focused on the promotion of Christian morality in the community through strengthening the family unit and keeping youth out of trouble.

To expand their community work, the Capuchin Fathers began a program of training the lay leaders called Delegates of the Word in 1967. They trained about ninety-six Delegates in the Jalapa area.

An active member of the Capuchin team in Jalapa was Father Evaristo Bertrand, whose patient community work, simple lifestyle, and attitude toward the poor won him a tremendous respect in the community.

In 1974, a group of young members of Jalapa parish formed new groups called "Espíritu Santo." Sixty to one hundred youths, both male and female, joined the new movement to peacefully "pursue a more just society." They visited the owners of large cattle ranches of the area with a Bible in one hand and the labor code in the other. They tried to persuade the ranchers to increase the workers' wages. They also intervened to free people arrested for interrogation. Their close contact with the inadequate justice system made the members of the group increasingly aware of torture and other violations of human rights. They met with local authorities and formed small groups to visit prisoners in local jails. These activities caught the attention of the National Guard and local officials, who blamed Father Evaristo and other priests in the area.

Finally, in 1976, Father Evaristo was arrested by a National Guard patrol and was expelled to Honduras. The members of the local Christian Base Communities petitioned the bishop of Estelí, Monsignor Carranza, to intervene and to ask the government to let Father Evaristo return to the community. The bishop flatly refused to get involved, saying that it was a matter of "national security."[88]

Intensification of political repression in the area restricted the open activities of Christian Base Communities and other organizations. By the end of 1978, the youth groups ceased to function. But, the overwhelming majority of the members of the groups joined clandestine political-military action led by the FSLN. A growing number of adult members of local communities began to function in a civilian network of support for the combatants.

Following the triumph of the revolution, some of the members of Jalapa communities emerged as high-ranking officers in the Sandinista army. Two out of four members of the local directorate of the FSLN, two out of three directors of the Municipal Junta, the coordinator of the Sandinista Defense Committees (CDS), the head of the militias, and several directors of the Sandinista Association of Rural Workers (ATC) are former members of Christian Base Communities of Jalapa.[89]

Another religious group influenced by the ideas developed by Vatican II and Medellín conference were Jesuits, who in 1969 formed a Church organization, *Centro de Educación y Promoción Agraria* (CEPA — Center for Agrarian Education and Promotion), for working in the rural area. CEPA's goal was to develop a project designed to help peasants meet their daily needs more effectively.

Later CEPA began publishing a bulletin, *Cristo Campesino*, which in a very simple language explained the realities and the problems of daily life in the country. CEPA also organized health and agricultural training courses in Carazo and Masaya, and later extended the program to the north. Another important program of CEPA was training the Delegates of the Word in Carazo and Estelí.

At the beginning, CEPA was an apolitical organization, designed to help the peasants elevate their living standards. However, with each step it took to help the campesinos improve their living conditions, CEPA had to confront hostile landowners and their advocate, the government. The difficult task of reaching individual campesinos and preparing them to defend their interests against aggressive landlords and government officials opened a discussion among the members of the organization in search of a better way to fulfill their tasks. In the early 1970s, CEPA reached the conclusion that "the peasants could not change their living conditions without an organized and collective political action."[90] Thereafter, a major part of the CEPA's energy was spent on organizing the campesinos to defend their interests collectively. In the mid-1970s, when repression intensified in the countryside and was extended to every kind of popular organization, rural Christian Base Communities and agricultural cooperatives formed by CEPA became a major target for the National Guard's attacks, and many of them were destroyed or driven underground. Repression and clandestine forms of operation politicized many peasant members of CEPA, and close contact was established between some CEPA members and the FSLN. Radicalization of CEPA brought political pressure from the conservative Catholic hierarchy, especially Bishop López Fitoria of Granada and Bishop Vega of Juigalpa. This pressure resulted in the withdrawal of many priests from the organization in 1976.[91] Another cause of declining membership in CEPA was the intensification of repression in 1977, and government persecution of the Jesuits, who decided to drop out of CEPA. Most of the remaining members of CEPA were lay activists.

When the Sandinistas formed the Association of Rural Workers (ATC) in 1977, some key CEPA workers joined the new organization and gained leadership positions. Some other members of CEPA joined the FSLN as combatants, and several of them were killed in battle by the National Guard. This new development caused the Church hierarchy to attempt to limit CEPA's activities and to discourage it from political radicalization and close relationships with the FSLN. When the restrictions began to act as major obstacles for CEPA's community programs, the organization decided to cut its formal ties with the hierarchy and to operate as an independent Christian organization.

Transformation of the Peasantry and the Rural Church

The rapid process of transformation of a peasantry that was widely regarded as passive, submissive, and religiously fatalistic into an active force of political opposition and, in many cases, an aggressive and combative group, has been a source of confusion and misinterpretation among historians and political scientists who try to analyze the situation in Central America, particularly in Nicaragua.[92]

A popular explanation, backed by many North American political analysts, and widely used in the mass media, blames the change on Communist agents infiltrating different institutions, such as the Catholic Church, and inciting violent rebellion among the peasantry through deceptive propaganda or by forcing peasants to join the fight by creating terror in the countryside. However, a careful study of Nicaraguan history from 1968 to 1979, and the role of different institutions and organizations such as the Catholic Church and the

FSLN in the rapid sociopolitical transformation of the country offers a different explanation based on the dialectical relations between social classes and their sociopolitical and cultural institutions.

It is true that historically the dominant view among the Nicaraguan peasantry regarding their economic and social misery was that it was inevitable and ordained by God. To explain the situation, the campesinos usually used familiar phrases such as, "God has made us poor and we don't have to change," or, "Christ was poor. He came to teach us to suffer."

Even the strongest supporters of the traditional Church today do not dispute the fact that the Catholic Church in Latin America had played a major role in creating passivity and fatalism among the population, and for centuries had provided an ideological justification for the sociopolitical system. In fact, awareness of this historical role and the self-criticism of the Latin American bishops was one of the basic factors in the Medellín conference, giving rise to a vigorous attempt to change the stand of the Church away from siding with the rich and the powerful, and toward taking sides with the poor.

As Father Smutko, a Nicaraguan Church activist, observes:

> Maybe it is a paradox that today in many parts of Latin America, the Catholic Church is deeply involved in an intense process of "consciousness-raising" to help the poor to liberate themselves from this fatalism and lethargy.[93]

At Medellín the bishops emphasized the need to educate the people about their basic human rights and to raise their awareness of social realities; but many of them could not predict that their attempts to promote the social teachings of the Church would act as an important force for social revolutions, and as a common ground for a close collaboration of Christians and Marxists in taking up arms and overthrowing sociopolitical structures. Father Smutko explains the Church's concept of consciousness-raising as

> a process by which a person comes to discover his dignity as a human being, his rights as a citizen, his possibilities to shape his proper destiny . . . especially by working together [with other people]. . . . *Concientización* offers the person the historical com-

mitment to transform his community and his society into a situation of more liberty, love, justice and fraternity.[94]

In Nicaragua, the process of consciousness-raising was not oriented toward encouraging the peasants to take up arms against Somoza. Rather, its aim was "development of a critical judgment among the campesinos, to increase their capacity to work together to form their own destiny and to overcome fatalism."[95] However, when the Church began fighting its own historical creature, fatalism, it eliminated a major obstacle which had prevented the campesinos from assuming their historical role. The peasants became aware of their dignity and their rights. They realized that the unjust social structure was not a natural state of being and could change. The theological development innovated by the progressive Church, on the intellectual level, when applied to a given historical situation, was transformed to an active social force which surpassed the social teachings of the Catholic Church. The priests who taught the peasants to realize their human dignity were now taken by surprise when the same peasants became fighters to defend their dignity. The Church was once again caught in a contradiction with no control over the outcome.

The reaction of different sectors of the Church to the new situation varied tremendously. While the Church hierarchy, isolated from the poor because of its social status, tried to confine the radicalization of the popular movement, the priests working and living with the people were deeply affected by the dialectical relations of the growing militancy of the peasantry and their own changing religious beliefs. The poor, initially awakened by the process of consciousness-raising in the Christian Base Communities, went much further than their own teachers in their commitment for social change. Now it was the priests' turn to learn from their own followers in fulfilling the teachings of liberation theology. One example of this was the famous Father Gaspar García Laviana, who joined the FSLN as a combatant and died while fighting Somoza as a guerrilla of the National Liberation War, and struggling against "institutionalized violence" as a priest.

Between the two extremes of the hierarchy trying to curb the radicalism of the movement, and the few priests who joined the FSLN as fighters, many priests working in the countryside vigorously supported the people in their fight against Somoza, and helped them emotionally and materially. A good example of this active support for the people was a public statement of the Capuchin Fathers in 1976 condemning the Somoza regime for gross violations of basic human rights and massacre of the peasants.

Public Condemnation of the Repression

In 1976, all of the Capuchin priests of Zelaya met for a retreat at *La Cartuja de Matagalpa* to discuss the reality of life in the Zelaya mountains, which had become characterized by the torture and execution of campesinos, without judicial process.

For about two years, the missionaries of Siuna, in Zelaya Province, Father Teodor Niehaus and Father David Zywiec, with great patience and in a very dangerous situation, had collected lists of the missing and tortured campesinos of the rural zone of Siuna. They gave the list to Bishop Salvador Schlaefer. The bishop met with General Anastasio Somoza three times in less than a year, each time with a longer list of the peasants of Waslala, Yoasca, Iyas, Zinica, and other peasant communities of Siuna, all victims of the National Guard. Somoza said that some of the disappeared peasants had certainly gone to other parts of the country. He also said that if there were abuses, he would investigate and talk to the Guard, because he did not want the poor peasants to suffer.[96] However, the number of victims kept growing and so did the concerns of the Capuchins. In a meeting of the rural zone in 1976, the missionaries unanimously signed a letter to the bishop and asked him to present the case to the Episcopal Conference, asking the bishops for a public condemnation of the massacres and disappearances. Later, the urban missions of Zelaya met in Waspán and repeated the same demand to the bishop. Thus when the missionaries arrived at *Cartuja* for the retreat almost all of them had already signed the letter of the rural zone or the urban zone, or both.

According to the Capuchins, the following types of torture were practiced on prisoners by the National Guard troops near the Sofana chapel in February 1976:

> The prisoners were kicked; beaten with rifles; struck on the head with military helmets; hung by the neck; had teeth extracted

from their jaw; were hung up by their feet; had their shoes removed and then were forced to walk over rough ground through thorn bushes; had rags stuffed in their mouths and were blindfolded; were tied by the neck and then pulled like animals; their faces were cut with knives. . . .

In the *comarcas* of Sofana, Boca de Dudu and Yucumalí, National Guard troops have burned houses without providing any compensation to the owners.

Since May 1, 1976 there have been occasions when National Guard helicopters have opened fire in the *comarcas* of Sofana, Boca de Piedra, Parasca, Yucumalí, and Dipina.

These events have interrupted the normal life of the campesinos in these zones. Fear is widespread in the *comarcas*. A number of families have fled and abandoned their land and houses. In May 1976 only seven families remained in Sofana *comarca* where six months earlier there had been more than 40 families. In Platano *comarca* only 12 families remained out of 40.[97]

Because of press censorship the report was not published in Nicaragua. However, it was printed in other countries, and mimeographed copies were circulated in Nicaragua. One year later, the list of the disappeared, now much longer, was presented by Father Fernando Cardenal to the United States Congress, which was investigating the violations of human rights in Nicaragua. Finally the Church hierarchy responded to the pressure of the Capuchin Fathers and other priests and lay persons by condemning the torture and assassination of the peasants, in the Pastoral Letter issued on January 8, 1977, by the Episcopal Conference signed by all the bishops. (See Chapter 7.)

Somoza's response was an intensification of repression in the rural area. Many of Zelaya's chapels and community centers were violated by the military. As Penny Lernoux, a Latin American expert, reports:

[They] used twenty-six chapels as barracks and torture centers and as places to rape the peasant women. Lay leaders were singled out for arrest and torture. One Zelaya Delegate of the Word was left tied up for several days in a chapel, then beaten and tortured for three months. . . . [98]

The same pattern of government repression and Church radicalization was repeated in other sectors of the country. In the northern zone of Matagalpa, Jinotega, and Yalí, Christian Base Communities, which were formed by Father Miguel Vasquez since 1972, grew in number and strength. They soon became a target for the Guard's repression, and their priests and Delegates of the Word were branded as Communists and guerrilla collaborators. In the case of Yalí, the thirty-two Christian Base Communities were called subversive by the Guard and the members were persecuted. Over the next three years, as Dodson and Montgomery observed,

> the estrangement of the people and the government deepened as churches were searched and occupied by the Guard and as individuals were imprisoned or killed, or disappeared. Religious meetings were broken up or banned altogether. By 1978, most Christians not only opposed the Somoza regime but were pro-Sandinista.[99]

CHAPTER 7

Intensification of the Political Conflict and Clarification of the Sociopolitical Alliance

The year 1977 began with a gloomy picture in Nicaragua, particularly in the rural areas. The repression and mass killings of peasants by the National Guard was now a matter of public knowledge, and the Catholic Church hierarchy was under tremendous pressure to take a public stand against Somoza.

On January 8, 1977, the Nicaraguan Episcopal Conference issued a New Year's message to the Nicaraguan people, focusing on the ongoing repression and strongly demanding an end to the violations of human rights in the country.

> The state of terror obliges many of our campesinos to flee in desperation from their homes and farm lands in the mountains of Zelaya, Matagalpa and Las Segovias. . . . It has been verified that many villages have been practically abandoned; houses and personal belongings have been burned and the people, desperate and without help, have fled.[1]

The bishops also complained about the religious repression in the rural areas.

In some towns of Las Segovia the commandants demand special permission for each religious meeting of Catholics. In other places in the mountains of Zelaya and Matagalpa, the patrols have occupied the Catholic chapels, using them for barracks. Some Catholic Delegates of the Word of God have been pressured to suspend their cooperation with the missionary priests. There are cases in which Delegates of the Word have been captured by members of the army, have been tortured and some have disappeared.[2]

While the basic emphasis of the message was the violation of human rights and the condemnation of heightening repression in the countryside, the bishops concluded that the recent national situation has resulted in, on the one side, "the accumulation of lands and riches in the hands of a few," and on the other, deprivation of the powerless campesinos of their farm lands through threats, under the state of emergency.

For frustrated Nicaraguans, who were witnessing the suffering of their people and had no place to turn for help, the bishops' message was a sign of hope, and was interpreted as the Church's support for the popular struggle to bring profound changes in the sociopolitical structure of the country. However, the bishops were careful not to align themselves with the radical opposition seeking a revolutionary change through armed struggle. Posing the question, "Can violence be the remedy on the path for a renewed change of our institutions?" the bishops denounced the "lawlessness" of "so-called freedom movements" which "stir passions, lead to person vendettas and end up as 'new lords' who take charge of government without regard for human rights."[3] The bishops were careful not to attack the foundation of the regime, and limited their demands in a general appeal for:

1. Guarantees of life and of work and a return of civil rights. 2. Proper trials for common crimes as well as for so-called political crimes. 3. Freedom to promote a more just and equitable order. [4]

Nevertheless, the government reacted harshly to the criticism of the existing situation. In the first half of 1977, the government officials intensified their attacks on the archbishop of Managua and other priests and Catholic institutions.

On May 22, 1977, in an interview with the press, Dr. Roberto Cranshaw Guerra, head of the police in Managua, publicly denounced the Catholic Church, and demanded a trial for "red cassock priests," including Father Molina of barrio Riguero and Archbishop Miguel Obando y Bravo.[5] However, the official attacks on the Church hierarchy diminished when faced with strong solidarity among the clergy, and the support of the people for the Church members.

The Somoza family was always particularly cautious in its relations with the Church hierarchy. Somoza tried to avoid a direct confrontation with the high clergy, and did not react to the Church's denunciation, hoping that it would be forgotten after a while. On several occasions, Somoza even agreed with the Church's criticism, asserting that the Liberal Party had a similar view and was trying to correct the existing problems. In addition, the Church hierarchy also took a conciliatory posture. In mid-1977, when Somoza became ill and left the country for medical treatment in the United States, the Nicaraguan bishops, Obando y Bravo, Pablo Vega, and Salvador Schlaefer, sent a telegram stating: "Facing the weak health [of the President], we elevate our prayers to God for [his] immediate recuperation. Attentively and cordially."[6] A few days later, Somocista Liberal Youth (Juventud Liberal Somocista) arranged a mass in the Church of San Francisco de Bolonia, and the Nationalist Liberal Party (Somocista) thanked "the bishops for their prayers for the health [of Somoza], a very precious factor for the Republic."[7] From July 31 until September 14, 233 masses were celebrated for the health of the president.

Another important event of 1977 was the formation of a political front, *Los Doce* (The Twelve), by the FSLN. This group acted as the liaison between the Frente and the bourgeois opposition, and later became the basis of the first revolutionary government. Sergio Ramírez, a member of *Los Doce*, and now the vice-president of Nicaragua, later recalled the formation of the group.

The group *Los Doce* was born around July of 1977. Organized by the Sandinista Front [it was] to carry out the political task of introducing the thesis of armed struggle to certain sectors of Nicaraguan society at this point of history. I was already a member of the FSLN before the formation of *Los Doce*. I directly participated in choosing the people and the organizations to be represented in the group, people from private enterprise, the Church, intellectuals, industrialists, and merchants. People who because of their honesty and their political position were supporting the Sandinistas.[8]

In 1977, Nicaraguan politics was also impacted by the new emphasis put on respect for human rights in the Carter Administration's foreign policy. The U.S. Embassy in Managua informed Somoza that approval of U.S. military support for Nicaragua in 1978 depended on an improvement in the human rights records of the Nicaraguan government. One of the immediate results of the new U.S. pressure was the lifting of press censorship in September 1977.

Under the new situation, the activities of the political opposition increased rapidly. In August, the Social Christian Party announced its decision to hold its congress on September 24 and 25. The Congress concluded with a call for termination of the dictatorship and the beginning of a democratic system in the country.

Another political organization which increased its activities was UDEL. It arranged meetings in different cities. When the press censorship was lifted, UDEL published a document with minimum demands: (1) lifting the state of siege and censorship of all communication media, (2) freedom for political and syndicate organizations, (3) appointment of a new officer with no relations to the Somoza family as the chief of the National Guard, (4) a judicial order which would guarantee political pluralism and participation of all sectors of society in the generation of all public powers, and (5) a general amnesty and exoneration for all political prisoners and exiles.

UDEL strongly criticized the regime for

corruption of basic democratic institutions, politicization of the administration of justice, identification of the interests of the state with those of the governor, dishonest competition with private enterprise and lack of union organizations, etc.[9]

Following the lifting of censorship, the new atmosphere of political liberalization created a high level of hope that the private sector could bring desirable changes to the political structure through peaceful reforms and legal avenues. Each of the groups in the political opposition was trying to broaden its own base and to gain a prominent place in the future negotiations with the regime. In this process, some of the old differences among political groups, which were suppressed in favor of unity under the situation of State of Siege and censorship, were now revived and even discussed openly in the press.

However, the new atmosphere of political competition and broad discussion was suddenly changed by the arrival of a new element, a series of successful armed attacks on National Guard positions by the FSLN in October 1977.

The October Offensive, National Dialogue, and the Role of the Church

On October 12, 1977, a group of Sandinista guerrillas assaulted the police station in Ocotal. The next day, another group of well-armed Sandinistas attacked the National Guard barracks in San Carlos, just north of the border with Costa Rica. According to the government report, six National Guard soldiers were killed and six others injured. Two days later, another attack occurred in Mozonte; and on October 17, there were others in Masaya and several neighborhoods of Managua.[10]

Meanwhile, the group *Los Doce*[11] issued a statement on October 14, demanding substantial changes toward creating a democratic system with the participation of the FSLN. This statement was important in the prevailing political atmosphere in the country. The rampant government corruption and repeated violations of human rights had added new forces to the opposition, and the bourgeois sectors of Somoza's opponents organized in UDEL had systematically refused to recognize and collaborate with the radical faction of the opposition, the FSLN. The statement of the *Los Doce*, almost all of them from well-known bourgeois families, and some of them wealthy businessmen, was an attempt to give the FSLN a legitimate standing in the political opposition and to bridge the widening gap between the moderate and the radical factions.

Successful armed actions of the FSLN and open support of the organization by the *Los Doce* was fundamentally a declaration for overthrowing the dictatorship and replacing the regime by a profoundly different sociopolitical order under the control of the FSLN fighters. However, although very attractive to some sectors of the frustrated Nicaraguan people, the FSLN alternative was not acceptable to the capitalist sector and its political organizations.[12]

The private sector was basically interested in finding peaceful ways to transform the dictatorship into a Western style democracy with the least disruption of the socioeconomic structure of the country. The FSLN's constant call on the lower classes to rise up and to take up arms to destroy the existing "repressive social structure" and to create a new society in which the "voiceless and oppressed" would participate in the government held a frightening message for the private sector.

Following the October offensive and the *Los Doce* declaration, the leaders of political groups immediately multiplied their efforts to create a consensus among the moderates to unite and to begin a political negotiation with Somoza to prepare the ground for a peaceful termination of the personal dictatorship in the country.

Archbishop Miguel Obando y Bravo had maintained a close contact with UDEL and had repeatedly declared his support for the political program of the organization, as opposed to the revolutionary armed struggle. On October 19, he issued a statement affirming that it was necessary to look for "civilized ways," and that it was time for different forces in the country to enter a constructive dialogue.[13] The timing of the statement, which was issued a few days after the successful armed operations of the FSLN and the open support of the *Los Doce* for the Sandinistas, was a significant indication of the uninterrupted opposition of the Church hierarchy to the armed struggle and any radical sociopolitical alternative to existing structures, a policy that the bishops had pursued unanimously and clearly since the end of 1972.

The archbishop's call for seeking a peaceful means of political transformation drew an immediate response from the major groups in the bourgeois opposition. UDEL was the first organization to announce that it would join the archbishop to establish a process of national agreement. Condemning violence, UDEL asserted:

> Peace can only be established if a process of political transformation is initiated, which converts Nicaragua to a society authentically democratic, pluralistic, and independent, constructed on the basis of administrative honesty, socio-economic justice, and respect for human rights.[14]

UDEL's example was soon followed by other political and business groups, including the Conservative Party of Nicaragua (Partido Conservador de Nicaragua — PCN), Authentic Conservative Party (Partido Conservador Auténtica — PCA), and INDE (Instituto Nicaragüense de Desarrollo). Later, the four main opposition groups, UDEL, PCN, PSC, and PCA signed a joint document to support a "Commission for Promoting National Dialogue" headed by Monsignor Obando.[15] The Chambers of Construction and Commerce also supported the Commission, in which the President of INDE, Alfonso Robelo, participated as a member. The other members of the Commission were Monsignor Manuel Salazar y Espinoza, the bishop of León and the president of the Nicaraguan Episcopal Conference; Monsignor Pablo Vega, the bishop of Juigalpa, Chontales, and the vice-president of the Episcopal Conference; and Dr. Félix Esteban Guandique, a well-known jurist.

The private sector's fear of armed struggle and the alternative introduced by the FSLN was well manifested in a *La Prensa* editorial on October 19, 1977. Declaring its support for the initiation of a National Dialogue, *La Prensa* strongly condemned any kind of violence: "Violence only destroys all democratic and civic opportunities for a solution to the national problems."[16]

Heavy emphasis on the peaceful, legal means of political transformation was also noticeable in the statement of the Conservative Party in support of the national dialogue. The party stressed "the necessity and obligation for an immediate search for accessible legal means to open a political change."[17]

Another factor in the private sector's insistence on a peaceful means of political transformation was the heightening economic crisis of the country, which was a result of increasing violence and political instability. As Pablo Antonio Cuadra, a prominent spokesman of the Nicaraguan private sector, observed in October 1977:

> The country cannot survive the existing political situation. Besides the loss of human life, and growing hatred and violence and dangerous radicalization of attitudes, the economy could not bear this permanent and double earthquake of lack of integrity and tranquility.[18]

The Commission soon found another important supporter. According to an Associated Press cable of November 18, 1977, the United States Ambassador in Managua, Mauricio Solaun, pressured Somoza to initiate dialogue with the forces of the opposition, with an eye toward democratization of the country.[19] According to the AP cable, Ambassador Solaun informed Somoza that a commission headed by the Under-Secretary of State Warren Christopher had approved only two of the seven credits asked for by the Nicaraguan government. The other credits were postponed for three months while the commission waited for the Nicaraguan government to show political progress and a respect for human rights.[20]

A week later, on November 25, Monsignor Obando y Bravo declared that General Somoza had agreed to begin talks to establish a meeting for national dialogue with the Commission. However, Somoza would not send his delegates until the end of the municipal elections planned for February 1978.[21]

Meanwhile, the "Coordinating Commission for National Dialogue" notified the opposition parties that they could begin the process of selecting their delegates and proposing an agenda for the dialogue. One of the groups announcing its conditions for the national dialogue was *Los Doce*. They declared that the first prerequisite for the national dialogue was the exclusion of Somoza.

> We have never sought a dialogue with Somocismo. On the contrary, we have made it clear that we cannot enter dialogue with Somoza . . . because [he] is the principle obstacle for a national understanding . . . learning from the long and dark history of Somocismo, dialogue with the dictator serves for his consolidation . . . and in this crucial moment for Nicaragua, when the dictator is weak and isolated, dialogue is the only political means for him to survive.[22]

Los Doce also stated, "In seeking a national solution, it is impossible to leave out the Sandinista Front."[23]

Another source of opposition to a dialogue with Somoza could be found among the progressive clergy, who published their views in religious publications such as *SID*[24]. In the November–December issue of *SID*, two articles appeared analyzing the political situation. One, prepared by the *Instituto Histórico Centroamericano* (IHC),[25] first gave a detailed chronology of events covering the period from July 1977 to December 1977, and then an analysis of the roots of the "National Dialogue," and the role of the Catholic hierarchy. The article held that the conflict between the Somoza group and the rest of the bourgeoisie in Nicaragua was not an antagonistic contradiction. According to the article, the bourgeois state basically has two functions: to guarantee the domination of the bourgeoisie in the society and to provide the necessary infrastructure for capitalist development of the economy. The first function is fulfilled through coercive force, in the case of Nicaragua, the National Guard and the judicial system. The second function is fulfilled through the socialization of a series of expenses which otherwise have to be assumed by individual capitalists, such as construction of roads, a communication system, and providing an education and health network.

In Nicaragua, the article maintained, both of the above-mentioned tasks of a capitalist state were fulfilled by the Somoza regime. However, by controlling the state apparatus and the National Guard for forty years, the Somoza group also secured its own dominance over the rest of the bourgeoisie, and this was the basis for intrabourgeois conflict in Nicaragua. According to the article, the armed actions of the FSLN in October 1977 made both factions of the bourgeoisie realize that if their internal conflict was not solved, they could lose control to a radical organization, the FSLN, which was traditionally representative of the interests of the exploited classes, mainly peasants, workers, and the urban marginal population. This was the main reason, according to the article, for the bourgeoisie's strong support for a national dialogue following the FSLN attacks on San Carlos and other cities in October. Another factor pressing for the national dialogue, from the author's point of view, was the Carter Administration's emphasis on human rights in U.S. foreign policy, and its pressure on Somoza to improve his government's record on the issue.

Therefore, the article continued, the Catholic Church hierarchy in offering itself as the mediator in the national dialogue, had accepted the responsibility for mediation between the two conflicting groups of the bourgeoisie, a process which had totally excluded the interests of the masses. This was the reason that the Church hierarchy had recognized only the official political parties as the most representative organizations in setting up the conditions for the national dialogue, which was aimed at solving the contradiction between the two factions of the bourgeoisie, threatened by the danger of an evergrowing mass movement.[26]

The other article in the same issue of *SID* took the theological justification of a national dialogue given by the hierarchy, and analyzed it point by point according to liberation theology. One of the concepts on which the hierarchy had put a heavy emphasis to justify its support for a national dialogue with Somoza was the necessity of maintaining peace in Nicaragua. The article had a different view of the issue. According to the author, peace in Latin America historically had meant tranquility in the framework of an unjust sociopolitical situation. In Medellín another concept of peace was offered to Catholics. Peace was defined as a strong and prolonged commitment to the elimination of hidden violence, not the tranquility of a static order which would crush all signs of rebellion. The article insisted that

> it is not possible to have peace without destroying the capitalist system which emphasizes economic profit over [the value of] human being. It is necessary to break the defense of oligarchic groups who resort to all means to weaken the protest movement. . . .[27]

Another important concept challenged by the article was the definition of democracy used by the private sector and the Church hierarchy. The author called this concept of democracy based on liberalism "a political caricature, and a lie." The article asserted that

> real democracy consists of taking and facing the political decisions from the angle of the people's point of view and not of the oligarchy, or money. It is decision making for the people, for the poor, for the workers, not arbitrarily from above, but by themselves. . . .
> If democracy means the power of the people, it is necessary that

the people take over the power and implement their own point of view. The people who love the Church have to struggle to produce this revolutionary change.[28]

The article also had a different concept of Christian love from that of the Church hierarchy. In contrast to the hierarchy, which had repeatedly condemned the class struggle on the basis of the doctrine of Christian universal love, the author stressed that it was necessary to love all men, but not in the same manner.

Loving the oppressed is defending and liberating him, loving the oppressor is accusing and fighting him. Liberation of the poor and the rich comes at the same time. Paradoxically, love is only really universal if it is class based.[29]

Therefore, from the author's point of view, to create a harmony in Latin American societies a revolution had to overthrow the existing political systems first, and in reality this could not happen through nonviolence.

In spite of strong criticism, the Church hierarchy continued its crusade against the advocates of the armed struggle, as well as its attempts to rally Nicaraguan Christians behind the supporters of the "National Dialogue," with the participation of Somoza. In a message to the people of Nicaragua published in *La Prensa* on December 21, 1977, Archbishop Obando y Bravo expressed a very strong anti-armed struggle line. The archbishop first categorized violence in two types.

One which attacks, the other which defends; one by the people who want to create conflict at any price, and the other by persons who want peace at any price. However, the price is always violence. And we reject both types of violence. . . .

The statement continued with strong approval of nonviolent methods, including dialogue. The archbishop agreed that dialogue by itself was not enough, and that it had to be combined with other concrete actions, but "always in the spirit of non-violence." He gave the name of "active non-violence" to methods such as dialogue and peaceful demonstrations. He called "active non-violence" a practice which "permits [the people] to be revolutionary without renouncing Christianity, and to be faithful to Christ, without renouncing the revolution."[30]

The importance of the archbishop's message can be only appreciated if we consider the fact that a major part of the guerrillas who attacked the National Guard positions in San Carlos on October 13 were members of the Christian community of Solentiname. For years Solentiname was a model for Christian organization and community commitment for the Nicaraguans who deeply respected the famous writer and poet Father Ernesto Cardenal, the founder of Solentiname. The progress of the community in all aspects of life, including the creation of a profound intellectual and artistic atmosphere in the midst of the simplicity of a campesino life, had been greatly publicized in Nicaragua and abroad.

The news of the participation of members of the Solentiname community in the armed struggle against Somoza served as a great example for revolutionary Catholics to strengthen their religious convictions by practicing their belief in their Christian obligation to create the Kingdom of God on earth, and for liberating themselves and their people from a sinful structure. Solentiname had become a symbol of authentic Christian commitment, and as such, it was in sharp conflict with the conservative ideas advocated by the Church hierarchy. Refuting Solentiname was an essential necessity for the traditional Church if it was to uphold its own brand of sociopolitical involvement as the only legitimate Christian option. Thus the archbishop's December message condemning armed struggle as anti-Christian was a direct attempt by him to discredit the Solentiname experience and example.

In contrast to Archbishop Obando, who from the very beginning condemned the attack on San Carlos and the other National Guard positions as an uncivilized act of violence,[31] members and supporters of the Solentiname community tried to explain and justify their action in a religious framework. In a letter to the Nicaraguan people published in *La Prensa* on October 18, 1977, Father Ernesto Cardenal described the participation of the Solentiname Christians in the armed struggle as a direct result of a profound understanding of the gospel.

One thing that politically radicalized us the most was the gospel. Every Sunday, with the campesinos we studied the gospel in the form of dialogue, and they, with an admirable simplicity and a theological profoundity, began to understand the essence of the gospel message: the announcement of the kingdom of God . . . [and] its establishment on earth, a just society, with no exploited or exploiter, with everything [shared] in common, similar to the communities of the early Christians. But above all, the gospel taught us that the word of God is not only for being listened to, but also for being put into practice. . . .

Therefore, the campesinos of Solentiname, being aware of the suffering of their brothers and sisters in other parts of the country, decided to act upon their learning of the gospel and to try to liberate their people. Father Cardenal explained:

In the beginning we preferred a non-violent revolution. . . . However, later, we came to the conclusion that in Nicaragua, a non-violent struggle is not practical. And Gandhi himself would have agreed with us. In reality, all authentic revolutionaries prefer non-violence to violence, but they do not always have the liberty to choose.

So, "following a long period of maturation of their beliefs," a group of young members of Solentiname decided to take up arms to act upon their profound Christian convictions. Why did they do so? Father Cardenal answered:

They did it only for one reason, for their love of the kingdom of God. For their ardent desire to create a just society, a real and concrete kingdom of God, here on earth.[32]

Another source of conflict in the Nicaraguan Church was the differing opinions as to the nature of the Somoza regime and the methods for dealing with it. The hierarchy, although openly critical of the repression, still recognized the legitimacy of the Somoza government and its constitutional authority. Therefore, to correct the social and political problems resulting from the government actions, the "civilized way" for the hierarchy was to open a dialogue with Somoza and to discuss the differences. The similarity between the political position of the hierarchy and the private sector opposition was obvious in every document published by the two in this period.

On the other hand, siding with the radical opposition, the Christian Base Communities and the progressive sector of the Catholic Church did not recognize the legitimacy of the Somoza regime, and rejected opening a dialogue with the dictator. This political position was well formulated in a statement issued by Father Miguel D'Escoto, a Maryknoll priest and a member of *Los Doce*. In his statement, Father D'Escoto called the Somoza regime a sinful structure, and he refused to recognize any authority for it: "Somocismo is slander, violation and greed. Somocismo is torture, avarice. . . ."[33] As a priest, Father D'Escoto saw it his obligation

> to denounce this sin, and to proclaim that fidelity to Christ means that, among other things, all the Nicaraguans should struggle to liberate their country from this moral leprosy.[34]

Another Catholic priest taking sides with the radical opposition in spite of the hierarchy's condemnation of armed struggle was Father Gaspar García Laviana. Born and raised in Spain, Father Gaspar was sent to Nicaragua by his community, Sacred Heart, as a missionary priest in 1970, and began working in the parish of San Juan Del Sur. From the beginning, he was deeply affected by the poverty and misery of Nicaraguan peasants. Later he established contact with the priests working in the northern zone, including Father Evaristo, and learned from their experience of organizing the poor peasants. Gaspar's enthusiasm to find better ways to help the poor peasants brought him into contact with CEPA (Centro de Educación y Promoción Agraria), and he participated in CEPA's efforts to create a national network of pastoral workers in rural Nicaragua (for more informatin in CEPA, see Chapter 6.) As a CEPA activist, Father Gaspar travelled extensively in Nicaragua to organize rural communities.

Working in Nicaragua for nine years Gaspar García experienced the suffering of the people, seeing "the wicked exploitation of the campesino who was crushed under the boots of landlords protected by the National Guard, the instrument of injustice and repression." All over the country, he witnessed

> the corruption, ruthless repression . . . the people who were moaning under the bayonets, and tortured in the prisons for re-claiming what was theirs, a free and just society, from which the robbery and assassination would disappear for ever.[35]

Father García finally reached the conclusion that the only way to liberate Nicaraguans was to join the fight as an FSLN combatant. He took up arms because, it was

> a just war, a war justified by Christians . . . and [his own] Christian conscience, because [it] represents the struggle against a situation odious to the Lord, . . . And because as the documents of Medellín indicate . . . the revolutionary insurrection is legitimate in the case of an evident and prolonged tyranny which violates fundamental rights of the people and dangerously damages the common good of the country. . . .[36]

In his letter to the Nicaraguan people on December 25, 1977, Gaspar García wrote:

> Somocismo is sin, and liberating ourselves from oppression is liberation from sin. And with a gun in my hand, full of faith, and full of love for my Nicaraguan people, I'll fight until my last breath for the arrival of the kingdom of justice in our country. . . .[37]

Meanwhile, a new wave of demonstrations and workers' strikes began throughout the country.[38] The private sector was still trying to find a common ground with Somoza for a compromise. On December 28, 1977, the opposition parties, UDEL, PCA, and PSC formulated their conditions for dialogue as follows:

> 1. To open extended investigations about numerous disappeared people. . . .

2. To arrange Common Tribunals (Tribunales Comunes) for numerous prisoners who have not been tried, and to free the ones kept with no charges against them.

3. To conduct investigations into the dissipation and embezzlement of public funds in different government and autonomous agencies.

4. To stop arbitrary procedures in applying the Radio and T.V. Code.

5. To stop creating obstacles for the activities of political organizations of the opposition.

6. To negotiate and ratify the pattern of legal representation submitted by numerous unions to the Ministry of Labor, in accordance with the law.

7. To stop the persecution against *Los Doce*.[39]

The representatives of the opposition noted that all their conditions were basically a demand for the government to fulfill its duties according to the law.

The private sector's strong rejection of armed struggle as a solution to national problems, and their emphasis on dialogue as the only way to terminate the dictatorship and repression were, once more, forcefully supported by the Catholic hierarchy in the bishops' New Year's message to the Nicaraguan people. In their message, the bishops first strongly criticized the government for repression and injustices prevailing in the country.

We cannot stay silent, when a major sector of our population suffers sub-human living conditions as a result of unjust distribution of wealth; when the civil guarantees are defined in words but totally absent in practice; when death and disappearance of many citizens (in the cities and the countryside) are framed in mystery; when a valuable portion of our people — the youth — considers taking up arms as the only patriotic solution; when public functionaries enrich themselves abusively, forgetting their mission to serve the people whom they represeent . . .[40]

However, the second part of the letter, suggesting solutions, had a very different tone. Quoting from previous documents of the Church, the bishops addressed the government: "We honor your function, recognize your role and just laws, respect what you do. . . ."[41]

Addressing the workers, the bishops reaffirmed that "the Church knows your sufferings, your struggles, and your hopes." However, "hatred does not save the world."

The main emphasis of the message was well formulated in the section addressing youth. The bishops called on youth to "struggle against egoism. Reject the instincts of violence and hatred which can originate wars and direct you toward evil." They insisted that when hatred and revenge is built "in the midst of gunfire," the uprising of a nation could create evil. They asserted: "The road of the gospel — which is the only valid announcement of peace for the people — is through love, not blood and violence."

In the conclusion of the message, the bishops spelled out the focus of their political position.

> In the situation in which our country lives, the only way to stop the spread of hatred and blood is to maintain an unreconcilable posture of support for a sincere and real dialogue. Only justice and love fit in a Christian posture.[42]

The strong antirepression line of the message was welcomed by most of the Nicaraguans, and it deeply affected the sentiments of the religious people, who were torn between the promises of the moderate opposition to correct the situation by peaceful means and dialogue with Somoza, and the radical opposition insisting on the necessity of armed struggle. The message created an atmosphere of hope and optimism in the country, and rallied undecided people behind the reformist option and the advocates of the "National Dialogue." A series of letters and telegrams supporting the bishops' position flooded the pages of *La Prensa*, and strengthened the camp of the bourgeois opposition.

Recognizing the propaganda value of the message for the bourgeoisie, the Sandinistas tried to counter the effects of the bishops' statement by one of their own. On January 9, 1978, in a communiqué distributed in Managua and published in *La Prensa*, the FSLN declared: "The dialogue is a lie against the people, because it is posed at a precise moment in which the dictator is fatally wounded."[43]

However, on January 10, it was Somoza's henchmen, not the FSLN, who effectively refuted the national dialogue in a direct action: the assassination of Pedro Joaquín Chamorro, the leader of the bourgeois opposition, and the first President of UDEL.

The Assassination of Pedro Joaquín Chamorro and the General Strike

Following the assassination of Pedro Joaquín Chamorro, demonstrators appeared daily in the streets and, in many cases, were attacked by the National Guard, which resulted in a violent reaction by the people. In some instances, such as in Managua on January 13, 1978, a street demonstration clashed with the National Guard, leaving one person dead and many others wounded. The demonstrators later attacked the buildings and business establishments which belonged to the Somoza family, burning some of them, including the Center for Plasma, El Porvenir textile factory, and Banco de Centroamérica.[44]

Another important development was the statement of UDEL on January 11 in which the organization declared: "The dictatorial government is responsible for the circumstances which led to the assassination of Pedro Joaquín Chamorro," and, therefore, UDEL would "pull out of the National Dialogue," which had lost its significance because of the abhorrent actions of the government, "resorting to repression as the only means to stay in power."[45] In addition, the PCA (Partido Conservador Auténtica) announced that the conditions for the dialogue did not exist anymore. And finally, the Coordinating Commission for the Dialogue informed the public that, facing the new situation, it would suspend all its activities indefinitely.

The reaction of some other political groups in the reformist camp was even stronger. Frustrated by the ineffectiveness of peaceful means of struggle in the face of a repressive and brutal dictatorship, the Socialist Party publicly agreed with the FSLN position on rejecting the Dialogue, and called for the formation of one single opposition front, including the FSLN, for confronting the regime and overthrowing the dictatorship.[46]

On January 13, the two most powerful workers organizations, the Central de Trabajadores de Nicaragua (CTN), and the Confederación General Del Trabajo-Independiente (CGT-I), declared an indefinite strike of their members as a protest against the assassination of Pedro Joaquín Chamorro and the recent imprisonment of most of the labor leaders and union affiliates.[47]

A few days later, on January 18, 1978, a communiqúe signed by CADIN (Cámara de Industria de Nicaragua), INDE (Instituto Nicaragüense de Desarrollo), the Chamber of Construction, the Chamber of Commerce, the Cooperative of Cotton Producers of Managua, and several other organizations also declared that they would call for a permanent work stoppage until favorable conditions prevailed. Four days later, the general strike began. A self-appointed "National Committee of the General Strike" was formed with the participation of leaders of different political parties and business organizations, calling on entrepreneurs, students, employees, and workers to stop working on January 22, 1978, to demand that those responsible for Chamorro's assassination be brought to justice. A day later, in some of the commercial centers, up to 85% of the businesses closed down.

An effective general strike with the participation of both the private sector and labor organizations could prove the best way to attain the main goals of the bourgeois opposition, which was to put pressure on Somoza to compromise, or even to resign, and to maintain the peace and tranquility vital for a smooth period of transition in political power. The broad cooperation of labor organizations and the middle and lower classes could be the best guarantee of an effective social support for the future government. It also could refute the necessity of armed struggle and radical social changes proposed by the FSLN.

On January 24, nine important private sector organizations, including INDE and CADIN, published a joint document repudiating the "mockery of Justice, which maintains a state of anxiety in the country." They declared their solidarity with the "peaceful protest" of all sectors of the society, manifested in a general strike. To prevent "more pain and uncertainty for the Nicaraguan family," they demanded justice, and expressed their support for "peaceful means" to establish a government which would guarantee "the freedom, and respect for the rights of the citizens."[48]

On the same day, UDEL strongly demanded the resignation of Somoza from the presidency.

1. The assassination of the martyr of democratic freedom, Pedro Joaquín Chamorro, in addition to rousing the consciousness of all Nicaraguans, which is expressed in a unanimous protest, is the culmination of a process of violence, corruption, and systematic violation of the human rights by assassination, disappearances, tortures and unjustified imprisonment of thousands of campesinos, workers, industrialists, priests and nuns, and the political and moral de-composition which has put our society on the edge of destruction.

2. General Anastasio Somoza Debayle is the principle responsible [person] of the [above] described process. He has weakened all basic institutions of democracy to protect his own personal interests, and has deprived the people of political liberty, [he] has limited the autonomy of the Congress and Judicial Power, [he] has promoted dishonest competition with the private sector. He has subjected the Army to a procedure which has undermined its institutions, prestige, and professionalism, and repeatedly has identified his private interests with those of the State, eroding public morale and opening a current of corruption which has reached alarming levels.

3. The policies applied by Somoza have prevented an equitable distribution of the benefits of the economic growth, and the problems of housing, unemployment, health and education continue on an alarming level with no solution, and [they] affect the majority of our people.

4. The above described situation does not have the backing of, or the legitimization among any sector of our society; and Somoza, deaf to all protests and reclamation, is not capable of guaranteeing the security of the Nicaraguans, and he [himself] is the principle root of the intranquility and contradictions.

5. Following the events of the atrocious assassination of our [UDEL] founder, the first President, Pedro Joaquín Chamorro Cardenal, and growing understanding of the dangerous rate of decomposition of our society, all sectors of our people, [workers, employees, businessmen, professionals, and students], have expressed their protest through a *General Stoppage of all the Activities*, which is unprecedented in our country and has to be understood as a demand for fundamental change in the direction of the. government.

In the light of all the above mentioned conditions, *Unión Democrática de Liberación*, UDEL, demands the resignation of General Anastasio Somoza Debayle from the Presidency of the Republic, and directorship of the National Guard, as the basic condition which would permit, in an organized peaceful way, formation of a government to initiate the establishment of a democratic system based on justice and liberty, an objective which requires and demands the support of all sectors of the nation.[49]

On January 25, the National Directorate of the Conservative Party of Nicaragua also demanded the resignation of the President and the appointment of a new group of people by the Legislature to take over the Executive with the support of the National Guard.

There is no other alternative but total unity to salvage the institutions [of the country], to rescue order, to restore confidence and to exercise justice.

The Somocist government is not capable of offering justice, or confidence. The Conservative Party declares that only resignation of the President of the Republic can grant an ultimate hope for peace and concordance. We call for an immediate meeting of the Legislative Power to recognize this resignation, and to designate his replacement. A new team of men being put in charge of the National Government to run the Executive Power, with the backing of the National Guard, can restore confidence and can prepare, in unity with other powers of the State, the new political and socio-economic framework which our present society demands.[50]

Following the declarations of UDEL and the Conservative Party demanding the resignation of Somoza, *La Prensa* published an editorial supporting this demand.

Conscious of the actual situation, *La Prensa* does not see any other solution but the one proposed by UDEL and the Conservative Party. We accept the concepts of their pronouncements, and firmly support their demands, adding . . . that the stated solution can bring peace and tranquility for our people. . . ."[51]

Meanwhile, other cities joined the general strike, and over 80% of all businesses closed down in Chinandega, Carazo, Boaco, Rivas, Ocotal, Nandaime, Jinotepe, Estelí, and Masaya. The "Strike Committee" declared that the general strike would continue until the resignation of Anastasio Somoza. The Conservative Party (PCN), the Social Christian Party (PSC), and the Authentic Conservative Party (PCA) also issued a joint statement demanding the resignation of Somoza. The Independent Liberal Party (PLI), and the Central of Nicaraguan Workers (CTN), and the Union of Popular Organizations (UNOP) did the same.[52]

Although the above documents were written by different organizations — UDEL, the Conservative Party, Business groups, and *La Prensa* — they all focused on the same themes: the peaceful nature of the General Strike, the participation of different sectors of the Nicaraguan society, and the resignation of the dictator through a constitutional process which would maintain "institutions" and rescue the "order," and return "confidence."

Another sector voicing similar demands was the Catholic hierarchy. Following the assassination of Chamorro, the Episcopal Conference published a document offering condolences to the Chamorro family, the Nicaraguan journalists, and the Nicaraguan people. In this document, the Episcopal Conference called on the authorities to investigate the assassination and to punish the guilty parties, leaving no doubts surrounding the case. The bishops warned the government that any leniency in solving this case could "open a painful road to violence which would be impossible to contain." They also warned the people "who seek arms and blood as a solution for the problems which could only be solved in an atmosphere of justice and national concordant."[53]

In an interview with *La Prensa* on January 27, Archbishop Obanda y Bravo expressed his "complete support for the General Strike as a peaceful means to re-claim justice."[54] Also, in a second document published on January 29 by the Episcopal Conference, the bishops reaffirmed that they were "in agreement with all who try to solve the national problems through peaceful means." Once more they asked the national government "to seek real and definite solutions to the problems . . . and to respond to the demands of the majority of the people. . . ."[55]

Somoza's reaction to the general strike was the initiation of more repressive decrees to force the people to cooperate with the government. He also put a close watch on the radio programming of private stations and closed down *Radio Católica*, the official voice of the Church. Facing the new situation, the radio reporters went on an indefinite strike and began to read the news for the people in churches. This action became known as Catacombs Reporting (Periodismo de Catacumbas), and the people packed the churches to hear the news.

Meanwhile, street demonstrations were increasing. According to *La Prensa*, most of the demonstrations were organized by the students and popular classes (lower and middle classes), and the common slogans were "United people will never be defeated," and "It's enough." In a few cases a new slogan was heard: "An armed people will never be crushed." The demonstrators were still hoping to gain the sympathy of the soldiers, and their slogan addressing the National Guard was *"Guardia* stop, don't kill your people." The communication media of the opposition were also trying hard to point out that the demonstrations were against Somoza, not the National Guard.[56]

In spite of increasing repression, the demonstrations continued. On January 31, in Matagalpa, a demonstration was attacked by the Guard, leaving six people dead and many more injured. Street barricades began to appear and soon became a part of daily life in Nicaragua. Violent demonstrations spread throughout the country. In Managua, women of a middle-class neighborhood, Altamira began hitting pots and pans as protest against the repression. Other middle-class neighborhoods of Managua followed the Altamira example. The National Guard entered the residential areas, beating up women and children. Soon after, street barricades appeared even in the middle- and upper-class neighborhoods.[57]

The spread of violence and an active resistance by the people were obvious signs of a new phase in the struggle. The impetus behind the general strike was now shifting toward street fighting and radicalization of many Nicaraguans, who increasingly chose to fight back against repression instead of using peaceful protest. The new developments put the private sector in a difficult position. On the one hand, they had called for an indefinite general strike until the resignation of Somoza, hoping that it would come shortly; on the other hand, the intransigence of the dictator and the determination of the people to fight back had created a dangerous situation which could lead to a civil war and destruction of many sociopolitical institutions which the private sector wanted to preserve.

In a declaration on February 1, 1978, UDEL expressed its concerns about the new situation.

> The organized struggle of the Nicaraguan people against the Somocista dictatorship, which is manifested in the General Strike . . . has been wrongly portrayed by the dictator in its intentions, scope and significance. In a desperate attempt to survive the present crisis, [the dictator] is trying to convince the National Guard and the Liberal Party that this struggle is against them and their institutions.

> Facing this scheme, UDEL declares, once more, that the struggle of the Nicaraguan people embracing all economic political, social, labor and religious sectors, is against Anastasio Somoza Debayle, because he constitutes the principle element of disruption and contradiction in our society; and the major obstacle to democratization of the country. . . . The situation is clear, and the Liberals, the military, and the public employees should understand that what the Nicaraguan people demand is resignation of Anastasio Somoza from the Presidency of the Republic and directorship of the National Guard to give way to the constitutional mechanism which permits a civic and democratic road solving national problems.[58]

In spite of the repeated attempts of UDEL and other private sector organizations to keep the General Strike in a peaceful framework, and to limit the demands to the resignation of Somoza, different sectors of the Nicaraguan people, particularly among the lower classes, had already begun to go much beyond a peaceful resistance and a mere replacement of the dictator without touching his social basis. On January 31, in Matagalpa, a group of protestors occupied the office of the head of the local police and burned all the police archives. In another demonstration against a Somocist member of the congress, the people of Matagalpa clashed with the National Guard, leaving one person dead and eight more wounded.[59]

Violent clashes with the National Guard increased the concerns of the private sector about the future of the general strike, and its later effects on the relationship between the army and the political opposition. In a editorial on February 3, 1978, *La Prensa* tried to assure the National Guard that its "noble" profession is recognized by the Nicaraguans, and that it only has to change from a partisan army, supporting the dictator, to a nonpartisan organization defending the "Nicaraguan family." *La Prensa* insisted that it was important for the National Guard, like any other Nicaraguan institution, "to reflect on every level," the desirability of "initiation of a change without Somoza." The editorial went on to stress the need for a professional and nonpartisan army in the process of political change in the country. Without it, *La Prensa* warned, "The Nicaraguans will experience the process of a frightening crisis in the judical system . . . and political crimes would increase and more blood would be shed."[60]

Collapse of the Bourgeois Leadership

The evident ineffectiveness of the general strike in pressuring Somoza to step down, and the rapid radicalization of the lower and middle classes, who increasingly had resorted to street fights against the National Guard, convinced the leaders of the bourgeois opposition that the strike had to be ended. On February 4, the private sector organizations, which had been closed since January 17, opened the business centers. The termination of the strike before the declared objectives were reached was a clear manifestation of the weakness of a moderate opposition which was pressed between the intransigence of the dictator and an uncontrollable radicalization of the lower classes. While Somoza did not bend to the pressure for compromise, the radical opposition (i.e., the FSLN and *Los Doce*) called for the continuation of the strike and active resistance. The leadership of UDEL could not control the tension even in its own ranks. A conflict broke out between representatives of the Socialist Party and the CGT-I who wanted the strike to continue, and the UDEL leadership who wanted it terminated before further damage to their credibility.

As the private sector lost ground in the leadership of the mass movement, the FSLN stepped in and filled the gap with a series of successful armed actions that gained strong support among the people. On the night of February 2, the FSLN attacked and seized the cities of Granada and Rivas. In Granada, the attack began at 9:30 P.M. from three different points of the city. An intense gun battle continued for two hours until the National Guard put down its arms. The FSLN retreated at 3:00 A.M., before the National Guard reinforcements reached the city. Thirty soldiers were killed in the action. A simultaneous successful attack on Rivas left forty soldiers dead.[61] The FSLN casualties were one wounded in Granada, three dead and one wounded in Rivas. On the same day, different towns of Nueva Segovia were attacked, leaving another twenty-nine National Guard soliders dead.

The public debate on political options intensified among Nicaraguans. Even Archbishop Obando had to acknowledge the existence of choices, and the Church's division over political alternatives. In an interview, the archbishop of Managua confirmed that he "always supports non-violent means." However, he added that

> there are theologians and moralists who believe collective armed resistance is permitted if three conditions exists: (a) existence of grave and evident injustice which legitimizes defense; (b) verified failure of all possible peaceful solutions; (c) a less grave danger of injustice caused by the armed struggle, comparing to the injustices which have caused it.[62]

Facing the successful attacks of the FSLN against the National Guard, the U.S. State Department broke its silence, affirming that "the demands for liberty, justice and democratization" could be realized by "moderation and conciliation in seeking peaceful solutions."[63] The statement continued to "condemn all kinds of attempts at violence." A few days later, the American Embassy in Managua insisted on the necessity of preventing violence and turning back to peaceful means to resolve the crisis.[64]

According to a United Press International cable printed in *La Prensa*, a spokesperson for the State Department, Terence Todman, declared that "a dialogue between the [Nicaraguan] government and the opposition groups was a way to accomplish a solution to the Nicaraguan crisis, preventing acts of violence." The statement continued to affirm that "Somoza had proposed the dialogue and Pedro Joaquín Chamorro had accepted it. And the violence was incited by the Sandinistas, and it was not supported by the others."[65]

Facing a new situation, the Catholic hierarchy attempted to modify its political position and its call for the resignation of Somoza. On February 22, a week after the State Department's call for the renewal of the dialogue, the Nicaraguan bishops, in a much criticized statement, declared their disapproval of usage of the church buildings for political protest or as centers for informing the public, as had happened during the general strike. The bishops proclaimed that these actions had been "disrespectful for the churches and had created desecration."[66]

Meanwhile, street demonstrations continued in different cities, and in many of them the demonstrators were carrying the FSLN flag. An obvious trend toward militant resistance was noticeable in the street demonstrations in major cities. In Monimbó, an indigenous neighborhood of Masaya, the protestors used homemade contact bombs against the National Guard. On February 21, the inhabitants of Masaya and Monimbó celebrated the forty-fourth anniversary of the death of Sandino in a commemorative mass and conference in *Central de Trabajadores de Masaya*. Somoza sent troops from Managua, and ordered National Guard helicopters to bomb residential areas of Masaya. That night, the people of Monimbó reacted to the attack, using firearms and homemade contact bombs. The fight continued for several days, leaving many civilians dead and many more injured. The National Guard prevented Red Cross workers from entering the barrio to help the wounded. The fight spread throughout Masaya, and most of the barrios set up street barricades against the National Guard. The government attacked from the air, indiscriminately bombing Masaya, particularly the indigenous inhabitants of Monimbó. Upon hearing about the fight in Monimbó and Masaya, residents in other major cities rose in protest, barricades were built, and street fights began all over the country.

The spontaneous insurrection in Monimbó proved that the people had chosen to strike back again Somoza, and they would not wait for the FSLN to schedule the struggle in accordance with its own timetable and state of preparedness. As Sergio Ramírez (a member of *Los Doce* and now vice-president of Nicaragua) reported later: "The insurrection of Monimbó was not planned by the FSLN."[67] The revolutionary vanguard was already behind the people's movement. The Sandinistas recognized the problem immediately and tried to direct the Monimbó struggle by sending in the few cadres they had in the area, including Camilo Ortega, younger brother of Daniel and Humberto Ortega, leaders of the *Terceristas*. However, the help was too little and too late. Camilo was killed in Monimbo, and the battle continued in an unorganized fashion.

The private sector was increasingly losing ground to the radical movement. Even inside its own ranks there was defection and a high level of political confusion. U.S. foreign policy, often inconsistent, hardly helped the private sector in strengthening its political standing. In contrast to strong support for the political opposition by the beginning of 1978, the Carter Administration, following the mass uprisings in February, shifted toward backing Somoza and strengthening his position with more military aid. The halt which was put on all military aid to Nicaragua on February 1 was lifted in mid-March, and the U.S. government released $12 million in U.S. aid to the country,[68] in spite of the reports of massive violations of human rights by Somoza during the mass uprisings, especially in Monimbó.

The changing policy of the U.S. government caused resentment among the Nicaraguan moderate opposition. In the beginning of June, UDEL issued a statement bitterly complaining about the U.S. aid given to Somoza.

> The recent announcement of the North American government concerning the grant of a new loan to Somoza has the disastrous effect of being a license [to Somoza] to continue violations of human rights, and to reject any peaceful means to bring about the democracy demanded by the people. . . . We protest the ambiguous and contradictory North American policies, which leave the statements about [protection of] human rights hollow.[69]

The most disappointing news for the Nicaraguan moderate opposition came in mid-July, when a letter to Somoza, written by President Carter, was leaked to the press. In this letter, dated June 30, 1978, President Carter had congratulated Somoza on some recent promises to improve the human rights situation in his country.[70] The letter acted as a strong catalyst for the more nationalist elements in the bourgeois opposition to distance themselves from Washington, and to seek an independent solution to the country's problems. Being convinced that the reformist opposition, now with no firm ally in Washington, had lost its chance to pressure Somoza to resign, many of the moderates began to think about collaborating with the Sandinistas as the only way to secure Somoza's resignation. The internal developments in the FSLN and the emergence of a new political line which had opened the organization to different ideologies created a new hope for some sectors of the political opposition.[71] They assumed that they could actually modify the radicalism of the left by joining it in the process of overthrowing Somoza and the formation of a new government.

The FSLN and the Bourgeoisie

Following the division of the *Frente* into different factions in 1975–76, the *Tercerista* (insurrectionist) Tendency was the one most flexible on the issue of tactical alliance with the bourgeoisie. In contrast to the GGP (Guerra Popular Prolongada) Tendency, which advocated a prolonged people's war, the insurrectionist faction was seeking a fast way to overthrow Somoza in a popular insurrection. For this purpose, they were willing to recruit support from the middle-class and even upper-class anti-Somoza elements. Recognizing the internal conflict in the bourgeoisie, which had resulted in the formation of a large capitalist block of opposition to the Somoza dynasty, the *Terceristas* had modified the Marxist politics of the original FSLN in an apparent attempt to attract more nationalist and progressive elements of the bourgeois opposition.[72]

Following the October offensive of 1977, one of the leaders of the *Terceristas*, Plutarco Elias Hernández, in an interview with the *New York Times* indicated that they had abandoned their struggle for a "Marxist victory through 'prolonged popular war'" in favor of a more immediate popular insurrection supported by broad sectors of the population." Hernández affirmed, "We must pass through the stage of democracy because socialism cannot be built overnight. . . . Those who think we'll be going straight to communism are wrong.

Our basic program is not Communist. It is a threat to no one who favors a just society."[73] According to Hernández, among the first actions planned by the Sandinistas, following the upcoming revolutionary triumph, was the expropriation of the vast business empire of the Somoza family. They also favored nationalization of the banking sector, sweeping land reform, emphasis on social welfare and education and establishment of diplomatic relations with socialist countries.[74]

Following the collapse of the general strike in February, which was an indication of the ineffectiveness of the peaceful methods of the bourgeois opposition to pressure Somoza to resign, some militant members of the political opposition began seeking an alternative. They even considered the *Tercerista* Tendency as a viable factor in the national political picture. In an analysis of the political situation of February 1978, *La Prensa* published an article in which the author, Reinaldo Antonio Tefel, a Christian activist, portrayed the *Tercerista* Tendency as "a very important element recently introduced into the national political picture." According to the article, the most important aspects of the new "element" were

> a new democratic revolutionary political line which does not insist on introduction of "dictatorship of the proletariat," but rather the establishment of a democratic national government with participation of all progressive sectors of the country.[75]

Another important aspect of the *Tercerista* Tendency, according to the author, was its insurrectionist policies, which were not "based on a long period of war, but rather, overthrowing the dictator in a short time." The writer asserted that the support which the *Terceristas* had obtained in Latin America, the United States, and among the popular sectors of the Nicaraguan society as well as the prominent citizens, *Los Doce*, had converted them to an important factor which should be considered by the political opposition.

The shift in U.S. foreign policy toward the reestablishment of friendly relations with Somoza and the lifting of the ban on U.S. aid in mid-March, followed by Carter's friendly letter to Somoza in June, angered many elements of the bourgeois opposition, and collaboration with the radical elements increased tremendously.

The time was ripe for the FSLN to test its policy of tactical class alliance. In spite of the repeated threat of arrest, the members of *Los Doce* returned from exile in mid-July, and joined the new coalition of anti-Somoza political forces, *Frente Amplio Opositor* (Broad Opposition Front). FAO included UDEL, the newly formed *Movimiento Democrático Nicaragüense* (MDN — Nicaraguan Democratic Movement, which was based in the professional and business community), the Social Christian Party, and three factions of the Conservative Party. Although one of the members of *Los Doce*, Sergio Ramírez, was chosen as one of the three members of FAO's political commission, *Los Doce* never "endorsed the FAO platform as the basis of a post-Somoza government."[76] and maintained that without the participation of the FSLN, no solution could be found for the national crisis. However, the mere presence of *Los Doce* in FAO was a sign of the FSLN recognition of the bourgeoisie as a partner in any future change of the government. This collaborative policy of the Sandinistas created hopes for the bourgeoisie that in any upcoming negotiation with Somoza, it could use the new class alignment as a strong card against Somoza. Once more, the moderate political opposition, represented by FAO, felt strong enough to demand the resignation of Tachito from the presidency and the directorship of the National Guard.

The new optimistic political atmosphere created by the formation of FAO, with participation of *Los Doce* and the support of the FSLN, was rapidly reflected in the political position of the Catholic hierarchy. The bishops, who, in February, had irritated the opposition by their statement opposing the use of church buildings for political purposes, rapidly changed their policy again, and supported the renewed demand of the opposition for resignation of Somoza, and formation of a new government.

In a document signed by the bishops on August 2, 1978, the hierarchy called for

> a new democratic revolutionary political line which does not insist on introduction of "dictatorship of the proletariat," but rather the establishment of a democratic national government with participation of all progressive sectors of the country.[75]

They insisted on the necessity of "freedom for political organizations," "judicial independence," "a clean administration," "reorganiza-

tion of the Army," and "the end of violent repression." The bishops
declared that

> peace without justice is a dream. Also the possibility of preventing
> the violent actions of the people who are tired of [unsuccessfully]
> trying other ways to accomplish justice, is a dream.[78]

However, the bishops once again condemned armed struggle to
change the situation.

> We repeat again that it is not too late yet. Peace is still pos-
> sible. We are all brothers under the same sky. God is our common
> father. Centuries of Christian faith and cultural values should not
> be swept away in a wave of hatred and madness, in a collective
> self-destruction.[79]

The bishops called on all "men of good will" to collaborate to create
"justice, love, and liberty. . . ."

Another document signed by Archbishop Obando y Bravo and
his advisory council, on August 3, 1978, clearly reflected the main
demand of FAO.

> In the context of a mutual concession, by its resignation, the
> [Somoza] Government could promote the formation of a national
> government, which by obtaining the support of the majority,
> would prevent Nicaragua from falling into a power vacuum and
> anarchy, a possible course in a process of change.[80]

Following the pastoral letter and the archbishop's message, *La
Prensa* waged a strong campaign to promote the archbishop's proposal for formation of a national government with the participation
of all sectors of Nicaraguan society.

> Our pastor, Miguel, rejects the violence and all kinds of
> escalation of armed activities, as a means to solve the crisis, and
> calls on us to work enthusiastically to construct a period of transi-
> tion with a national government which regains the credibility and
> the confidence of all Nicaraguans. . . . The creation of a national
> government is a compromise which implies mutual concessions,

and as the Archbishop had indicated, the [Somoza] government can promote the formation of the [new] government by its resignation which would provide the conditions for democratization and restoration of peace and justice in Nicaragua.[81]

However, both the bishops' statements and the *La Prensa* editorials had based their support for the formation of a national government on the assumption that FAO, as the representative of the majority, would form the backbone of the new regime. Although *Los Doce*, supportive of the FSLN, had participated in FAO, there was no direct representation of the Sandinistas in the organization, and the leadership clearly was in the hands of the representatives of the bourgeoisie.

The *Terceristas*, while emphasizing collaboration with the bourgeois opposition, were not willing to support an alliance in which the leadership would be in the hands of the bourgeois organizations. They had previously maintained that

> the popular political forces (i.e., the FSLN itself, the trade unions, the various mass organizations, and the Communists) should enter a tactical alliance with the bourgeois opposition forces, and form together with them the post-Somoza transitional government. So that the popular forces should win the upper hand in this 'democratic popular government,' and be able to transform an originally mixed economic system into a socialist economic order on the basis of the nationalized Somoza property, they should be organized already before the uprising in as united and comprehensive a fashion as possible.[82]

This policy resulted in vigorous attempts by the FSLN to mobilize their supporters in different organizations on all levels, from neighborhood committees to peasant associations.

The culmination of this organizational effort was the formation, in the early summer of 1978, of the *Movimiento Pueblo Unido* (MPU — Movement of United People), which was

> the political alliance of the revolutionary organizations, revolutionary parties and popular associations of the working class, campesinos, youth, students, progressive women, intellectual, and other broad democratic sectors.[83]

Twenty-two different organizations participated in the MPU, including the *Central General de Trabajadores (CGT), the Asociación de Trabajadores del Campo* (ATC), *Frente Estudiantil Revolucionario* (FER), *Partido Socialista Nicaragüense* (PSN), and the *Partido Comunista de Nicaragua* (Pc de N).

For the FSNL, the MPU had three purposes:

> (1) To develop organizational work within the mass movement, among both workers and peasants; (2) To consolidate the unity of all democratic and revolutionary sectors; (3) To push forward with the popular armed insurrection.[84]

The MPU focused on organizing popular sectors on all levels, especially in the neighborhood committees (Comités de Defensa Civil) and workplaces. The grassroots organizations soon spread all over the country and created an enormous support base for the revolution.

Confident of its strong support base, the FSLN launched a bold military action. On August 22, the FSLN forces occupied the National Palace, and took the members of Congress hostage. Somoza, having some of his relatives and close friends and advisors among the hostages, surrendered to the pressure, and released Sandinista political prisoners, as demanded by the FSLN. The organization's political statement was also read on radio and television, and was printed in the press. This successful action was met with strong support among the people, who took to the streets to celebrate and to cheer the FSLN commando unit and the released political prisoners leaving the country for Panama.

Following the National Palace occupation, FAO called for another general strike. However, the people, once more, resorted to street demonstrations and clashed with the National Guard. In Matagalpa, demonstrations escalated into a general insurrection, and the people took over the city The National Guard sent reinforcements, and attacked the city with tanks and fighter planes, and finally recaptured Matagalpa on September 3.

The FSLN leadership, not yet prepared for a general insurrection, had to bend under popular pressure, and on September 9 it called for a national insurrection. Within twenty-four hours, a bloody battle began on all fronts. The popular forces, mostly unarmed, were fighting an uneven war against the National Guard, which was supported by aircraft and tanks. The fighting continued until the end of September, and thousands of people were slaughtered during the battle and the subsequent "mopping up" operation by the National Guard. Although Somoza sealed off the cities to the press, the reports of savage atrocities reached the international press through eyewitnesses.[85]

The September insurrection had the characteristics of a mass movement organized by a revolutionary organization. For the first time, the leadership of the movement was completely in the hands of the FSLN, and the organization had total support among the people. Although the offensive was initiated by the *Tercerista* faction, the other two tendencies supported it and threw all their forces into the battle.

The collaboration of all three tendencies, and the active participation of the people, made the modern opposition, the Somoza regime, and the U.S. government realize that the struggle had advanced much beyond an antidictatorial movement, and was in the process of endangering the basic social structures of the country. Although Somoza successfully crushed the insurrection, he had to use the maximum force at his disposal. On the other hand, most of the casualties were civilians, and the FSLN units pulled out to the mountains, basically intact. Moreover, thousands of young people who had fled the cities to escape the National Guard reprisal now joined the FSLN, and began military and political training in the mountains. It was obvious that in the case of a renewed uprising, Somoza could not match the mass movement supported by an ever-growing guerrilla force.[86]

The Last Attempt to Stop the Revolution: the United States, the Nicaraguan Bourgeoisie, and the Catholic Hierarchy

The feasibility of a sweeping revolution fostered another attempt by the U.S. government to mediate a compromise between Somoza and the moderate opposition. However, a sector of the nationalist bourgeoisie, angered by the continuation of the U.S. military aid to Somoza, viewed the mediation as another attempt by the United States to maintain Somoza in power. In an editorial, *La Prensa* wrote:

> When all diverse sectors of the Nicaraguan people demanded the termination of all economic, military and diplomatic aid to Somoza, they were not asking for any kind of foreign intervention against Somoza, rather the cessation of foreign intervention in favor of Somoza. In the political and institutional framework of Nicaragua, all foreign aid is only used to consolidate the repressive basis of the dictatorship. . . .
>
> We cannot forget that the Somocist dictatorship has its roots in the direct North American intervention. And the maintaining of power by the Somoza family [with the aid of the United States] is the continuation of this intervention.[87]

La Prensa went on to critcize

> the ambiguous and contradictory positions of the U.S. government, which in the pretext of the principle of non-intervention, refuses to cut its ties with the Somocist dictatorship.[88]

By now, the private sector's leaders knew that they could not overthrow the dictator by themselves. The general strike and repeated denunciations had shown that these resources were not enough to secure Somoza's resignation. On the other hand, the leaders also understood that if the radicals overthrew Somoza in a popular struggle, the very existence of the bourgeoisie and its position as the dominant class would be endangered. Therefore, faced with the two choices of either letting the popular classes, who were becoming more and more supportive of the Sandinistas, win the battle, or, in cooperation with the United States, to come to agreement with the dictator, the bourgeoisie took the second option.

FAO accepted the mediation of the United States, Guatemala, and the Dominican Republic, and began planning for a transition government which would take over following the resignation of Somoza. When on October 25, the United States announced its plans for a provisional government including Somoza's *Partido Liberal Nacionalista* and the National Guard, the group *Los Doce* pulled out of the talks and resigned from FAO. This action was a strong blow to the credibility of FAO, and some other member organizations soon followed the example of the *Los Doce*. Meanwhile, the three tendencies of the FSLN, which had agreed in December on the coordination of their operations, began internal discussions on the organizational unity of the *Frente*. The new perspective of a unified revolutionary organization supported by the vast majority of the people who had participated in the September uprising, strongly reinforced the possibility of a fast triumph for the FSLN.

The new developments in the revolutionary camp had a catalytic impact on the divisions in the reformist block. On the one hand, the right-wing sectors of the political opposition came closer to the U.S. government in a desperate attempt to stop the revolution. On the other hand, the groups which had left FAO now rushed to ally themselves with the FSLN to share in the upcoming victory.

The Church hierarchy, which had backed the mediation and FAO's leadership, continued its support for the process, and maintained its alliance with the remaining groups of FAO. The alignment was strengthened in meetings among the Catholic hierarchy, FAO leadership, and the private sector business organizations represented by COSEP (Consejo Superior de la Empresa Privada). In one such meeting, held on November 22, 1978, the hierarchy and COSEP "urged FAO to continue its struggle to find a peaceful solution to the conflict."[89] Following the meeting, the representative of COSEP said, "We all agree on the urgency of a change in the government. But, as Nicaraguans, we fervently search for a peaceful alternative to lessen the major damages as have [already] received."[90]

However, the process of disintegration of FAO continued. In November, the *Central de Trabajadores de Nicaragua* (CTN), pulled out of FAO and criticized the organization and the Mediation Commission. The CTN charged that "the Commission is conducting the negotiations toward a pact with Somoza, and the member organizations of FAO are falling into the trap [planned by] the Commission."[91]

The efforts to form a transitional government soon collapsed because of Somoza's insistence of remaining in power until the end of his presidential term in 1981. The next, and the last, proposal of the Mediation Commission was a public referendum in which the people would vote for the resignation of Somoza or the continuation of his presidency. FAO agreed to the new plan.[92] However, Somoza's representatives in the planning meetings began insisting on the continuation of his presidency, and the talks finished with no results.

The FSLN, now with a clear perspective on organizational unity, was prepared to absorb the new allies who had left FAO. A new opposition front, *Frente Patriótico Nacional* (FPN — National Patriotic Front), was formed on February 1, 1979. The participants were *Movimiento Pueblo Unido* (MPU, formed by the FSLN in summer of 1978), *Partido Liberal Independiente* (PLI), *Los Doce, Central Trabajadores de Nicaragua* (CTN), *Partido Popular Socialcristiano* (PPSC), *Frente Obrero*, and *Sindicato De Radioperiodistas de Managua*.

The program of the FPN had a strong anti-Somoza, anti-imperialist tone, rejecting any pacts with the regime, and any mediation by the United States. The program called for (1) national sovereignty, (2) effective democracy, and (3) justice and social progress.[93] In a clear reference to the mediation, the FPN strongly rejected "all kind of foreign intervention which tries to impose formulas for our social, economic, and political life."[94] The rest of the program addressed the "overthrow of Somoza," "dissolution of the existing Congress," "creation of a new National Army," "confiscation of all properties belonging to the Somoza family," "realization of an integral agrarian reform," and "nationalization of all natural resources." The hegemony of the FSLN political line was clearly manifested in the FPN program. A final development which guaranteed a triumph for the FSLN in the upcoming insurrection was the formation of a single directorate on March 7, 1979.

The imminent triumph of the Sandinistas and their overwhelming support among the Nicaraguans preparing for a final offensive did not change the archbishop's hard line on the armed struggle. In an interview with *La Prensa* on April 8, 1979, Monsignor obando y Bravo asserted: "Violence seeks the death of the other [person], the gospel always seeks life [for other]." He concluded that these two were incompatible, and that theologically "violence is always unjust because it is against liberty." He advised the Christians to take "the same attitude towards violence as towards any other evil, and resist the temptation to justify violence."[95]

Repeated failure in any negotiation with Somoza exhausted the bourgeois opposition, and the rate of defection in FAO climbed rapidly. However, the right-wing leadership was still trying to reach a pact with Somoza. In April 1979, FAO and the Church hierarchy formed a "Reflection Committee" under the leadership of Archbishop Obando, and tried to reestablish their credentials in Nicaraguan political life and to emerge as a real force capable of stopping the rapidly growing revolutionary ranks.

The rapid turn of events finally changed the attitude of both the bourgeois opposition and the Catholic hierarchy toward the Sandinistas and the armed struggle. In June, with the revolutionary triumph only weeks away, and all attempts to negotiate a peaceful settlement with Somoza proven futile, FAO, which was now basically the representative of the big bourgeoisie and the non-Somocist financial oligarchy, made another effort to preserve the bastion of the Somoza regime. They offered to support the revolution if the postrevolutionary government would consist of seven members: one each from the National Guard, Somoza's Liberal Party, the FAO, the entrepreneurs, the free professions, and the trade unions, with the FPN and the FSLN being represented by only one joint representative.[96] This plan was rapidly rejected by the FSLN.

Meanwhile, the rush among the bourgeois groups to project a "revolutionary spirit" continued. Even the ultraconservative members of the big bourgeoisie adopted a revolutionary posture. The fervor also affected the Church hierarchy, and in a message to the Nicaraguan people on June 2, 1979, the bishops told the people that they had been "urging radical changes in the structure of [the] sociopolitical life" since 1971.[97] Referring to Somoza's intransigence to implementation of any changes, the bishops complained:

> Today we see that the dikes have broken because of the incessant cries from the populace and the lack of response from the established system. It would seem that it has no other purpose except to kill and annihilate, disregarding even the ethics of war.[98]

Following years of a strong stand against revolutionary violence, and of branding the revolutionaries as "non-Christians," the bishops were finally forced to accept the social reality. They recognized the undeniable "moral and juridical legitimacy" of the revolutionary uprising," when there is manifest, long-standing tyranny which does great damage to fundamental personal rights and dangerous harm to the common good of the country."[99]

The long-time strong anti-Marxist stand of the hierarchy finally was replaced with an unprecedented ideological tolerance in the process of a desperate attempt to secure a share for the bourgeois opposition in the upcoming revolutionary triumph.

> The current times demand that we supersede all party factions, every ideological difference and particular interest, and search at least temporarily, for new foundations that will assure our destiny as a nation. We consider as indispensable the acceptance of pluralism of ideas and political postures. . . .[100]

Although the bishops were among the last groups of Nicararguans to endorse the revolution, and there were serious questions as to the sincerity of their position, the FSLN warmly welcomed their support. In an attempt to unite all sectors of the population to overthrow the dictator, past differences were set aside momentarily, and the Nicaraguan people appeared united behind the revolution. Both the bourgeoisie and the Catholic hierarchy, in spite of their rigorous attempts to stop the revolution, were pictured as revolutionary both in Nicaragua and in the international community.

However, the few months of rapid transition and highly charged revolutionary atmosphere was only a short, although important, moment in the long history of the country and its institutions. The historical forces continued to develop, and the age-old division of the society, among different social classes, and of the Church, among diverse sectors of clergy, each with its own sociopolitical alliances, persisted, and resulted in further development of the ongoing struggle in Nicaragua.

Epilogue

The *Frente Sandinista de Liberación Nacional* entered Managua on July 19, 1979. The triumph of the revolution crushed the last hopes of the ultraconservative members of the upper class and their allies, the Catholic hierarchy and the United States government, who were all trying to encourage the other Latin American countries to intervene militarily to stop the revolutionary victory. With Somoza in Florida, the National Guard totally disintegrated by the popular insurrection, and the leaders of the Somocist Liberal Party fleeing the country en masse, the Sandinista triumph seemed total. In this atmosphere, the *Frente's* announcement of the formation of the Junta of the National Reconstruction Government, with a strong representation of the business community, and a cabinet chiefly composed of the private sector, came as a surprise. The pragmatism of the *Frente* leadership was demonstrated once again.

Faced with a national economy in shambles, the major means of production destroyed in a long violent war, a ransacked national treasury with only $3.5 million remaining from the last phase of Somoza's looting, and the highest per capita foreign debt in Latin America totaling $1.6 billion, the *Frente's* job of reconstructing the country would be a long and difficult task. The new regime had to secure the support of the private sector and the financial assistance of the capitalist countries of Western Europe and the United States. However, to obtain the much needed aid, the Sandinistas had to pay a heavy price, offering to the bourgeoisie a major part of executive power. The willingness of the *Frente* to share its hard-won victory with the right-wing private sector, which had used all the forces at its disposal to prevent a Sandinista triumph, caused bitter criticism among leftists and high hopes among rightists.[1] The leaders of the private sector, having lost their hope of stopping the revolution, now were given a chance to influence it from within. For five months following the July triumph, the class harmony and the optimistic view about the revolutionary process among all sectors of Nicaraguan society amazed international observers. Businessmen and Marxists were working together to reconstruct the country, with the aid of both Western capitalist countries and the Socialist block.

The atmosphere of collaboration and optimism also penetrated the conservative Catholic hierarchy, which on November 17, 1979, issued a pastoral letter surprisingly supportive of the revolutionary process.

> If socialism means — as it ought to mean — the preeminence of the interests of the majority of Nicaraguans and a model of a nationally planned economy, solidly and increasingly participant, we have nothing against it. A social project that guarantees the common use of the goods and resources of the country and allows — on the basis of the satisfaction of the fundamental necessities of every one — the improvement of the human quality of life seems just to us. If socialism implies . . . the participation of the worker in the product of his labor, the overcoming of economic alienation, there is nothing in Christianity that is in contradiction to this process. . . .
>
> If socialism means power exercised from the perspective of the vast majority, and increasingly shared by an organized people — in the sense that there is progress toward a true transfer of power to the popular classes — again it will encounter nothing but support and approval from our faith.
>
> If Socialism brings cultural processes that awaken the dignity of our masses and give them the strength to assume responsibilities and demand their rights, then we are dealing with a process of humanization that is convergent with the human dignity proclaimed by our faith.[2]

The supportive attitude of the Church hierarchy encouraged Christian activists, who had played a major role in the triumph of the revolution, and now were busy in building a new Nicaragua. Four priests accepted high positions in the executive branch of the government, and the religious groups sent their representatives to the Council of the State, the legislative body of the new government. The Christian Base Communities were highly active in ongoing mass mobilization both during and following the triumph.

However, the close collaboration between the Sandinistas and the private sector did not last long, nor did the support of the Church hierarchy for the revolutionary process. In the first few months following the triumph, the Sandinistas concentrated on converting the spontaneous mass support for the revolution into an organized and politically aware mass participation in the process. The neighborhood Sandinista Defense Committees (Comités de Defensa Sandinista — CDS), the Sandinistas Workers Federation (Central Sandinista de Trabajadores — CST), the Rural Workers' Association (Asociación de Trabajadores del Campo — ATC), the Association of Nicaraguan Women (Asociación de Mujeres Nicaragüenses 'Luisa Amanda Espinoza' — AMNLAE), and the Sandinista Youth 19th of July (Juventud Sandinista 19 del Julio) flourished and gained prominent roles in the mass mobilization through the country. The *Frente* soon proposed an increase in the number of seats in the Council of the State[3] from thirty-three to forty-seven to give the newly formed mass organizations a proper representation in the process of political decision making. The bourgeoisie, frightened of losing its grip over the state apparatus, bitterly complained about the Sandinistas' attempt to break away from pluralism. A sharp conflict began inside the government and intensified with the implementation of each new revolutionary program. The success of the first major national campaign, the literacy crusade, which cut the illiteracy rate from 50.7% to 12.3%, deepened the bourgeoisie concerns over the penetration of revolutionary ideas into the most remote areas of rural Nicaragua. Although the director of the literacy campaign was a Jesuit priest, Father Fernando Cardenal, and the teachers were 100,000 volunteer middle-class high school and university students, the leaders of the private sector accused the *Frente* of an attempt to indoctrinate the masses with Marxist ideas.

The Catholic hierarchy, which in its pastoral letter of November 1979, had pledged its support for, "cultural processes that awaken the dignity of our masses and give them the strength to assume responsibilities and demand their rights,"[4] suddenly shifted its position completely, and joined the business community in accusing the Sandinistas of trying to brainwash the people with Marxism and to destroy Christian values in Nicaragua. Again, like the bourgeoisie, the hierarchy failed to mention the predominantly Catholic leadership of the literacy campaign and its middle-class base.

The next sharp political conflict appeared when the Sandinistas proposed to nationalize the productive units left idle by their counterrevolutionary owners who had fled the country or had refused to keep their factories and farms in a productive condition. The private sector again complained that this was Marxist and would destroy the basis of the national economy. On April 22, 1980, the main spokesman of the business community in the Government Junta, Alfonso Robelo, resigned from his posts and later joined the Somocist forces in other Central American countries in their plan to overthrow the revolutionary government.[5]

The Catholic hierarchy's reaction was immediate and clear. Ignoring their own statement of support for "the preeminence of the interests of the majority of Nicaraguans and a model of nationally planned economy, solidly and increasingly participant,"[6] the hierarchy called the FSLN action materialistic Marxism and anti-Christian. Less than a month after Robelo's resignation, the bishops issued a statement, asking the priests with government positions to resign. According to the bishops the "exceptional circumstances" which had justified the priests' direct collaboration with the government had passed.

On July 14, 1980, just back from a meeting with Pope John Paul II in Brazil, Archbishop Obando declared that the leaders of the FSLN were Marxist, and that "Christian faith and Marxism could not coexist." He also asserted that "a Catholic people like the Nicaraguans" could not "be governed by a Marxist leadership."[7]

The war was declared. The right-wing bourgeoisie began to mobilize its forces to overthrow the Sandinista government. In its intense counterrevolutionary activities, the private sector soon found strong support. In 1981 the Reagan Administration came to power in the United States, renewing cold war rhetoric, and focusing on Nicaragua as the chief battleground between "communism," and the so-called "free world."

The clear alliance between the Nicaraguan bourgeoisie and the United States government transformed the historically strong anti-imperialist sentiments among the popular sectors to a powerful class feeling, and a new era began in Nicaragua. The popular antidictatorial movement, which overthrew Somoza in a confusing atmosphere of unity among all sectors of the society, now turned into a class struggle with its proper slogans and clear demands. Overcoming their initial illusions about securing the private sector's support for the reconstruction of the country, the Sandinista leadership tightened its control over political power. The lower classes, the rural and urban workers, small peasants, the urban marginal population, the lower sectors of the middle class, progressive intellectuals, the youth, the students, and progressive women all organized in their respective associations, and threw their decisive support behind the government and its social programs. The progressive clergy again played a significant role in mass mobilization and mass organizations. In many urban barrios and rural communities the membership overlapped in the mass organizations and the Christian Base Communities, and priests and nuns appeared as active organizers in the new social movement. On the other hand, the Church hierarchy, following the lead of its long-time ally, the ultraconservative bourgeoisie, moved increasingly to the right and identified itself with the counterrevolutionary forces and their North American supporters in a long and bloody battle against the Sandinista regime.

Although the right-wing private sector enjoys massive political, financial and military assistance from the United States, it suffers from a major weakness: the lack of active support inside Nicaragua. To create the necessary popular base, the bourgeoisie heavily relies on the Catholic hierarchy, the only organized antirevolutionary group with deep-rooted influence among the people.

To penetrate the popular classes and to break the base of support for the revolution, the hierarchy has used different methods, including (1) removing the progressive priests from their parishes and replacing them with conservative clergy loyal to the traditional Church; (2) encouraging Christians to abandon mass organizations and prorevolutionary activities; (3) running a constant antirevolutionary propaganda campaign through pastoral letters, public statements, and the opposition mass media; (4) mobilizing mass religious celebrations and manipulating the religious events and prayer sessions to publicize their antigovernment views; (5) emphasizing a spiritual approach to life, belief in miracles, and separation of religious life from social activities; (6) constantly attempting to discredit, and dissolve if possible, the organizations of the progressive clergy (e.g., the Association of Clergy [ACLEN], Centro Ecuménico de Antonio Valdivieso, Instituto Histórico Centroamericano, and Confederación de Religiosos [CONFER]); (7) trying to weaken the pluralistic image of the revolutionary government by pressing for the resignation of priests holding government positions.

In 1980, to fulfill his task of mobilizing mass support for the counterrevolutionary sector, Archbishop Obando formed a new organization, *Comisión de Promoción Social Arquidiocesana* (COPROSA). The initial funds for the organization's program were solicited from the Agency for International Development (AID), $493,000, and the Catholic Relief Services (itself heavily financed by the AID), $100,000.[8]

To shatter the early international recognition of the new Nicaraguan government as a pluralistic power, the Church hierarchy increased its pressure on the priests collaborating with the revolutionary government to resign their official positions. On June 1, 1981, the bishops published a harsh ultimatum to the priests.

> If the priests presently occupying public offices and exercising party functions were not to abandon those responsibilities immediately and return full time to their priesty duties, we would consider them to be openly defying and formally disobeying the legitimate ecclesiastical authority; they would thus be subject to the sanctions of the Church laws.[9]

This ultimatum was met with extensive opposition from the Christian Base Communities, who organized to voice their dissatisfaction with the Episcopal Conference's position, and to urge the bishops to enter a dialogue with the priests. The FSLN also showed a swift reaction, and sent a high-ranking delegate to the Vatican to discuss the situation.

The priests in the government also firmly defended their commitment to the revolution. In their response to the hierarchy's ultimatum they asserted:

> We declare our unbreakable commitment to the Popular San-

dinista Revolution, in loyalty to our people, which is the same as saying, in loyalty to the will of God.[10]

Finally the Church hierarchy bent under pressure and allowed the priests to maintain their government positions. However, they demanded that the priests abstain from performing priestly duties in public or private, including the celebration of Mass. The issue was not solved and the tension continued.

Another consistent policy of the conservative bishops, particularly Archbishop Obando and Bishop Vega, was weakening the mass base of the revolution, especially among the Christians. The Christian Base Communities, with their long history of active support for the revolutionary process, became a target of the hierarchy's attacks. Since 1980, the conservative bishops have waged a vigorous campaign to portray the Christian Base Communities as a newly organized force trying to establish a "National Church," as opposed to the legitimate worldwide Church. They have asserted that the Christian Base Communities have actually separated themselves from the hierarchy and have established a parallel Church.[11] The progressive sector, however, strongly denies that a parallel Church has been established. From their point of view, the struggle is between an emerging model of Catholicism which tries to adapt the Church to the demands of the time and the ongoing social transformation, and a traditional model, which attempts to maintain its long-time privileges by standing in the way of social progress.

In its attack on the Christian Base Communities, the Church hierarchy has found a close ally in Pope John Paul II. A long-time conservative and an staunch anticommunist, the Pope considers any support for a socialist alternative in the Third World countries as a gain for the enemy. His bitterness toward progressive movements intensifies particularly when they gather support among Christians. Liberation theologians, with their strong socialistic tendencies, have been victims of vicious and systematic attacks by the Vatican. And the Christian Base Communities, as the example of "God's people" in the process of building the Kingdom of God, as understood by the progressive Christian thought, were marked for annihilation.

The complete agreement between the ultraconservative bishops, such as Obando y Bravo and Pablo Vega, and the Pope was strikingly evident in a letter written by the Pope to the Nicaraguan bishops in June 1982. In his letter, the Pope referred to the new movement as the "people's Church," and warned the bishops of the danger that it poses for the authority of the "lawful pastors."

> A "people's Church" opposed to the Church presided over by the lawful pastors is a grave deviation from the will and plan of salvation of Jesus Christ. It is so from the point of view of the Lord's and the apostles' teaching in the New Testament and in the ancient and recent teaching of the Church's solemn magisterium. It is also a principle, a beginning, of fracture and rupture of that unity which he left as the characteristic sign of the Church itself, and which he willed to entrust precisely to those whom "the Holy Spirit established to rule the Church of God" (Acts 20:20).[12]

The Pope expressed his fear of a "people's Church," which in his words, "set the 'rights' of the aforementioned 'bases' over the authority" of the hierarchy. And since the term "people" takes on a "sociological and political content, it means a Church embodies in the popular organizations. . . ."[13] The Pope, with these pronouncements, clearly affirmed the class alliance of the Catholic leadership with the bourgeoisie, and joined their common fear of an organized people.

The Pope continued his crusade against the Christian Base Communities in his visit to Nicaragua in March 1983. In his speech in Managua, the Pope repeated the phrase "popular Church," in a surprisingly harsh tone, and then branded it as an "absurd and dangerous" project.

Encouraged by the Vatican's support, the Nicaraguan conservative hierarchy used all the power in its disposal to weaken the progressive sector of the clergy and the Christian Base Communities. Many progressive priests have been removed from their parishes and replaced with conservative clergy to reinforce the traditional elements of Christian thought and to discourage Christian support for the revolutionary process. One of these cases occurred in summer of 1982 in the Santa Rosa parish of Managua. The archbishop ordered Monsignor Arias Caldera, a progressive priest working with the poor of the parish for years, to leave his position. The members of the parish opposed this action, and tried to negotiate with the archbishop for the return of their priest. Obanda refused to reconsider his decision, and when the parishioners held a prayer vigil to protest the hierarchy's policy, Obando sent the auxiliary bishop of

Managua, Bosco Vivas, to remove the Blessed Sacrament of the Santa Rosa Church. Tension intensified and a skirmish occurred. The next day, the archbishop excommunicated those parishioners who had participated in the prayer vigil. All these actions of the hierarchy, in their attempts to weaken Christians who are supportive of the revolutionary process, has resulted in a sharp polarization among Catholics, and an increasing isolation of the hierarchy from the bases of the Church.

The most striking demonstration of the close alliance of the Catholic hierarchy with the counterrevolutionary bourgeoisie and its main supporter, the Reagan Administration, is the bishops' long-time refusal to condemn the CIA's not so secret activities in Nicaragua, and the U.S. government's total support for a bloody war imposed on the country by ex-National Guard members based in Honduras. On May 17, 1983, long after the CIA covert war against Nicaragua was exposed in the international news media and the United States Congress, and the Reagan Administration had openly asked the Congress to finance the counterrevolutionary forces, Archbishop Obando denied any knowledge about the subject. When interviewed in Rome by an Associated Press reporter, "the Archbishop said that he had received no reliable information about any U.S. government plans against Nicaragua."[14]

In 1983, the Nicaraguan government proposed the law of Military Service, to strengthen the defense of the country against increasing penetration from Honduras and Costa Rica, and to combat a growing atmosphere of terror created by constant sabotage and attacks on remote communities and towns by the counterrevolutionary forces. The Bishops' Conference strongly opposed the Military Service law, and proposed conscientious objection to it, while stating that, "no one can be punished, persecuted, or discriminated against for choosing such a solution."[15]

In 1984, when the news of war in Nicaragua and the mining of Nicaraguan harbors by the CIA occupied the daily headlines, the Bishops' Conference published a pastoral letter signed by the nine bishops, which called for a dialogue among all Nicaraguans, even those who have taken up arms against the government. The bishops did not mention the mining of the harbors; however, the sentence "Materialistic and atheistic education is mining the consciences of our youth"[16] was included in the letter.

Although many of the political attacks of the hierarchy against the government have been launched by the Bishops' Conference, and most of these letters are signed by all the bishops, there is still a significant division among the bishops concerning political issues. Although, the emphasis on Church unit, both by the Nicaraguan hierarchy and the Vatican, has muted any public manifestations of differences among the bishops, it has not completely suppressed it. For instance, in June 1981, when the Episcopal Conference published the ultimatum to the priests with government positions, Bishop Ruben López of Estelí and expressed his disagreement with the statement and asserted that he had not been informed of its content before publication.

Bishop Barni of Matagalpa and Bishop Schlaefer of the Atlantic Coast have maintained cordial relations with the government. In 1981, Schlaefer delivered the closing statement at the Council of the State, and Barni opened the Council in 1982.

Bishop Vilchez, a new member of the Episcopal Conference, has expressed his support for the participation of the masses in the Popular Militias. In an interview with *Barricada*, on October 3, 1982, he said, "If the United States invades Nicaragua, Nicaraguans have the right to defend themselves."[17] Also in August 1983, when the Episcopal Conference published its communiqué opposing the law of Military Service, in an interview with *El Nuevo Diario* Bishop Santi stated that he had not been informed of the content of the communiqué, expressed his belief in the duty of Christians to defend their country.[18]

The Pope's visit to Nicaragua, and his insistence on the unity of the Church under the leadership of Archbishop Obando, has left the Nicaraguan bishops in a difficult position as far as publicly expressing their views and voicing their opposition of Obando's intransigent anti-Sandinista policies. However, these differences have become clear on one major issue, namely, the attack of the counterrevolutionary bands on the Nicaraguan population, and the killing and torturing of civilians by these groups.

The Contras have found solid support among several members of the Church hierarchy, particularly Obando and Bishop Pablo Vega. In contrast to Obando and Vega, some other bishops have been outraged by the brutality of the Contras in dealing with defenseless civilians. In July 1983, when two kidnapped Christian activists from Estelí, Felipe and María Barreda, were tortured and killed by the Contras, Bishop Ruben López publicly condemned the kidnappings and assassinations of many Christians by Somoza bands. The bishop praised the Barredas "because their lives had been exemplary of Christian love and they had offered their lives, as had many others, so that the new Nicaragua might be born."[19]

The strongest statement against the war and U.S. policies in Nicaragua was issued on December 20, 1984, by Pablo Schmitz, the North American auxiliary bishop of the Atlantic Coast. He noted, "As a Christian, a Capuchin, and a priest, I cannot agree with this war being waged by the forces of imperialism against the Nicaraguan people."[20]

However, in contrast to the more liberal bishops, the conservative hierarchy, represented by Obando and Vega, has increasingly identified itself with war efforts of the Contras and the Reagan Administration. The archbishop intensified his antirevolutionary activities following his selection as the Cardinal of Central America in April 1985. This appointment was interpreted as the Vatican's total support for Obando's political position. The first Mass celebrated in America by the new Cardinal was on June 13, 1985, in Miami. Present in the celebration were leaders of the Contras, including Adolfo Calero, the top leader of the FDN (Nicaraguan Democratic Forces, the main Contra group, well known for its torturing and killing of Nicaraguan civilians), and Edén Pastora (at the time, the leader of ARDE, another Contra group based in Costa Rica). Obando, who was so consistent on the doctrine of nonviolence in the late 1970s, and who had repeatedly branded Nicaraguan revolutionaries as anti-Christian because of their use of armed struggle, has flatly refused to denounce the violent actions of the Contras against the civilian population, which has produced more than twenty thousand victims.

Another staunch supporter of the Contras is Bishop Pablo Vega. Pablo Vega, the bishop of Jinotega, has been one of the most conservative members of the hierarchy since the 1960s. Following the triumph of the revolution, he was one of the first bishops to attack the Sandinistas, and to join hands with the bourgeoisie in mourning the "glorious past." In a homily in El Sauce (Chinandega) on June

16, 1984, Bishop Vega stated: "Our country, our right to the land, and our right to free participation have been, for our people, only a yearning, a nostalgia, and a past with no hope of returning."[21]

Vega became internationally active in the collection of political and material support for the Contras. He travelled to the United States several times, usually during the Congressional debates on aid for the Contras. In his meetings and interviews, he resorted to flat lies to discredit the Nicaraguan government, and to convince the international community that a repressive government was in power in Nicaragua. In his visit to the United States in 1984, he accused the revolutionary government of the assassination of three priests, a lie, which he later retracted upon his return to Nicaragua.

When the Nicaraguan government set the date for the presidential election for November 4, 1984, the conservative bishops tried to gain the support of all the bishops to condemn the election. When the consensus was not achieved, Bishop Vega, as the president of the Bishops' Conference, wrote a belligerent letter on October 25, ten days before the election. Vega wrote in his letter, "Everyday the reality is more threatening, each day more oscillating: between 'repressive violence' and 'vengeful violence.'"[22]

To discredit the government, Vega has accused the Sandinistas of being puppets of the Soviet Union and Cuba. He uses this accusation to justify his support for the Contras. He describes them as a force to balance Soviet and Cuban influence in the country. In an interview conducted in 1984 by Dr. Max Azicri, a political scientist from the University of Pennsylvania, when Vega was pressed to take position on the Contras' acts of killing and torturing the campesinos, he referred the interviewer to the ideological influence of Soviets and Cubans and said, "To kill the soul is worse than to kill the body, says the Lord."[23]

Vega did not stop at attacking the revolution verbally. He also used his power as a bishop to deprive the revolution from any support in the religious community. One of the numerous cases of a clear abuse of religious power for political ends by Bishop Vega occurred in July 1984. A Catholic priest, Father Pedro Belzunegui, celebrated Mass at the burial of some youths killed by the Contras in San Juan del Norte. Father Belzunegui noted:

Christ said: Blessed are the poor, who suffer and cry, but also cursed are those who make them suffer. Because of this, from this Church, we want to say: Forever cursed be the criminal CIA that clothes itself in the blood of our brothers and sisters.

Pablo Vega, the bishop of Father Belzunegui, used his influence to move the priest to Guatemala, and called him "a propagandist about things that are none of his business."[24]

The constant support of the conservative hierarchy for the Contras and U.S. aggressive policies in Nicaragua has outraged the progressive sector of the clergy, and resulted in a harsh confrontation in the Church. In February 1986, when the news reached Nicaragua about the indirect participation of Cardinal Obando y Bravo and the more active involvement of Bishop Vega in giving a religious boost to Reagan's campaign to give $100 million to the Contras, Father Miguel D'Escoto, a Maryknoll priest and the Foreign Minister of Nicaragua, in a public speech addressed himself to Cardinal Obando in a personal and direct way, telling the Cardinal that his hands were stained with blood and that he had betrayed the people by approving aid to the counterrevolutionaries.[25]

Finally the public pressure and the insistence of the more liberal bishops resulted in a letter of the Bishops' Conference on April 6, 1986, in which, for the first time, it stated, "We judge that all forms of aid, whatever the source, that leads to destruction, pain and the death of our families or to hatred and division among Nicaraguans are condemneable."[26]

Although the division in the Nicaraguan Catholic Church has intensified tremendously since the triumph of the revolution, and the political lines have been drawn between the hierarchy and the progressive clergy, the organizational separation has not occurred yet, and both sectors claim to belong to one institution, the Catholic Church.

Leaving aside the rhetoric and constant exchanges of allegations and accusations couched in religious assertions and slogans, the heart of the conflict lies in a deep division between a hierarchy allied with the private sector and large landholders, which is waging a war against a government representing the lower classes' interests, and a progressive clergy, which has identified itself with the popular classes and is participating in the ongoing class struggle in the country.

Notes

Chapter 1. The Catholic Church in Nicaragua

1. Royal Patronage was a series of rules and regulations governing the Church-State relationship in Iberia, and later in Latin America. It was based on old Iberian customs, and on special concessions to the Iberian Catholic kings by the papacy in the fifteenth and early sixteenth centuries. According to royal patronage, the kings had the right to appoint and recall bishops and archbishops; to license the clergy, both secular and regular, in the new colonies; to control the communication between the clergy and the papacy; to regulate the finances of the Church; to decide on the boundaries of bishoprics and parishes; and to exercise many other controlling powers over Church structure and functions.

2. José Dolores Gámez, *Historia de Nicaragua* (Managua: Tipografía De "El País," 1889), 176–78.

3. Edgar Zúñiga, *Historia eclesiástica de Nicaragua* (Managua: Editorial Unión, 1981), 88–89.

4. Ibid., 97.

5. N. Wilson et al., "Investigación para la historia de la iglesia en Nicaragua" (Thesis, Universidad Centroamericana, Facultad de Humanidades y Ciencias, July 1975), 55.

6. For more details, see ibid., 55–57; and Arellano, *Breve historia*, 49–52.

7. He was later released and returned to Nicaragua to join the movement.

8. Zúñiga, 304.

9. Wilson, 59.

10. Pablo Antonio Cuadra, "Ensayo histórico-cultural sobre la Iglesia Católica en Nicaragua," in *El catolicismo contemporáneo de hispanoamérica*, ed. Richard Pattee (Buenos Aires: Editorial Fides, 1948), 348.

11. Ibid.

12. Ibid., 349.

13. William Walker, *War in Nicaragua* (New York: S.H. Goetzel & Co., 1860), 143.

14. Gámez, 621.

15. Jerónimo Pérez, *Obras históricas completas* (Managua: Banco Central, 1975), 180.

16. Cuadra, 350.

17. *History of Central America*, vol. 8 of *The Works of Hubert Howe Bancroft* (San Francisco: The History Company Publisher, 1887), 484.

18. Wilson, 69.

19. See Sergio Ramírez Mercado, *El pensamiento vivo de Sandino* (San José: EDUCA, 1979), 5-25. Also, Dr. Ofsman Quintana, a Nicaraguan historian, points out the position of Secretary Knox as the lawyer for the Fletcher family, owners of the Rosario and Light Mines Company, as an indication of the role of the North American capital in the overthrow of Zelaya. See Ofsman Quintana, *Apuntes de historia de Nicaragua*, 8th ed. (Managua: FANATEX, 1977), 235-36.

20. *New York Times*, September 10, 1912.

21. Harold Norman Denny, *Dollars for Bullets, The Story of American Rule in Nicaragua* (New York: Dial Press, 1929), 100.

22. Cuadra, 351.

23. Dana G. Munro, *The Five Republics of Central America* (New York: Oxford University Press, 1918), 232.

24. Ibid., 245.

25. Ibid., 238.

26. The Department of State, *The United States and Nicaragua, A Survey of the Relations From 1909 to 1932*, Latin American Series, no. 6 (Washington

D.C.: U.S. Government Printing Office, 1932), 29. Also see Gregorio Selser, 34-44; and Munro, *The Five Republics*, 253.

27. Munro, *Intervention and Dollar Diplomacy in the Caribbean, 1900*-1921, 413-17.

28. Munro, *Five Republics*, 258.

29. January 2, 1927, NA RG (National Archive Record Group) 59, 817.00/4350. Cited in Millet, 52.

30. Selser, 105.

31. Bishop Pereira y Castellón to Cardinal James Gibbons, October 9, 1912, reproduced in Oscar González Gary, *Iglesia católica y revolución en Nicaragua*, vol. 1 (México, 1986), 127-32.

32. Ibid.

33. José Román, *Maldito país* (Managua: ed. Unión Cardoza, 1983), 45, cited in Giulio Girardi, *Sandinismo, marxismo, cristianismo in la nueva Nicaragua*, vol. 1 (Managua: Centro Ecuménico Antonio Valdivieso, 1986), 45.

34. Donald C. Hodges, *Intellectual Foundations of the Nicaraguan Revolution* (Austin: University of Texas Press, 1986), 7.

35. Ibid., 40.

36. For an interesting discussion on Sandino's spiritualism and theosophy, see Oscar González Gary, *Iglesia católica y revolución en Nicaragua*; and Donald C. Hodges, *Intellectual Foundations of the Nicaraguan Revolution*.

37. Introducción al pensamiento sandinista (Managua: Editorial Juan De Dios Muñoz, n.d.), 37.

38. W.W. Cumberland, *Nicaragua, An Economic and Financial Survey* (Washington: United States Government Printing Office, 1928), 11.

39. Neil Macaulay, *The Sandino Affair* (Chicago: Quadrangle Books, 1967), 211, quoted from Bolanos, *Sandino*, 70-71.

40. Francisco Gaitán, "Vida organizada de la G.N. de Nicaragua," mimeographed copy (Managua, 1952), 39-49, reproduced in Oscar González Gary, 148-49.

41. Wilson, 438.

42. *Baricada*, no. 44 (Managua, May 19, 1984), cited in González Gary, 145.

Chapter 2. Economic Formation and Sociopolitical Conflict

1. Consejo de Planificación Nacional, Dirección de Planificación Nacional, *Plan nacional de reconstrucción y desarrollo, 1975*-1979, anexo estadístico, (Managua: n.p., Dec. 1975), II, 4–6.

2. Ibid., 20.

3. Ibid., 4–6, 26.

4. The figures for 1965 are compiled from Banco Central De Nicaragua-Ministerio de Economia, Industria y Comercio, *Compendido estadístico, 1965*-1974 (Managua: Banco Central, 1976), 471. The figures for 1975 and 1979 are compiled from *Plan nacional de reconstrucción y desarrolo, 1975*-1979, 26.

5. Oficina de Planificación, *Estudio de desarrollo agropecuario* . . . , Cuaderno no. 4.

6. Nancy Beth Jackson, "The Adaptation of Technology in Nicaragua" (Ph.D. Diss., University of Miami, 1973), 39.

7. René Herrera Zúñiga, "Nicaragua: el desarrollo capitalista dependiente y la crisis de la dominación burguesa, 1950–1980," *Foro internacional, 80*, XX, no. 4 (April–June 1980), 617–18.

8. Lethander, 171–73.

9. CEPAL et al., *Tenencia de la tierra y desarrollo rural en Centroámerica* (San José: Editorial Universitaria Centoamericana, 1973), 48, 70.

10. Herrera Zúñiga, 618.

11. Overseas Economic Survey, *Nicaragua* (London: His Majesty's Stationary Office, 1951), 5.

12. Harry Wallace Strachan, "The Role of the Business Groups in Economic Development: The Case of Nicaragua; (Ph.D. Diss., Harvard University, 1973), 184.

13. Estudios e Informes de la CEPAL, *Nicaragua: el impacto de la mutación política* (Santiago de Chile: n.p., 1981), 4.

14. *Foro internacional, 80*, 619.

15. CEPAL, 5.

16. Departamento de Estudios Económicos, Banco Central de Nicaragua, *Nicaragua, comercio exterior, 1977*, 177.

17. Nicaragua, Banco Central, *Informe annual, 1980*, Cuaderno no. 1 (Managua: n.p., 1980), n. page.

18. George Black, *Triumph of the People, The Sandinista Revolution in Nicaragua* (London: Zed Press, 1981), 40.

19. *A Modern Nicaragua* (Managua: n.p., 1955), 7. Quoted in John D. Martz *Central America, the Crisis and the Challenge* (Chapel Hill: University of North Carolina Press, 1959), 169.

20. U.S. Department of Commerce, Bureau of International Commerce, *Investment in Nicaragua* (Washington D.C.: U.S. Government Printing Office, 1962). Cited in Lethander, 218.

21. Black, 39.

22. Quoted in Black, 39.

23. Black, 39.

24. Wheelock, 128.

25. *Foro internacional, 80*, 619.

26. Lethander, 118; and Consejo de Planificación Nacional, Dirección de Planificación Nacional, 6.

27. CEPAL, 12.

28. Ibid., 8. From Banco Central de Nicaragua, y Ministerio de Económia, Industria y Comercio, *Datos de la tercera encuenta de situación de empleo*, (Managua: n.p., 1975).

29. Black, 69.

30. Pedro Belli, Instituto Centroamericano de Administración de Empresa (Managua, 1975), 15.

32. Belli, op. cit., 15.

33. *Anuario estadístico de Nicaragua* 1979, 131.

34. CEPAL, 12.

35. Ibid.

36. *Pastoral colectiva de episcopado nicaragüense* (Managua: Editorial Católica, 1950), 5, quoted in Arellano, 85.

37. Herrera Zúñiga, 622.

38. FJD was formed in the late 1940s by some young Liberal dissidents who had broken with Somoza in 1944 over his intention for reelection.

39. Arellano, 91.

40. Ibid.

41. Stephen Schlesinger and Stephen Kinzer, *Bitter Fruit, The Untold Story of the American Coup in Guatemala* (Garden City, New York, 1982), 174.

42. Ibid., 214.

43. Barron Buenaventura, *La santa iglesia, su historia* (Madrid: Edición S.M., 1959), 164. This book was taught in the private Catholic high schools in Nicaragua during the 1960s and 1970s.

44. Black, 44.

Chapter 3. The Response of Latin American Catholics to Socioeconomic Problem

1. A different version of this chapter was published in *Latin American Perspectives*, vol. 13, no. 3 (Summer 1986):37–57.

2. Leo XIII, *Rerum Novarum*, 1891.

3. John XXIII, *Mater et Magistra*, 1961.

4. Daniel H. Levine, ed., *Churches and Politics in Latin America* (Beverly Hills: Sage Publications, 1979), 21.

5. According to a report by the North American Congress on Latin America (NACLA), between 1950 and 1973 more than 428,000 foreign officers and enlisted men (including 64,000 Latin Americans) were trained under the Military Assistance Program in the United States and Panama, with thousands of others receiving U.S.-sponsored in-country training. For more information on this subject, see "U.S. Military Training," *NACLA* X, no. 1 (January 1976):11.

6. Jenny Pearce, *Under the Eagle, U.S. Intervention in Central America and the Caribbean* (Boston: South End Press, 1982), 53; and Michael T. Klare, *Supplying Repression: U.S. Support for Authoritarian Regimes Abroad* (Washington: Institute for Policy Studies, 1977), 20.

7. Statement by Don Etchison before House Subcommittee on Human Rights in Nicaragua, Guatemala, and El Salvador, June 1976, in

Human Rights in Nicaragua, Guatemala, and El Salvador: Implications for U.S. Policy, hearings before the Subcommittee on International Organizations of the Committee on International Relations, House of Representatives, 94th Congress, 2nd Session, June 8 and 9, 1976. (Washington D.C.: U.S. Government Printing Office, 1976), 127.

8. Jenny Pearce, 55.

9. U.S. Congress, *Human Rights in Nicaragua* . . . , 126.

10. Ibid.

11. The working document for the Bishops Conference was published by the CELAM two months before the Medellín meeting.

12. Segundo Galilea, "Liberation Theology began with Medellín," *LADOC* V, no. 58 (May 1975):4.

13. Gutiérrez, 228.

14. For an extensive discussion on this subject, see George V. Pixley, *God's Kingdom: A Guide for Biblical Study* (Maryknoll, N.Y.: Orbis Books, 1981).

15. Rom. 13:1-3.

16. CELAM, *The Church in the Present-Day Transformation of Latin America in the Light of the Council* (Bogotá: General Secretariat of Consejo Episcopal Latinoamericana, 1970), II, 48. Document of Justice was written by the Committee of Justice and Peace, headed by the Brazilian Bishop Aráujo Sales of Salvador (Bahía).

17. CELAM, 1970, II, 48.

18. See Levine, 1979, 30.

19. Leo XIII, *Rerum Novarum*, 1891.

20. Leo XIII, *Rerum Novarum*, 1891.

21. Rom. 12:4-6.

22. John XXIII, *Mater et Magistra*, 1961.

23. Paul VI speech quoted in Mutchler, 1971, 114.

24. Ibid., 115.

25. Ibid., 116-17.

26. CELAM, 1970, II, 45.

27. The document on Peace was written by the Subcommittee on Peace directed by Bishop Carlos Parteli, the archbishop of Montevideo and president of the Uruguayan Conference of Bishops.

28. CELAM, 1970, II, 55.

29. Gutiérrez, 1973, 273.

30. Ibid., 273.

31. Ibid., 276.

32. CELAM, 1970, II, 63.

33. Ibid., 61.

34. Quoted in McCormick, 1968, 691.

35. Pixley, 1983, 378-93.

36. Juan Luis Segundo, *Americas* (April 27, 1968):574.

37. Pixley, 1983.

38. Robert M. Grant, 1977, 113.

39. González Ruiz, 1970, 78.

40. Robert Adolfs, 29-54.

41. Pius XI, *Quadragesimo Anno*, quoted in Guerry, 1961, 76.

42. Pope Pius XII, Christmas Allocution, 1942, quoted in Guerry, 1961, 32.

43. Pius XII, Allocution to Italian Workers, March 11, 1945, quoted in Guerry, 141.

44. González Ruiz, in *When All Else Fails* . . . , 1970, 78.

45. John XXIII, *Mater et Magistra*, 1961.

46. *Mater et Magistra.*

47. Segundo, *Americas* (1968):577.

48. Dussel, 1976, 136.

49. Dussel, 1976, 137.

50. Segundo, 1974, 115.

Chapter 4. *Implementation of Liberation Theology in Nicaragua, 1968–72*

1. Roberto Argüello Hurtado, "La pastoral y la política," *El Pensamiento centroamericano* XXVIII, no. 139 (April 1972):26.

2. González Gary, 229–30.

3. Ernesto Cardenal, *The Gospel in Solentiname*, trans. Donald D. Walsh (New York: Orbis Books, 1976), vii.

4. Phillip Berryman, *The Religious Roots of Rebellion, Christians in Central American Revolutions* (New York: Orbis Books, 1984), 22.

5. Tenant C. Wright, S.J., "Ernesto Cardenal and the Humane Revolution in Nicaragua," *Americas* (December 15, 1979).

6. González Gary, 240.

7. Berryman, 61.

8. Noel A. García, "La Realidad de la Iglesia en Nicaragua," in *De cara al futuro de la iglesia en Nicaragua*, proc. of the Primer Encuentro Pastoral, Managua. 20 Enero/1 Febrero (Managua: Editorial Hospicio, 1969), 39.

9. Ernesto Castillo, "Realidad humana de Nicaragua," in *De cara* . . . , 158.

10. Pablo Antonio Vega, "Realidad humana en Nicaragua (comentario)" in *De cara* . . . , pp. 160–61. In contrast to this early view of the priestly activity as nonpolitical, Bishop Vega later became very much involved in anti-Sandinista politics following the revolution and was expelled from Nicaragua on July 4, 1986, for his public support of armed actions of the CIA-supported counterrevolutionary groups.

11. For excerpts from *Testimonio*'s articles, see Arellano, 106–17.

12. *Testimonio*, no. 8, quoted in Arellano, 110.

13. Quoted in Arellano, 110.

14. Ibid., 113.

15. González Gary, *Iglesia católica y revolución en Nicaragua*, 243.

16. Ibid.

17. Ibid., 244–45.

18. Uriel Molina, "El sendero de una experiencia," *Nicaráuac*, Revista del Ministerio de Cultura de Nicaragua, no. 5 (April–June 1981):18.

19. Ibid., 22.

20. Ibid., 24.

21. Ibid.

22. "The Principles Guiding The Church's Political Activity," a Pastoral Letter issued on March 19, 1972, by the bishops of Nicaragua, translated and published in *LADOC* III, no. 30 (September 1972).

23. Ibid.

24. A political agreement between Somoza's Liberal Party and the Conservative Party, represented by Agüero. According to the pact, 40% of the legislative seats and judicial appointments would go to the Conservatives, and the executive power would be transferred to a triumvirate of one Conservative and two Liberal members in return for the Conservatives' consent and participation in writing a new constitution, which would allow Somoza to be reelected in 1974.

25. Roberto Argüello Hurtado, "La pastoral y la política," *El pensamiento centroamericano*, XXVIII no. 139 (April 1972):27.

26. Pedro Joaquín Chamorro, *El pensamiento* (April 1972):28.

27. Pastoral Letter, March 19, 1972.

28. Ibid.

29. Text of the Somoza-Agüero Political Pact, quoted in Julio Icaza Tijerino, *El Pensamiento* (April 1972):30.

30. Icaza Tijerino, *El Pensamiento* (April 1972):29–30.

31. Argüello Hurtado, 27; and Arellano, 124.

32. Tommie Sue Montgomery, "Cross and Rifle: Revolution and the Church in El Salvador and Nicaragua," *Journal of International Affairs* (1982):208–21.

33. Pablo Antonio Vega, "El socialismo, la iglesia, y Cardenal," *La Prensa*, July 18, 1971.

34. *Violence*. A formal conference given by Monsignor Miguel Obando y Bravo in July 1972 at the National Autonomous University in Managua, translated and published by *LADOC* IV (December 1973):20.

35. Ibid.

36. Ibid., 25.

37. Ibid., 22.

Chapter 5. The 1972 Earthquake and the Aftermath

1. Francisco Lainez, *Terremoto 72, elites y pueblo* (Managua: Editorial Unión, 1977), 101–2.

2. Ibid., 128.

3. Ibid., 135.

4. Black, 60.

5. Lester A. Sobel, ed., *Latin America, 1973* (New York: Facts on File, 1974), 184–85.

6. "Washington's Baby," *NACLA* X, no. 2, (February 1976):23, quoted from *Inforpress*, #46, p. 3A, and *Latin America 1973*, 185.

7. John A. Booth, *The End and the Beginning: The Nicaraguan Revolution* (Boulder, Colorado: Westview Press, 1982), 89.

8. Julio López et al., *La caída de somocismo y la lucha sandinista en Nicaragua* (Costa Rica: EDUCA, 1979), 83.

9. Pedro Joaquín Chamorro, "Empresa privada y empresa pública," *La Prensa*, May 8, 1968.

10. Ibid.

11. Booth, 81.

12. *Latin America 1973*, 185.

13. "Mensaje y comunicado al pueblo católico," Nicaraguan bishops, 1973, mimeographed copy.

14. A statement by the archbishop of Managua, Nicaragua, Monsignor Miguel Obando, published as a pamphlet dated April 1974, *LADOC* no. 59 (June 1975).

15. Ibid.

16. "Declaración de la Conferencia Episcopal de Nicaragua reunida en sesión extraordinaria," Managua, May 27, 1974, *Boletín informativa de la arquidiócesis de Managua*, no. 24 (1974):19.

17. Ibid.

18. This constitution was written by the Constituent Assembly formed by the Somoza's Liberal Party and Agüero's faction of the Conservative Party in 1971, following the arrangement of the Political Pact between Somoza and Agüero. See chapter 2 for more details.

19. "Observations to Help Reflection and Dialogue on the Subject of the Citizen's Political Duty," a Pastoral Letter issued by the Nicaraguan Bishops Conference on August 6, 1974, *LADOC* 44, no. 59 (June 1975).

20. Ibid.

21. Booth, 105.

22. *¿Qué es el Partido Socialcristiano Nicaragüense?* 1961, mimeographed copy.

23. Booth, 107.

24. *¿Que es . . . ?*

25. Unión Democrática de Liberación (UDEL), *Programa mínimo* (Managua: n.p., December 1974).

26. Ibid.

27. Ibid.

28. Pedro Joaquín Chamorro, "Labor Verses Business," *La Prensa*, n.d., rpt., *Revista del pensamiento centroamericano*, no. 158 (January–May 1978):54–55.

29. Ibid.

30. For more details, see chapter 3, the section on Class Struggle and the Traditional Church.

Chapter 6. The FSLN and the Progressive Church

1. Jaime Wheelock Román, *Frente sandinista: hacia la ofensiva final* (Havana: Editorial de Ciencias Sociales, 1980), 59.

2. Wheelock, *Frente sandinista . . .* , 60.

3. *Historia del FSLN* (Frente Estudiantil Revolucionario, 19?), mimeographed copy.

4. At this early stage of formation, the FSLN was basically a Marxist group with strong nationalistic tendencies. The main goals of the organ-

ization were to mobilize the lower classes, workers and peasants, in a revolutionary organization to overthrow the government; to socialize the socioeconomic structures of the country; and to provide a total independence for Nicaragua.

5. Carlos Fonseca Amador, *Nicaragua, hora cero* (Managua: Secretaria Nacional de Propaganda y Educación Política, FSLN, 1979), n. page.

6. *Historia del FSLN*, 9.

7. Fonseca, *Nicaragua, hora cero.*

8. For more information on these meetings, see Margaret Randall, *Christians in the Nicaraguan Revolution.*

9. "Proclama del FSLN," 1969, in Carlos Fonseca, *Obras*, vol. 1, "Bajo la bandera del sandinismo" (Managua: Ed. Nueva Nicaragua, 1982), 267.

10. See Fonseca.

11. Black, 85.

12. *Apuntes de historia*, 243.

13. For more details on the three tendencies, see Claribel Alegría and D.J. Flankoll, *Nicaragua: la revolución sandinista* (México: Edición Era, 1982); and John A. Booth.

14. Quoted in Margaret Randall, 134.

15. Interview with the author, September 11, 1981, Managua.

16. Randall, 169.

17. Interview with the author.

18. Interview with the author.

19. Ibid.

20. Ibid.

21. Ibid.

22. Fernando Cardenal, younger brother of Ernesto Cardenal, joined the Society of Jesus in 1952; he studied theology in Nicaragua, Guatemala, and Mexico, where he was ordained in 1967. His next stop was Colombia, where he worked in a poor neighborhood of Medellín for nine months. Returning to Nicaragua, in July 1970, he was appointed vice-rector of the Central American University in Managua. But in December of the same year, he was expelled from the university for supporting the demands of a

student strike. Thereafter, he devoted himself in organizing retreats and courses for Christian youth. For more information on the religious life and political activities of Fernando Cardenal, see Teófilo Cabestrero, *Ministros de dios, ministros del pueblo* (Spain: Editorial Desclée De Brouwer, S.A., 1983.)

23. Alegría, 213.

24. Ibid., 214.

25. Ibid., 216.

26. "Movimiento cristiano y la revolución popular sandinista," *Gaceta Sandinista* I, no. 4 (December 1975, San Francisco).

27. Ibid.

28. Ibid.

29. Quoted in Randall, 163–65.

30. Ibid.

31. Ibid.

32. FSLN, "Por la incorporación de las grandes masas cristianas al proceso revolucionario," *La Gaceta Sandinista*, no. 2 (Managua, October 1975), quoted in Oscar González Gary, 290.

33. Quoted in Randall, 187.

34. Molina, *Nicaráuac*, no. 5, p. 30.

35. Quoted in Randall, 193.

36. Ibid., 193.

37. *Gaceta Sandinista*, 1975.

38. Quoted in Randall, 194.

39. Ibid., 177.

40. Ibid., 167.

41. Uriel Molina, *Nicárauac*, no. 5, p. 28.

42. *La Prensa*, May 22, 1977.

43. Ibid.

44. Ibid.

45. The Maryknoll Sisters belong to a North American religious

order based in New York. They began their missionary work in Nicaragua in the mid-1950s, in Siuna, a small mining community in the northern mountains, then moved to Managua in 1968–69.

46. Following the earthquake the area was chosen as one of the three sites for a government project to relocate displaced residents of Managua. The project was called *Operación Permanente de Emergencia Nacional* (OPEN).

47. *Apuntes de la Historia* . . . , II, 242.

48. For more information on this guerrilla action, see the section on the FSLN in the 1970s, in the current chapter.

49. "Mensaje No. 2, de: unidad de combate 'Juan José Quezada,' a: el pueblo nicaragüense" in *Apuntes de historia* . . . , 250.

50. Ibid.

51. Luis Samandu, and Ruud Jansen, "Nicaragua: dictadura somocista, movimiento popular e iglesia, 1968–1979," "Estudios Sociales Centroamericanos, no. 33 (December 1982, San José, Costa Rica), 202.

52. Quoted in Dodson and Montgomery, 169.

53. Ibid.

54. An interview with one of the Maryknoll Sisters, by the author, Managua, September 13, 1981. Maryknoll Sisters interviewed in Managua wanted to remain anonymous because they frequently travel to other Central American countries where the progressive Church, including the Maryknoll Order, is persecuted by the governments.

55. Ibid.

56. Ibid.

57. Ibid.

58. Maryknoll's Constitution quoted in "To the People of Nicaragua", a letter written by the Maryknoll Sisters in Nicaragua, December 28, 1977, mimeographed copy.

59. Interview with the author, September 13, 1981.

60. The Maryknoll house in the barrio was subjected to unexpected visits by the National Guard, and the sisters were branded as subversives. Although not arrested or physically abused at the time of the struggle against the water company in 1976, some of them were badly beaten by the National Guard in a later stage of the struggle in 1977.

61. Interview with the author, September 13, 1981.

62. Penny Lernoux, 93.

63. "To the People of Nicaragua," mimeographed copy.

64. Interview with the author, September 13, 1981.

65. Rosa María Pochet, 88.

66. Consejo de Planificación Nacional, Dirección de Planificación Nacional, *Plan nacional de reconstrucción y desarrollo, 1975*-1979 (Managua: n.p. December 1975), I, 126.

67. Compiled from Instituto Nacional de Estadística y Censos, *Anuario estadístico de Nicaragua, 1979* (Managua: n.p., 1979).

68. *Anuario estadístico de Nicaragua, 1979*, 105.

69. Ibid.

70. "From the Other Side," *North American Congress on Latin America (NACLA)* X, no. 2, (Feb. 1976):3.

71. Instituto Nacional de Estadística y Censos, 47–48. In both of these studies, the urban population includes all people living in towns with more than 1,000 inhabitants.

72. Ibid.

73. Richard Walter Oscar Lethander, "The Economy of Nicaragua," (Ph.D. Diss., Duke University, 1968), 99.

74. Instituto Nacional de Estadística y Censos, 168–88.

75. Ibid., 141–42.

76. Consejo de Planificación Nacional, 10.

77. The use of the term *indigenous* in the Nicaraguan context is misleading. A process of disease, war, and slave trading had largely destroyed the cultural and tribal customs and traditions, as well as the social structures of the original occupants of the region at the time of European penetration. Through a process of intermarriage and cultural dissemination, certain communities have maintained links to the original culture, while preserving the possibility of population growth. Portions of language, dress, social organization, and cultural traditions may have been altered or forgotten, but these communities have generally maintained some regional or cultural ties which still emphasize or reflect those earlier

characteristics of indigenous ancestors. These groupings are generally referred to as indigenous, although they may only partially reflect blood or cultural ties to the past.

78. T. Matamoras, *La republica de Nicaragua* (Managua: n.p., 1906), 29.

79. Instituto Histórico Centroamericano "Nicaragua's Resettlement Project," *Envío*, no. 10 (March 15, 1982).

80. Philip A. Dennis, "The Costeños and the Revolution in Nicaragua," *Journal of Inter American Studies* 23 (August 1981):271–96.

81. "Nicaragua's Resettlement Project," 1.

82. Ibid.

83. Ibid.

84. Delegates of the Word are lay persons who are trained and authorized to perform many of the sacramental functions.

85. Gregorio Smutko, "Cristianos de la Costa Atlántica en la revolución," *Nicaráuac*, no. 5 (April–June 1981):52.

86. Gregorio Smutko, "Informes implicaciones políticas de los programas de acción social de la iglesia católica en Centroámerica," *Boletín Del Archivo General de la Nación* (Managua, Nicaragua, 1980), 9–35.

87. "El clero por el socialismo," *Proceso*, no. 148, March 9, 1979, quoted in Samandu, 205.

88. For a detailed description of the work in Jalapa and of Father Evaristo, see Smutko, *Boletín* . . . ; and Rosa María Pochet and Abelino Martínez, *Nicaragua, iglesia: ¿manipulación o profecía?* (San José, Costa Rica: Editorial DEI, 1987). Father Evaristo remained in Honduras asnd began forming Christian Base Communities there until 1978, when he was expelled from Honduras under pressure from Somoza. He lived in Costa Rica until the triumph of the Nicaraguan Revolution and his return to the country.

89. Pochet, 133.

90. Anabel Torres et al., "Lucha ideológica en el campo religioso y su significado Político," Managua, August 17, 1981, unpublished paper, p. I-4.

91. Manuel Rodríguez García, *Gaspar vive*, 122.

92. While Nicaraguan peasants had fiercely resisted oppressive forces from the very beginning of the colonial period well into the modern times

on a sporadic basis, they never developed a political movement on a national level. One of the major obstacles to the radicalization of the peasantry was the pacifying role of the Catholic Church, which preached submission to political authority and social structure as one of the maxims of piety.

93. Smutko, *Boletín*, 17.

94. Ibid.

95. Smutko, *Nicaráuac*, no. 5, p. 52.

96. Smutko, *Nicaráuac*, 55.

97. "Terror in Nicaragua," Capuchin Communications Office, Milwaukee, WI. Published in *LADOC* (May–June 1977).

98. Lernoux, 86–87. According to Smutko (*Nicaráuac*, no. 5), before the end of the insurrection of 1979, the list of the victims of the National Guard in Zelaya increased to 350. An ex-official of the Guard stationed in Waslala estimated that the Guard had killed about 1,000 peasants in the province of Zelaya in the last years of the war.

99. Dodson and Montgomary, 172.

Chapter 7. Intensification of the Political Conflict and Clarification of the Sociopolitical Alliance

1. "New Year's Message of the Conference of Bishops of Nicaragua," *LADOC* VII, no. 5 (May–June 1977):11–15.

2. Ibid.

3. Ibid.

4. Ibid.

5. For more details on Cranshaw's interview, see chapter 6.

6. Instituto Histórico Centroamericano, *Encuentro*, no. 14 (July–December 1978):8.

7. Ibid.

8. Alegría, 267.

9. Ibid.

10. *La Prensa*, October 19, 77.

11. This group was composed of twelve individuals with different professional and political backgrounds. However, they were all well known in Nicaragua for their long-time commitment against the dictatorship. The group included two lawyers (Ernesto Castillo and Joaquín Cuadra), two businessmen (Emilio Baltodano and Felipe Mantica), two priests (Fernando Cardenal and Miguel D'Escoto), an academic (Carlos Tunnermann), a writer (Sergio Ramírez), an agronomist (Ricardo Coronel), an architect (Casimiro Sotelo), a banker (Arturo Cruz), and a dental surgeon (Carlos Gutiérrez).

12. In the contemporary Nicaraguan political vocabulary, the terms bourgeoisie, private sector, and capitalists have been used often interchangeably, all meaning wealthy landowners, large industrialists, financial and commercial magnates, and their intellectual representatives such as writers, journalists, and other professionals supporting a capitalist alternative for the country, in contrast to socialism.

13. *La Prensa*, October 19, 1977.

14. UDEL's statement published in *La Prensa*, October 19, 77.

15. A document signed by UDEL, PCN, PSC, and PCA, published in *La Prensa*, October 26, 1977.

16. *La Prensa*, October 19, 1977.

17. A statement signed by the Conservative Party, published in *La Prensa*, October 26, 1977.

18. *La Prensa*, October 22, 1977.

19. *La Prensa*, November 18, 1977.

20. *La Prensa*, November 18, 1977.

21. *La Prensa*, November 29, 1977.

22. A statement of the *Los Doce* published in *La Prensa*, December 24, 1977.

23. Ibid.

24. *SID* (Servicio de Información y Documentación) was the information bulletin of the Jesuit Community in Altamira, Managua.

25. The IHC is a Jesuit-based research institution in La UCA, (Central American University, at Managua). Since the mid-1970s, the IHC has been one of the religious organizations run by the progressive Church sectors. Although never affiliated with the FSLN, during the intensification of

the political struggle in Nicaragua, 1977–79, the IHC supported the radical alternative put forward by the FSLN. And since the triumph of the revolution in 1979, the *Instituto* has been very supportive of the social programs of the revolutionary government to alter the old social structure of the country. The identification of the IHC with the revolutionary process has made it a target of the attacks by the Catholic hierarchy, which finally, in 1982, announced that it would not approve of the institution and would not recognize it as a religious organization affiliated with the Church.

26. "Acontecimientos nacional," *SID* (November–December 1977):3–9.

27. "Dialogo nacional, una aportación desde la fe cristiana," *SID* (November–December 1977):16–25.

28. Ibid.

29. Ibid.

30. *La Prensa*, December 21, 1977. The same day that *La Prensa* published the archbishop's message, other news made the headlines. The National Guard had attacked the parish church in OPEN 3 the night before, and after using force to disperse a peaceful sit-in of the youth in the Church, had attacked a group of priests and nuns in the barrio, sending some of them to the hospital.

31. See the archbishop's October 19 statement in *La Prensa*, discussed earlier in the current chapter.

32. *La Prensa*, October 18, 1977.

33. *La Prensa*, December 10, 1977.

34. Ibid.

35. Gaspar García Laviana, "A Letter to the Nicaraguan People," December 25, 1977, rpt., *Nicaráuac*, no. 5 (April–June 1981):67–68.

36. Ibid.

37. Ibid. Father García was killed in battle on December 11, 1978.

38. In late December 1977, seven thousand hospital workers began a strike. Also, the AGROTEX textile factory was almost paralyzed by the workers' strikes. Both strikes continued into 1978.

39. *Encuentro*, no. 14 (July–December 1978):14–15.

40. Nicaraguan Episcopal Conference, "Mensaje al pueblo de dios al

iniciarse el año 1978," January 6, 1978, *Encuentro*, no. 14 (July–December 1978):99–102.

41. Ibid.

42. Ibid.

43. An FSLN communiqué published in *La Prensa*, January 9, 1978.

44. *La Prensa*, January 13, 1978.

45. A statement signed by UDEL and published in *La Prensa*, January 11, 1978.

46. Socialist Party's Statement of January 11, 1978, published in *La Prensa*, January 21, 1978.

47. *La Prensa*, January 13, 1978.

48. *La Prensa*, January 24, 1978.

49. UDEL's statement published in *La Prensa*, January 25, 1978.

50. Statement of the Conservative Party, published in *La Prensa*, January 25, 1978.

51. *La Prensa*, January 25, 1978.

52. *Encuentro*, no. 14 (July–December 1978):19.

53. *La Prensa*, January 17, 1978.

54. Ibid., January 27, 1978.

55. Ibid., January 29, 1978.

56. *Encuentro*, no. 14 (July–December 1978):21.

57. Ibid.

58. A statement signed by the National Council of UDEL on January 31, 1978, and published in *La Prensa*, February 1, 1978.

59. *La Prensa*, February 1, 1978.

60. *La Prensa*, February 3, 1978.

61. *Encuentro*, no. 14 (July–December 1978):23.

62. *La Prensa*, February 9, 1978.

63. Ibid., February 7, 1978.

64. Ibid., February 11, 1978.

65. *Encuentro*, no. 14 (July–December 1978):25.

66. "De la Conferencia Episcopal de Nicaragua," Matagalpa, February 22, 1978, mimeographed copy.

67. Quoted in Pilar Arias, *Nicaragua: revolución relatos de combatientes del frente sandinista* (México: Siglo Veintiuno, 1980), 156. For more details on the February 1978 insurrection in Monimbó and the absence of the FSLN in its initial phase, see Arias, 153–56; and Julio López et al., *La caída del somocismo y la lucha sandinista en Nicaragua* (Costa Rica: Editorial Universitaria Centroamericana – EDUCA, 1979), 179–80.

68. *Latin America* (New York: Facts on File, 1978), 114.

69. A statement signed by the leadership of UDEL and its member organizations published in *La Prensa*, June 2, 1978.

70. *Washington Post*, Aug. 1, 1978.

71. For information on the internal developments of the FSLN, see Chapter 7.

72. For more details on the *Terceristas* political analysis, see Julio López et al., *La caída del somocismo y la lucha sandinista en Nicaragua*, 229–32.

73. *New York Times*, October 26, 1977.

74. Ibid.

75. *La Prensa*, February 19, 1978.

76. George Black, 138.

77. Conferencia Episcopal de Nicaragua, "A los hombres de buena voluntad," *Encuentro*, no. 14 (July–December 1978):109.

78. Ibid., 110.

79. Ibid.

80. "Mensaje del señor arzobispo y su consejo presbiteral en las actuales circunstancias que vive el país," August 3, 1987, *Encuentro*, no. 14, 112–14.

81. *La Prensa*, August 4, 1978.

82. FSLN, "El Frente Amplio, el pueblo a la cabeza," *Lucha Sandinista* (Somewhere in Nicaragua, May 1978), quoted in Harald Jung, "Behind the Nicaraguan Revolution," *New Left Review*, no. 117 (September–October 1979):80.

83. "Programa inmediato del Movimiento Pueblo Unido-MPU," in Julio López et al., 360.

84. George Black, 122.

85. See the *New York Times* and the *Washington Post* of September 1978, and *Latin America 1978.*

86. López, et al., 189.

87. *La Prensa*, September 12, 1978.

88. Ibid.

89. Ibid., November 23, 1978.

90. Ibid.

91. Ibid., November 19, 1978.

92. Ibid., November 30, 1978.

93. "Acta constitutiva del Frente Patriótico Nacional," in López et al., 373.

94. Ibid.

95. *La Prensa*, April 8, 1979.

96. Harald Jung, 87.

97. "1979 Message to the People From the Nicaraguan Bishops," *LADOC* X, no. 2 (November–December, 1979):15.

98. Ibid.

99. Ibid., 16.

100. Ibid., 18.

Epilogue

1. The *Frente* offered a seat in the five-member Government Junta to Violeta Chamorro, the widow of the reformist leader of UDEL, Pedro Joaquín Chamorro, and another seat to Alfonso Robelo, a wealthy capitalist and the main negotiator of FAO in the last joint efforts of the U.S. government and the Nicaraguan bourgeoisie to reach an agreement with Somoza to prevent a revolutionary triumph.

2. "Compromiso cristiano para una Nicaragua nueva," Carta pastoral del Episcopado Nicaragüense, November 17, 1979, Editorial Unión, 8-9.

3. The Council of the State was the advisory and legislative body of the revolutionary government prior to the election of November 1984.

4. Pastoral letter of November 17, 1979.

5. The other member of the Junta representing the private sector, Violeta Chamorro, had resigned in early April, citing health problems as the reason for her resignation.

6. Pastoral Letter, November 17, 1979.

7. "¿Pueblo católico y gobierno marxista?" *En Marcha*, Boletín Informativo del Partido Conservador Demócrata de Nicaragua, Managua, July 31, 1980.

8. For details of the COPROSA formation and operation, and its relations to U.S. foreign policy, see Ana María Ezcurra, *Agresión Ideológica Contra la Revolución Sandinista* (México: Nuevomar, 1983.)

9. *Envío*, vol. 4, issue 43 (January 1985):2b.

10. "Primera respuesta de sacerdotes," June 8, 1981, in *Sacerdotes en el gobierno nicaragüense: ¿Poder o servicio?* (San José, Costa Rica: DEI, 1981), 12.

11. The author's interview with Father Bismark Carballo, spokesman for the archbishop, and the director of the *Radio Católica*, the official voice of the Church hierarchy, Managua, September 10, 1981.

12. "La carta del papa," Episcopal Conference, June 29, 1982, quoted in Laura Nuzzi O'Shaughnessy and Luis H. Serra, *The Church and Revolution in Nicaragua* (Athens, Ohio: Ohio University Center for the International Studies, 1986), 33.

13. Ibid.

14. Instituto Histórico Centroamericano, *Envío*, no. 30 (December 1983):20.

15. Ibid., 21b.

16. *Envío*, vol. 4, issue 38 (August 1984):5c.

17. Quoted in O'Shaughnessy, 28.

18. Ibid., 40.

19. Quoted in O'Shaughnessy, 39.

20. *Envío*, vol. 4, issue 43 (January 1985):8b.

21. Quoted in *Envío*, vol. 4, issue 38 (August 1984):8c.

22. *Envío*, vol. 5, issue 50 (August 1985):3b.

23. Quoted in ibid., 4b.

24. Ibid. Bishop Vega's intensive political activities against the government resulted in his exile from Nicaragua in July 1986.

25. *Envío*, vol. 5, issue 58 (April 1986):28.

26. Ibid., 31.

Bibliography

Books

Alegría, Claribel and D.J. Flakoll. *Nicaragua: la revolución sandinista, una crónica política/1855–1979.* México: Era, 1982.

Arellano, Jorge Eduardo. *Augusto César Sandino, escritos literarios y documentos desconocidos.* Managua: n.p., 1980.

————. *Breve historia de la iglesia en Nicaragua (1523–1979).* Managua: n.p., [1979.]

Ayón, Tomás. *Historia de Nicaragua desde los tiempos más remotos hasta 1852.* 3 vols. 2nd Ed. Managua: n.p., 1956.

Bancroft, Hubert Howe, "History of Central America." Vol. 8 of *The Works of Hubert Howe Bancroft.* San Francisco: The History Company Publisher, 1887.

Berryman, Phillip. *The Religious Roots of Rebellion, Christians in Central American Revolutions.* New York: Orbis Books, 1984.

Black, George. *Triumph of the People, The Sandinista Revolution in Nicaragua.* London: Zed Press, 1981.

Bonino, José Miguez. *Revolutionary Theology Comes of Age.* London: SPCK, 1975.

Booth, John A. *The End and the Beginning: The Nicaraguan Revolution.* Colorado: Westview Press, 1982.

Buenaventura, Barron. *La santa iglesia, su historia.* Madrid: Edición S.M., 1959.

Cabestrero, Teófilo. *Ministros de dios, ministros del pueblo.* Spain: Editorial Desclée de Brouwer, S.A., 1983.

_____. *Revolucionarios por el evangelio.* Spain: Editorial Desclée de Brouwer, 1983.

Calderón Ramírez, Salvador. *Últimos días de Sandino.* México: Ediciones Botas, 1934.

Cardenal, Ernesto. *The Gospel in Solentiname.* Trans. Donald D. Walsh. New York: Orbis Books, 1976.

Castañeda, Jorge G. *Nicaragua, contradicciones en la revolución.* México: Tiempo Extra, 1980.

Centroamérica: cristianismo y revolución. san José, Costa Rica: Departamento Ecuménico de Investigaciones, 1980.

Centro de Investigación y Estudios de la Reforma Agraria (CIERA). *La mosquitia en la revolución.* Managua: Centro de Publicaciones del CIERA, 1981.

CEPAL et al. *Tenencia de la tierra y desarrollo rural en Centroamérica.* San José: Editorial Universitaria Centroamericana, 1973.

Cole Chamorro, Alejandro. *145 años de historia política.* Managua: n.p., 1967.

Cumberland, W.W. *Nicaragua, an Economic and Financial Survey.* Washington D.C.: United States Government Printing Office, 1928.

Curso sobre la problemática actual. Managua: UNAN, [1981].

De Castilla, Miguel. *Educación y lucha de clases en Nicaragua.* Managua: Universidad Centroamericana, 1980.

Denny, Harold Norman. *Dollars for Bullets, The Story of American Rule in Nicaragua.* New York: Dial Press, 1929.

The Department of State. *The United States and Nicaragua, A Survey of the Relations From 1909 to 1932.* Latin American Series, No. 6. Washington D.C.: Government Printing Office, 1932.

Departamento Ecuménico de Investigaciones (DEI). *Apuntes para una teología nicaragüense.* Proc. of the Encuentro de Teología, Managua, Nicaragua, 8–14 September 1980. San José, Costa Rica: DEI, 1981.

_____. *Teología desde el tercer mundo.* Proc. of five international conferences of the Asociación Ecuménica de Teólogos del Tercer Mundo (Dar Es Salam, Tanzania — 1976; Accra, Gana — 1977; Wennappuwa, Sri Lanka — 1979; Sao Paulo, Brazil — 1980; Nueva Delhi, India — 1981). San José, Costa Rica: DEI, 1982.

Diederich, Bernard. *Somoza and the Legacy of U.S. Involvement in Central America*. New York: E.P. Dutton, 1981.

Dussel, Enrique. *A History of the Church in Latin America, Colonialism to Liberation (1492-1979)*. Trans. Alan Neely. Michigan: Wiliam B. Eerdmans Publishing Company, 1981.

————. *History and the Theology of Liberation, A Latin American Perspective*. Trans. John Drury. New York: Orbis Books, 1976.

El evangelio en la revolución. Managua: Instituto Histórico Centroamericano, 1979.

El pensamiento vivo de Sandino. San José, Costa Rica: EDUCA, 1979.

EPICA Task Force. *Nicaragua: A People's Revolution*. Washington D.C.: n.p., 1980.

Estado y clases sociales en Nicaragua. Proc. of II Congreso de la Asociación Nicaragüense de Científicos Sociales. [February 1982]. Managua: Centro de Investigaciones y Estudios de la Reforma Agraria (CIERA), 1982.

Estudio e Informes de la CEPAL. *Nicaragua: el impacto de la mutación política*. Santiago de Chile: n.p., 1981.

Ezcurra, Ana María. *Agresión ideológica contra la revolución sandinista*. México: Nuevomar, 1983.

Fe cristiana y revolución sandinista en Nicaragua. Proc. of the Seminario Fe Cristiana y Revolución Sandinista en Nicaragua. 24–28 September 1979, Managua, Nicaragua. Managua: Instituto Histórico Centroamericano, 1980.

Fonseca Amador, Carlos. *Nicaragua: hora cero*. n.d.; rpt. Managua: Secretaria Nacional de Propaganda y Educación Política, FSLN, 1979.

Gámez, José Dolores. *Historia de Nicaragua*. Managua: Tipografía de El País, 1889.

Gibellini, Rosino. Ed. *Frontiers of Theology in Latin America*. Trans. John Drury. New York: Orbis Books, 1975.

Gilly, Adolfo. *La nueva Nicaragua, antiamperialismo y lucha de clases*. México: Editorial Nueva Imagin, S.A., 1980.

Girardi, Giulio. *Sandinismo, marxismo, cristianismo en la nueva Nicaragua*. Managua: Centro Ecuménico Antonio Valdivieso, 1986.

González Gary, Oscar. *Iglesia católica y revolución en Nicaragua.* México: Razo Impresores, 1986.

Guerry, Emil. *Social Doctrine of the Catholic Church.* Trans. Miriam Hederman. New York: Alba House, 1961.

Grant, Robert M. *Early Christians and Society, Seven Studies.* San Francisco: Harper and Row, 1977.

Gutiérrez, Gustavo. *A Theology of Liberation, History, Politics, and Salvation.* Trans. Sister Caridad Inda and John Eagleson. New York: Orbis Books, 1973.

_____. *The Power of the Poor in History.* Trans. Robert R. Barr. New York: Orbis Books, 1983.

Hennelly, Alfred T. *Theologies in Conflict.* New York: Orbis Books, 1979.

Herring, Hubert. *A History of Latin America, From the Beginnings to the Present.* 3rd ed. New York: Alfred A. Knopf, 1968.

Hodges, Donald C. *Intellectual Foundations of the Nicaraguan Revolution.* Austin: University of Texas Press, 1986.

Incer, Jaime. *Geografía ilustrada de Nicaragua.* Managua: n.p., 1975.

Introducción al pensamiento sandinista. Managua: Editorial Juan De Dios Muñoz, n.d.

Klare, Michael T. *Supplying Repression: U.S. Support for Authoritarian Regimes Abroad.* Washington D.C.: Institute for Policy Studies, 1977.

Lainez, Francisco. *Terremoto 72, elites y pueblo.* Managua: Editorial Unión, 1977.

López, Julio, O. Núñez, C.F. Chamorro, and P. Serres. *La caída de somocismo y la lucha sandinista en Nicaragua.* Costa Rica: EDUCA, 1979.

La Patria de Pedro, El pensamiento nicaragüense de Pedro Joaquín Chamorro. Managua: La Prensa, 1981.

Las iglesias en la práctica de la justicia. San José, Costa Rica: Departamento Ecuménico de Investigaciones, 1981.

Lernoux, Penny. *Cry of the People.* New York: Penguin Books, 1980.

Levine, Daniel H. ed. *Churches and Politics in Latin America.* Beverly Hills: Sage Publications, 1979.

Los cristianos interpelan a la revolución. Managua: IHCA-CAV, 1981.

Macaulay, Neill, *The Sandino Affair.* Chicago: Quadrangle Books, 1967.

Martz, John D. *Central America, the Crisis and the Challenge.* Chapel Hill: University of North Carolina Press, 1959.

Metz, Rene, and Jean Schlick, eds. *Liberation and the Message of Salvation.* Proc. of the Fourth Cerdic Colloquium, Strasbourgh, 10–12 May 1973. Trans. David Gelzer. Pittsburgh, Pennsylvania: The Pickwick Press, 1978.

Millet, Richard. *Guardians of the Dynasty.* New York: Orbis Books, 1977.

Munro, Dana G. *Intervention and Dollar Diplomacy in the Caribbean, 1900*–1921. Princeton, New Jersey: Princeton University Press, 1964.

————. *The Five Republics of Central America.* New York: Oxford University Press, 1918.

Mutchler, David. *The Church as a Political Factor in Latin America.* New York: Preager Publishers, 1971.

Nicaragua, el pueblo frente a la dinastía. Madrid: EDOC-Espana, 1978.

Nicaragua: la hora de los desafíos. Lima: Centro de Estudios y Publicaciones, 1981.

Núñez Soto, Orlando. *El somocismo y el modelo capitalista agroexportador.* Managua: UNAN, Dep. de Ciencias Sociales, n.d.

Ortega Arancibia, Francisco. *Cuarenta años (1838–1878) de historia de Nicaragua.* Managua: Banco de America, 1975.

Ortega Saavedra, Humberto. *50 años de lucha sandinista.* Habana, Cuba: Editorial de Ciencias Sociales, 1980.

Overseas Economic Survey. *Nicaragua.* London: His Majesty's Stationary Office, 1951.

O'Shaughnessy, Laura Nuzzi, and Luis H. Serra. *The Church and Revolution in Nicaragua.* Athens, Ohio: Ohio University Center for International Studies, 1986.

Pérez, Jerónimo. *Obras históricas completas.* Managua: Banco Central, 1975.

Pearce, Jenny. *Under the Eagle, U.S. Intervention in Central America and the Caribbean.* Boston: South End Press, 1982.

Pixley, George V. *God's Kingdom: A Guide for Biblical Study.* Maryknoll, N.Y.: Orbis Books, 1981.

Pochet, Rosa María and Abelino Martínez. *Nicaragua, iglesia: ¿manipulación o profecía?* San José, Costa Rica: Editorial DEI, 1987.

Quijano, Carlos. *Nicaragua: un pueblo, una revolución.* México: Editorial Pueblo Nuevo, 1978.

Quintana, Ofsman. *Apuntes de historia de Nicaragua.* 8th ed. Managua: FANATEX, 1977.

Ramírez, Sergio. *El pensamiento vivo de Sandino.* San José: EDUCA, 1979.

Randall, Margaret. *Christians in the Nicaraguan Revolution.* Trans. Mariana Valverde. Vancouver: New Star Books, 1983.

Ricard, Pablo, ed. *Materiales para una historia de teología en América Latina.* Proc. of VIII Encuentro Latinoamericano de CEHILA, Lima (1980). San José, Costa Rica: Departamento Ecuménico de Investigaciones, 1981.

Rodríguez, Mario. *Central America.* Englewood Cliffs, N.J.: Prentice Hall, 1965.

Rodríguez, René M., and Antonio Acevedo Espinoza, eds. *La insurrección nicaragüense, 1978–1979.* Managua: Banco Central de Nicaragua, 1979.

Rodríguez García, Manuel. *Gaspar Vive.* San José, Costa Rica: Artes Graficas de Centroamérica, 1981.

Rosset, Peter, and John Vandemeer, eds. *The Nicaragua Reader, Documents of a Revolution Under Fire.* New York: Grove Press, 1983.

Sánchez, Mayo Antonio. *Nicaragua: año cero.* México: Editorial Diana, 1979.

Schlesinger, Stephen, and Stephen Kinzer. *Bitter Fruit, The Untold Story of the American Coup in Guatemala.* Garden City, New York: Doubleday & Company, 1982.

Selser, Gregorio. *Sandino.* Trans. Cedric Belfrage. New York: Monthly Review Press, 1981.

Sobrino, Jon, and Juan Hernández Pico. *Teología de la solidaridad cristiana.* Managua: IHCA-CAV, 1983.

Torres, Sergio, and John Eagleson, eds. *The Challenge of Basic Christian Communities.* New York: Orbis Books, 1981.

Universidad Nacional Autónoma de Nicaragua (UNAN), Departamento de Ciencias Sociales, Sección de Historia. *Apuntes de historia de Nicaragua.* 2 vols. Managua: 1980.

U.S. Department of Commerce, Bureau of International Commerce. *Investment in Nicaragua.* Washington D.C.: U.S. Government Printing Office, 1962.

Walker, Thomas, ed. *Nicaragua in Revolution.* New York: Praeger Publishers, 1982.

———. *The Christian Democratic Movement in Nicaragua.* Tucson, Arizona: The University of Arizona Press, 1970.

Walker, William. *The War in Nicaragua.* New York: S.H. Goetzel & Co., 1860.

Weber, Henri. *Nicaragua: The Sandinist Revolution.* Trans. Patrick Camiller. London: Veso Editions and NLB, 1981.

Wheelock Román, Jaime. *Frente Sandinista: hacia la ofensiva final.* Havana: Editorial de Ciencias Sociales, 1980.

———. *Nicaragua: imperialismo y dictadura.* Havana: Editorial de Ciencias Sociales, 1980.

———. *Raíces indígenas de la lucha anticolonialista en Nicaragua.* 4th ed. México: Siglo Veintiuno, 1980.

Woodward, Ralph Lee. *Central America, A Nation Divided.* New York: Oxford University Press, 1976.

Zúñiga, Edgar. *Historia eclesiástica de Nicaragua.* Managua: Editorial Unión, 1981.

Articles, Dissertations, Papers, Letters, Documents, Pamphlets

"Acontecimientos nacional." *SID* (November–December 1977): 3–9.

"Acta constitutiva del Frente Patríatico Nacional." In López, Julio, et al., *La caída del somocismo y la lucha sandinista en Nicaragua,* 372–78. Costa Rica: EDUCA, 1979.

Alaniz Downing, Luis Alberto. "Productividad y tenencia de la tierra en la agricultura nicaragüense." Thesis, Universidad Autónoma de Nicaragua, May 1981.

Argüello Hurtado, Roberto. "La pastoral y la política." *El Pensamiento Centroamericano* XXVIII, 139 (April 1972): 26–27.

Banco Central de Nicaragua-Ministerio de Economía, Industria y Comercio. *Anuario estadístico 1972.* Managua: Banco Central, n.d.

_____. *Anuario estadístico 1973*. Managua: Banco Central, n.d.

_____. *Anuario estadístico 1975*. Managua: Banco Central, n.d.

_____. *Censos nacionales 1971, población, característica económicas*. Vol. III. Managua, Banco Central, October 1974.

_____. *Compendio estadístico 1965-1974*. Managua: Banco Central, 1976.

_____. *Industria manufactura, situación actual y perspectivas*. Managua, Banco Central, 1975

_____. *Informe annual, 1980*. Cuaderno 1. Managua: n.p. 1980.

Biderman, Jaime. "The Development of Capitalism in Nicaragua: A Political Economic History." *Latin American Perspectives* X, no. 1 (Winter 1983): 7-33

Bonpane, Blase. "The Church and Revolutionary Struggle in Central America." *Latin America Perspectives* VII, no. 2 and 3 (Spring and Summer 1980): 178-89.

Capuchin Communications Office, Milwakee. "Terror in Nicaragua." *LADOC* (May-June, 1977): 6-8.

"Carta de los padres capuchinos al presidente Somoza, June 13, 1976." *Encuentro*, no. 14 (July -December 1978): 90.

"Carta de Monseñor Salvador Schlaefer, May 20, 1975." *Encuentro*, no. 14 (July-December 1978): 91.

Castillo, Donald. "Situación económica y alianzas políticas." *Revista Mexicana de Sociología* XII, no. 2 (April-June 1980): 501-21.

Castillo. Ernesto. "Realidad humana de Nicaragua." In *De Cara al futuro de la iglesia en Nicaragua*, 141-59. Proc. of the Primer Encuentro Pastoral, 20 January-1 February, 1969. Managua: Editorial Hospicio, 1969.

CELAM (Consejo Episcopal Latinoamericano). *The Church in the Present-Day Transformation of Latin America in the Light of the Council*. Bogotá, 1970.

"Central American Fixer." *NACLA* X, no. 2 (February 1976): 13-16.

Centro Ecuménico de Antonio Valdivieso. *Amanecer* (January 1982-December 1987).

_____. *CAV* (January 1982-December 1987).

CEPAD (Comité Evangélico Pro-Ayuda al Desarrollo). *Anuario 1979*. Managua: Editorial Unión, 1980.

Chamorro, Pedro Joaquín. *El Pensamiento Centroamericano* XXVIII, no. 139 (April 1972): 28.

——. "Empresa privada y empresa Pública." *La Prensa* 8 (May 1968): 2.

Comisión Evangélica Latinoamericana de Educación Cristiana. *Hablan los obispos de Nicaragua*. Cuadernos de Capatación, 5. Lima: CELADEC, 1979.

——. *Reflexión cristiana y revolución sandinista*. Cuadernos de Capatación, 15. Lima: CELADEC, 1979.

Conferencia Nacional de Religiosos de Nicaragua (CONFER). *Orientaciones sociales de la iglesia a la luz del magisterio pontificio*. Managua: Universidad Centroamericana, 1979.

——. *El nuevo rostro de Cristo en la alfabetización*. Managua: CONFER, 1980.

Consejo de Planificación Nacional, Dirección de Planificación Nacional. *Plan nacional de reconstrucción y desarrollo*. Managua: n.p., December 1975.

Consejo Superior de la Empresa Privada (COSEP). *Análisis sobre la ejecución del programa de gobierno de reconstrucción nacional para 1980*. Managua: n.p., 1980.

Cuadra, Pablo Antonio. "Ensayo histórico-cultural sobre la iglesia católica en Nicaragua." In *El catolicismo contemporáneo de hispanoamérica*, edited by Ricard Pattee, 335–53. Buenos Aires: Editorial Fides, 1948.

De La Pena, Sergio. "Nicaragua: una revolución andando." *Investigación Económica* 154 (October–December 1980): 89–92.

Dennis, Philip A. "The Costeños and the Revolution in Nicaragua." *Journal of Inter American Studies* 23 (August 1981): 271–96.

Departamento de Estudios Económicos, Banco Central de Nicaragua. *Nicaragua, comercio exterior, 1977*.

Departamento Ecuménico de Investigaciones (DEI). *Los cristianos estan con la revolución*. San José, Costa Rica: DEI, 1980.

——. *Sacerdotes en el gobierno nicaragüense: ¿poder o servicio?*. San José: DEI, [1981].

"Dialogo nacional. una aprotación desde la fe cristiana." *SID* (November–December 1977): 16–25.

Dodson, Michael, and T.S. Montgomery. "The Churches in the Nicaraguan Revolution." In *Nicaragua in Revolution*, edited by Thomas Walker, 161–80. New York: Praeger Publishers, 1982.

"El imperio económico de la familia Somoza." *Nicaragua, reforma o revolución* I, la crisis de sistema capitalista (December 1978.)

Escobar, José Benito. "Ideario sandinista." In *Sandino, el rebelde de America.* Managua: Editorial Unión, 1979.

Federación Nicaragüense de Educación Católica (FENEC). *Documento de respuestas de FENEC a la consulta nacional.* Managua: Editorial Unión, 1981.

Flora, Jan L., et al., "The Growth of Class Struggle: The Impact of the Nicaraguan Literacy Crusade on the Political Consciousness of Young Literacy Workers." *Latin American Perspectives* X, no. 1 (Winter 1983): 45–62.

Frente Estudiantil Revolucionario (FER). *Historia del FSLN.* N.p., n.d. Mimeographed copy.

"From The Other Side." *North American Congress on Latin America (NACLA)* X (February 1976): 3.

FSLN. "Comunicado oficial de la dirección nacional del FSLN sobre la religión." Managua: Mimeographed copy. [1980]

FSLNTP. *La crisis interna y las tendencias.* No. 1, Collección 4 de Mayo. Los Angeles, California: n.p., 1978.

Galilea, Segundo. "Liberation Theology Began with Medellín." *LADOC* 5(58): 1–6.

García Gutíerrez, Edgard D. *Proceso de industrialización en Nicaragua: periodo 1958–1968 y la integración económica centroamericana.* Managua: UNAN, 1969. Mimeographed copy.

García Noel A. "La realidad de la iglesia en Nicaragua." In *De cara al futuro de la iglesia en Nicaragua*, 34–51. Proc. of the Primer Encuentro Pastoral, 20 January–1 February, 1969. Managua: Editorial Hospicio, 1969.

García Laviana, Gaspar. "A Letter to the Nicaraguan People." December 25, 1977; rpt., *Nicaráuac*, no. 5 (April–June 1981): 67–68.

Gilly, Adolfo. "Estado y lucha de clases en la revolución Nicaragüense." *Investigación Económica* 154 (October–December 1980): 93–106.

Gorman, Stephen M. "Power and Consolidation in the Nicaraguan Revolution." *Journal of Latin American Studies* 13 (May 1981): 133–49.

Herrera Zúñiga, René, "Nicaragua: el desarrollo capitalista dependiente y la crisis de la dominación burguesa, 1950–1980." *Foro Internacional, 80* (México, El Colegio de México) XX, no. 4 (April–June 1980): 612–45.

Hynds, Patricia. "CIA Uses Religion: The Ideological Struggle Within the Catholic Church in Nicaragua." *Covert Action Information Bulletin*, no. 18 (Winter 1983): 16–20.

Icaza Tijerino, Julio. *El Pensamiento Centroamericano* XXVIII, no. 139 (April 1972): 29–30.

Instituto Histórico Centroamericano. *Envío* (June 1981–December 1987).

———. *Fe cristiana y revolución sandinista*. Managua: IHC., n.d.

———. "Sucesos nacionales." *Encuentro*, no. 14 (July–December 1978): 7–29.

Instituto Nacional de Estadística y Censos. *Anuario estadístico de Nicaragua, 1979*. Managua: n.p., 1979.

Instituto Nicaragüense de Desarrollo (INDE). *Informe anual 1979*. Managua: n.p. 1979.

———. *Ánalisis económico 1981*. Managua: INDE, 1981.

Irarrazaval, Diego. "Religiosidad y lucha nicaragüense." *CAV*, no. 5–6 (September 1981): 1–8.

Jackson, Nancy Beth. "The Adaptation of Technology in Nicaragua." Ph.D. Diss., University of Miami, 1973.

John XXIII. *Mater et Magistra*. Boston: St. Paul Editions, 1961.

Jung, Harald. "Behind the Nicaraguan Revolution." *New Left Review*, no. 117 (September–October 1979): 69–89.

Lacayo Ocampo, Leonardo. "Nace el gran Managua de una misión imposible." *La Prensa*, 24 December, 1975, 2.

"La coyuntura política." *Nicaragua reforma o revolución* III (December 1978): 131–38.

"La empresa privada de Nicaragua define su posición frente a Somoza." *Estudios Centroamericanos* 33, no. 355 (May 1978): 345–52.

Laird, Larry Kieth. "Technology Versus Tradition: The Modernization of Nicaraguan Agriculture." Ph.D. Diss., University of Kansas, 1974.

La Prensa, June 1977–June 1979.

La revolución de Nicaragua. Cuadernos Universitarios, 26, 27, 28. León, Nicaragua: Universidad Nacional Autónoma de Nicaragua, 1980.

Latin America (1973–1978).

Lethander, Richard Walter Oscar. "The Economy of Nicaragua." Ph.D. Diss., Duke University, 1968.

Los Doce. "Statement." *La Prensa*, 24 December 1977.

McCormick, Richard A. "Notes on Moral Theology." *Theological Studies* 29(4).

Ministerio de Planificación. *Plan de reactivación económica en beneficio del pueblo.* Managua: Secretaria Nacional De Propaganda y Educación Política, FSLN, 1980.

Molina, Uriel. "El sendero de una experiencia." *Nicaráuac* 5 (April –June 1981): 17–37.

Montgomery, Tommie Sue. "Cross and Rifle: Revolution and the Church in El Salvador and Nicaragua." *Journal of International Affairs* (1982): 208–21.

"Movimiento cristiano y la revolución popular sandinista." *Gaceta Sandinista* (San Francisco, California) I, no. 4 (December 1975).

New York Times, September 10, 1912.

New York Times, October 26, 1977.

Nicaraguan Episcopal Conference. "Carta pastoral de los obispos de Nicaragua sobre el deber del testimonio e de la acción cristiana en el orden político." Managua, June 29, 1971.

_____. "The Principles Guiding the Church's Political Activity." (A Pastoral Letter, issued on 19 March, 1972.) *LADOC* III, no. 30 (September 1972): 1–7.

_____. "Mensaje y comunicado al pueblo católico." [Managua], 1973. Mimeographed copy.

_____. "Declaración de la Conferencia Episcopal de Nicaragua reunida en sesión extraordinaria, May 27, 1974." *Boletín Informativo de la Arquidiócesis de Managua,* no. 24 (1974): 19.

_____. "Observations to Help Reflection and Dialogue on the Subject of the Citizen's Political Duty." (A Pastoral Letter, August 6, 1974.) *LADOC* 44, no. 59 (June 1975): 23-28.

_____. "New Year's Message, 1977." *LADOC* VII, no. 5 (May-June, 1977): 1-5.

_____. "Mensaje al pueblo de dios al iniciarse el ano 1978." January 6, 1978; rpt., *Encuentro,* no. 14 (July-December 1978): 99-102.

_____. "En la hora presente, mensaje de los obispos católicos de Nicaragua ante la grave crisis de la nación, January 28, 1978." *Encuentro* (July-December 1978): 103-4.

_____. "De la conferencia episcopal de Nicaragua." Matagalpa, February 22, 1978. Mimeographed copy.

_____. "A los hombres de buena voluntad." *Encuentro, Revista de la Universidad Centoamericana,* no. 14 (July-December 1978): 108-11.

_____. "1979 Message to the People from the Nicaraguan Bishops." *LADOC* X, no. 2 (November-December 1979): 15-19.

_____. "Compromiso cristiano para una Nicaragua Nueva." (A Pastoral Letter issued by the Nicaraguan Bishops, November 17, 1979.) Mimeographed copy.

_____. "Jesucristo y la unidad de su iglesia en Nicaragua, October 22, 1980." *Revista del Pensamiento Centroamericano,* no. 168-69 (July-December 1980): 64-92.

Obando y Bravo, Miguel. "Violencia." (A formal conference given by Monsignor Miguel Obando y Bravo in July 1972 at the National Autonomous University in Managua.) *LADOC* IV (December 1973): 20-27.

_____. "Should the Church be in Politics?" a statement by the Archbishop of Managua, Mons. Miguel Obando, published as a pamphlet dated April 1974. *LADOC,* no. 59 (June 1975): 29-31.

_____. "Mensaje del señor arzobispo y su consejo presbiteral en las actuales circunstancias que vive el país." 3 August 1978; rpt., *Encuentro, Revista de la Universidad Centoamericana,* no. 14 (July-December 1978): 112-14.

_____, and Manuel Salazar Espinoza. "A Letter to the Constituent National Assembly." *Boletín Informativo de la Arquidiócesis de Managua,* no. 17 (October 1973): 11–12.

Oficina Ejecutiva de Encuestas y Censos. *Anuario estadístico 1976.* Managua: Oficina Ejecutiva de Encuestas y Censos, 1977

_____. *Anuario estadístico 1977.* Managua: Oficina Ejecutiva de Encuestas y Censos, 1978.

Oyanguren, Mariano Fiallos. "The Nicaraguan Political System." Ph.D. Diss., University of Kansas, 1968.

Partido Socialcristiano Nicaragüense. "¿Qué es el Partido Socialcristiano Nicaragüense? (1961). Mimeographed copy.

Pixley, George V. "Biblical Embodiments of God's Kingdom: A Study Guide for the Rebel Church." In *The Bible and Liberation,* edited by Norman K. Gottwald. Maryknoll, NY: Orbis Books, 1983.

"Programa inmediato del Movimiento Pueblo Unido-MPU." In López, Julio, et al., *La caída del somocismo y la lucha sandinista en Nicaragua,* 360–72. Costa Rica: EDUCA, 1979.

"¿Pueblo católico y gobierno marxista?" *En Marcha* (Boletín Informativo del Partido Conservador Demócrata de Nicaragua), 1. Managua, July 31, 1980.

"Reflection Groups in Managua Defend Peasants." *LADOC* VIII, no. 5 (May–June 1978): 27–37.

Sacasa Guerrero. *El Pensamiento Centroamericano* XXVIII, no. 139 (April 1972): 35.

Samandu, Luis, and Ruud Jansen. "Nicaragua: dictadura somocista, movimiento popular e iglesia, 1968–1979." *Estudios Sociales Centroamericanos,* no. 33 (December 1982): 189–220. San José, Costa Rica.

"Sandino and the Rise of Somoza." *NACLA* X, no. 2 (February 1976): 4–8.

Segundo, Juan Luis. "Social Justice and Revolution." *Americas* (April 27, 1968): 574–77.

_____. "Capitalism-Socialism: A Theological Crux." In *The Mystical and Political Dimension of the Christian Faith,* edited by Claud Geffre and Gustavo Gutíerrez. New York: Herder and Herder, 1974.

Smutko, Gregorio. "Cristianos de la Costa Atlántica en la revolucción." *Nicaráuac,* no. 5 (April–June 1981): 49–65.

————. "Informes implicaciones políticas de los programas de acción social de la iglesia católica en Centroamérica." *Boletín Del Archivo General de la Nación*, 9–35. Managua, Nicaragua, 1980.

Strachan, Harry Wallace. "The Role of the Business Groups in Economic Development: The Case of Nicaragua." D.B.A. Diss., Harvard University, 1973.

Telpiz, Benjamin. "The Political and Economic Foundations of Modernization in Nicaragua: The Administration of José Santos Zelaya, 1893–1909." Ph.D. Diss., Howard University, 1973.

The Maryknoll Sisters in Nicaragua. "To the People of Nicaragua," 28 December, 1977. Mimeographed copy.

"The Revolutionary Challenge." *NACLA* X, no. 2 (February 1976): 26–34.

Torres, Anabel, et al., "Lucha ideológica en el campo religioso y su significado político." Managua, August 17, 1981. Unpublished paper.

UDEL. "Statement." *La Prensa*, 19 October 1977.

————. *Programa mínimo*. Managua: n.p., December 1974.

U.S. Congress, House Subcommittee on Human Rights. *Human Rights in Nicaragua, Guatemala, and El Salvador: Implications for U.S. Policy.*. Hearings Before the Subcommittee on International Organizations of the Committee on International Relations. 94th Congress, 2nd Session, June 8 and 9, 1976. Washington D.C.: U.S. Government Printing Office, 1976.

Vega, Pablo Antonio. "El socialismo, la iglesia, y Cardenal." *La Prensa*, July 18, 1971.

————. "Realidad humana en Nicaragua. (comentario)" In *De cara al futuro de la iglesia en Nicaragua*, 160–66. Proc. of the Primer Encuentro Pastoral, 20 January–1 February, 1969. Managua: Edirorial Hospicio, 1969.

Washington Post, August 1, 1978.

Wilson, N., et al. "Investigación para la historia de la iglesia en Nicaragua." Thesis, Universidad Centroamericana, Facultad de Humanidades y Ciencias, 1975.

Wright, Tennant C. "Ernesto Cardenal and the Humane Revolution in Nicaragua." *Americas* (December 15, 1979): 387–88.

Index

Accessory Transit Company, 6
Acción Nacional Conservadora. See ANC
AFL-CIO, 104
Agency for International Development
(AID), 204
Agrarian Reform Law, 73–74
Agricultural clubs, 147–148
Agüado, Enoc, 37, 99–100
Agüero, Father Diego de, 1
Agüero, Fernando, 43–44, 83
Alliance for Progress, 115
AMNLAE, 201
ANC, 108
Anti-Fascist United Front, 38, 102
Arbenz, Jacobo (president of
Guatemala), 42
ARDE, 209
Arias Caldera, Monsignor, 117, 206
Arles, Council of, 61
*Asociación de Mujeres Nicaragüenses "Luisa
Amanda Espinoza". See* AMNLAE
Association of Nicaraguan Women. *See*
AMNLAE
Association of Clergy (ACLEN), 204
Assumption, Sisters of, 127
Asunción order. *See* La Asunción order
ATC, 151–152, 192, 201
Atlantic Coast, 125
Atlantic zone, 142–147
Authentic Conservative Party (*Partido
Conservador Auténtico*), 44, 101, 165,
176, 180

Baltodano, Alvaro, 78, 132–133
Baltodano, Monica, 128
BANAMERICA, 91
Banco de Centroamérica, 176
BANIC, 91
Barni, Monsignor (bishop of
Matagalpa), 208
Barreda, Felipe and María, 209
Barrios, Justo Rufino (President of
Guatemala), 9
Beadle, Elias, 21
Beers, the house of Joseph W., 12
Belzunegui, Father Pedro, 210–211
Bertrand, Father Evaristo, 150, 172
Bishops' Conference. *See* Episcopal
Conference of Nicaragua
Bluefields (city), 145
Boaco (province), 142
Bocay, River, 145
Bogota, Colombia, 56
Bonanza (mining town), 146
Borge Martínez, Tomás, 99, 113–114,
117–118, 131, 133
Borge y Castrillo, Monsignor
(auxiliary bishop of Managua), 67
Bosco Vivas, Monsignor (auxiliary
bishop of Managua), 207
Broad Opposition Front. *See* FAO
Bryan-Chamorro Treaty, 13
Buchanan (president of the United
States), 7
Bustamente y Guerra, José, 4–5

Buitrago, Father Noel, 76

Cabildo Abierto, 4
CADIN, 177
Calderón y Padilla, Monsignor (bishop
   of Matagalpa), 75
Calderón, Margarita, 17
Calero, Adolfo, 209
Cámara de Industria de Nicaragua. See
   CADIN
Câmara, Dom Helder (bishop of
   Recife), 59
Capuchin Fathers, The, 77, 95, 135,
   149–150, 155–156; in Zelaya,
   147–149, 209
Carazo, province, 142, 151
Cardenal, Father Ernesto, 68, 85,
   117–118, 135, 170–171
Cardenal, Father Fernando, 76, 128,
   133, 135, 141, 156, 201
Carrión, Luis, 78, 134
Carter Administration, 186
Castañda, Pedro de, 3
Castillo Armas, Carlos (dictator of
   Guatemala), 42
Castillo Quant, José María, 122
Castillo, Ernesto, 71–73
Catacombs Reporting (Periodismo de
   Catacumbas), 181
Cathedral of Managua: the occupation
   of, 76
Catorce de Septiembre, barrio, 130
Cauleli, Vincente, 135
CAUS, 104
CDS, 151, 201
Center for Agrarian Education and
   Promotion. *See* CEPA
Center for National Distribution of
   Food, 88
Center for Plasma, 176
Center for Union Action and Unity.
   See CAUS
Central American Business
   Administration Institute (Instituto

Centroamericano de Administración
   de Empresas — INCAE), 91
Central American University (UCA), 91
Central American Common Market,
   25, 31–35, 42, 115
Central de Trabajadores de Nicaragua.
   See CTN
Central de Trabajadores de Masaya, 185
Central Sandinista de Trabajadores. See CST
Central Zone, 142–147
Centro de Acción y Unidad Sindical. See
   CAUS
Centro de Educación y Promoción Agraria.
   See CEPA
Centro de Investigación y Documentación de
   Costa Atlántica — CIDCA, 145
Centro Ecuménico de Antonio Valdivieso, 204
CEPA, 151–152, 172
CGT-I, 98, 102–104, 122, 177, 192
CGT, 104
Chamber of Construction, the, 177
Chamber of Commerce, the, 177
Chamorro, Emiliano, 12, 38
Chamorro family, 39
Chamorro, Fruto, 6
Chamorro, José Antonio (vicar of
   Granada), 4
Chamorro, Pedro Joaquín, 44, 92–94, 98,
   108, 113–114, 141; Assassination of,
   176
Chavarría, José David, 132
Chávez Núñez, Monsignor, 67, 75
Chibchas, 146
Chinandega (province), 142
Chontales (province), 142
Christian Base Communities, 53, 68,
   75, 118, 150–151, 153, 157,
   204–206; Radicalization of, 124–142
Christian Youth Club, 135
Christians for Socialism (in Chile), 79
Christopher, Warren (Under-Secretary
   of State), 166
CIA, 207
CIDCA, 145

Ciudad Sandino, 135. *See also* OPEN 3
Civil Corps for Reconstruction, 88
Class collaboration, Catholicism and, 54, 57
Class struggle, Liberation Theology and, 55–61; Catholicism and, 53–55
Clayton-Bulwer Treaty, 6
Comisión de Promoción Social Arquidiocesana (COPROSA), 204
Comités Cívicos Populares. See Popular Civic Committees
Comités de Defensa Sandinista. See CDS
Communist International, 38
Communist Party of Nicaragua, (PC de N), 102, 192
Comunidades Eclesiales de Base (CEB). *See* Christian Base Communities
Concientización, 141. *See also* consciousness-raising
Confederación General del Trabajo Independiente. See CGT-I
Confederación de Religiosos (CONFER), 204
Consciousness-raising, 68–69, 147–149, 154. *See also Concientización*
Consejo de Unidad Sindical. See CUS
Consejo Superior de la Empresa Privada. See COSEP
Conservatives, x
Conservative Party of Nicaragua. *See* Nicaraguan Conservative Party
Conservative National Action (Acción Nacional Conservador – ANC), 44, 101
Constituent National Assembly, 43, 88
Constitutionalist Liberal Party (PLC), 99
Contras, 208–210
Contreras, Hernando, 3
Contreras, Pedro, 3
Contreras, Rodrigo de, 2
Cooperative of Cotton Producers of Managua, the, 177
Coordinating Commission for National Dialogue, 166, 176
COSEP, 195

COSIP, 91, 93–94
Council for Union Unity. *See* CUS
Council of the Indies, 2
Council of the State, 208
Cranshaw Guerra, Roberto, 135, 161
Cristo Campesino, 151
Crusades, 61
CST, 201
CTN, 98, 102–104, 122, 176, 180, 195–196
Cuadra Pasos, Carlos, 38
Cuadra family, 39
Cuadra, Joaquín, 78
Cuadra, Pablo Antonio, 166
Cuban Revolution, 45
CUS, 104

D'Escoto, Father Miguel, 172
Delegados de la Palabra (Delegates of the Word), 147–148, 150–151, 157, 159. *See also* Delegates, the
Delegates, the, 147–148
Democratic Conservative Party (Partido Conservador Democrático), 44, 101
Democratic Youth Front. *See* FJD
Díaz, Adolfo, 12, 14
Disloyal competition, 93
Ducalu, barrio, 130

Earthquake, The 1972, 87, 126, 135
el Observador, 73
El Porvenir texile factory, 176
Encomendero, ix, 1–3
Encomienda, ix, 2
Episcopal Conference of Central America and Panama, 41; First Pastoral Letter, 41
Episcopal Conference of Nicaragua, 155–156, 180, 207–208, 211
Espíritu Santo, 150
Esteban Guandique, Dr. Félix, 165
Estelí (province), 142

Estrada, General Juan J., 11–12
Ethelburg Syndicate of London, 11
Exodos, 51

Family of God, 150
FAO, 189–198
FER, 120, 122, 192
First National Pastoral Meeting, 71–73
FJD, 40, 99, 113
Fonseca Amador, Carlos, 99, 114, 118
FPN, 196–197; the program of, 197
Fragoso, Monsignor (bishop of
     Crateus, Brazil), 60
Freire, Paulo, 53
Frente Amplio Opositor. See FAO
Frente Estudiantil Revolucionario — FER.
     See FER
Frente Juvenil Democrático. See FJD
Frente Obrero, 196
Frente Patriótico Nacional. See FPN
Frente Sandinista de Liberación Nacional.
     See FSLN
Frente. See FSLN
FSLN communiqué, 136
FSLN, xii–xiii, 44, 78–80, 95, 97,
     102, 111–124, 148–149, 152–153,
     161, 163–164, 176, 182–187,
     191–199; and the Bourgeoisie, 187;
     and the Catholic Church, 117–119;
     Student Movement and, 113–114

Gaceta Sandinista, 129–131
García Jerez, Monsignor Nicolás
     (bishop of León), 3–4
García Laviana, Father Gaspar, 59,
     154, 172–173
García y Suárez, Monsignor Marco
     Antonio (bishop of Granada), 84
García, Father Noel, 71
Garrison, Cornelius, 6
General Confederation of Workers.
     See CGT
General Confederation of Workers —
     Independent. *See* CGT-I
General Strike, 177–183, 188

Gibbons, Cardinal James, 16
González Dávila, Captain, 1
González y Robleto (Archbishop of
     Managua), 41, 67
Granada (province), 142
Guerra Popular Prolongada — GGP. See
     Prolonged People's War
Guerrilla operation of December 27,
     1974, 136
Guillén, Dulce María, 129
Gutiérrez, Gustavo, 51, 58
Gutiérrez, Roberto, 78, 130

Ham, Clifford D., Colonel, 13
Hanna, Matthew E., 23
Hartman, Maria, 124–127
Hernández, Plutario Elias, 187
Hilario Herdocia, José, 7
Holy War, 61
Hueck, Cornelio, 90

IHC, 167
Imperialism, 56
Incer, Roberto, 33
INDE (Instituto Nicaragüense de
     Desarrollo), 93–94, 165, 177
Independent Liberal Party (PLI), 83,
     98–99, 113–114, 180, 196
Institutionalized violence, 58–61, 74,
     80, 85–86, 154
Instituto Histórico Centroamericano. See IHC
Instituto Nicaragüense de Desarrollo.
     See INDE
Instituto Social Juan XXIII de la
     Universidad Centroamericana, 71
Investigation and Documentation Center
     of the Atlantic Coast. *See* CIDCA

Jalapa communities, 151; city, 149
Jesuit priests, 9, 135, 151; Expulsion
     of, 9
Jícaro, 149
Jinotega, province, 142
John Paul II, Pope, 202

John XXIII, Pope, xi, 46–47, 64
Junta of the National Reconstruction
  Government, 199
Just War, Doctrine of, 61
Justice, Document on, 52
Juventud Patriótica Nicaragüense. See
  Nicaraguan Patriotic Youth
Juventud Sandinista 19 del Julio. See
  Sandinista Youth, 19th of July

Kennedy, John F., 115
Knox, Secretary of State, 12

La Asunción order, 70, 135
La Gaceta Sandinista. See *Gaceta
  Sandinista*
la Jara, Father José de, 70
Labor Code, 103
Land-Lease Agreement, 37
Lansing Plan, 14
Larreznaga, barrio, 130
las Casas, Friar Bartolomé de, 2
Latin American Episcopal Council
  (Consejo Episcopal
  Latinoamericano) — CELAM, 56
Leo XIII, Pope, 46, 53, 54, 63, 109
León (province), 142; City of, 3
Leyes Nuevas. See New Laws
Lezcano y Ortega, José Antonio
  (archbishop of Managua), 13, 21, 24
Liberals, x; anticlerical policies of the, x
Liberal Party, 161. *See also* Nationalist
  Liberal Party
Liberation Theology, 25, 45–66, 118
Literacy crusade, the, 201
López Fitoria (bishop of Granada), 152
López Pérez, Rigoberto, 40, 99, 114
Los Doce, 161–164, 183, 188–189, 195

Madriz (province), 142
Magnetic-Spiritual School, 18
Managua (city), 163, 181; province, 142
Mano Blanca, 135
March 19 Pastoral Letter. *See* Pastoral
  Letter of March 19, 1972

Maryknoll Constitution, the, 139
Maryknoll order, 70; Sisters, 127,
  135–141
Masaya (city), 163; province, 142, 151
Matagalpa (city), 181–182; province, 142
Mater et Magistra, 46, 64
Mathews, General, 23
Mayorga, Salvador, 78
Mayorga, Silvio, 99, 114
MDN, 189
Medellín Conference, xi, 25, 50, 51,
  57, 147, 151–152, 168; documents
  of, xii, 50, 59–60, 141; teachings,
  73, 75; working documents of, 57
Mediation Commission, 195
Mejía, Father Francisco, 75
Miguelena, Father Benito, 3–5
Military Service, law of, 208
Miskito Indians, 125, 148
Molina, Father Uriel, 68, 73, 77–79, 118,
  125, 127, 131–132, 135, 141, 161
Moncada, José María, 19, 24
Monimbó, 185–186
Moño, Father José Antonio, 3
Morazán, Francisco, 5
MOSAN, 104
Movement of United People. *See* MPU
Movimiento cristiano. See Revolutionary
  Christian Movement
Movimiento Democrático Nicaragüense.
  See MDN
Movimiento Pueblo Unido. See MPU
*Movimiento Sindical Autónoma de
  Nicaragua.* See *MOSAN*
Mozonte, 163
MPU, 191–192, 196

National Church, 205
National Committee of the General
  Strike, 177
National Dialogue, 163–169, 176
National Emergency Committee, 88
National Housing Institute, 90
National Palace, 192
National State of Emergency, 88

Nationalist Liberal Party, 82, 89, 161

New Laws, 2

New Testament, 51, 60

New Year's message, January 8, 1977, 159

NICARAAO, S.A., 90

Nicaraguan Conservative Party, 37, 44, 101, 165, 179–180

Nicaraguan Corporation for Investment (Corporación Nicaragüense de Inversiones), 91

Nicaraguan Democratic Movement. *See* MDN

Nicaraguan Democratic Forces (FDN), 209

Nicaraguan Episcopal Conference, 159 *See also* Episcopal Conference of Nicaragua

Nicaraguan Patriotic Youth (JPN), 114

Nicaraguan Social Christian Party. *See* Social Christian Party

Nicaraguan Socialist Party (PSN), 38, 98, 101, 112, 116, 122, 176, 183, 192

Nicaraguan Workers Center. *See* CTN

Nicarao, barrio, 130

Niehaus, Father Teodor, 155

Nonviolence, Universality of, 60

Nueva Segovia (province), 142

Obando y Bravo, Miguel (Archbishop of Nicaragua), xii–xiii, 75, 80, 95–97, 137, 161, 164–166, 190, 196, 202, 205–211

October Offensive, the, 163

Office of Program Coordination, 88

Old Testament, 51, 60

Olds, Robert (Under-Secretary of State), 14

OPEN 3, barrio, 127; The Process of Radicalization in, 135–141

Ortega, Camilo, 186

Ortega, Daniel, 186

Ortega, Humberto, 186

Pacific zone, 142–146

Pancasán, armed actions in, 119; the campaign of, 119

Partido Comunista de Nicaragua. See Communist Party of Nicaragua

Partido Conservador Auténtico. See Authentic Conservative Party

Partido Conservador Democrático. See Democratic Conservative Party

Partido Liberal Constitucionalista. See Constitutionalist Liberal Party

Partido Popular Social Cristiano. See PPSC

Partido Socialcristiano Nicaragüense. See Social Christian Party

Pasos family, 39

Pastora, Edén, 209

Pastoral Letter, March 19, 1972, 80–84; January 8, 1977, 156; November 17, 1979, 200

Paul VI, Pope, 56, 80

PC de N. *See* Communist Party of Nicaragua

Peace, Document of, 58

People's Church, 206

Peralta, Manuel Morales, 73

Pereira y Castellón, Simeón (bishop), 11, 16

Pio X, Pope, 13

Pius IX, Pope, 63

Pius XII, Pope, 41, 63–64

PLI. *See* Independent Liberal Party

Popular Church, 206

Popular Civic Committees, 120

Popular Mass, Nicaraguan, 70

Popular Militias, 208

Populorum Progressio (encyclical), 80

PPSC, 196

Primer Congreso Eucarístico, 24

Private property, Catholic Church and, 64; Liberation Theology and, 65

Proletarian Tendency, 123

Prolonged Popular War, 120, 123, 187

PSCN. *See* Social Christian Party

PSN. *See* Nicaraguan Socialist Party

Puerto Cabeza (town), 125

Quadra, Vincente (president of
    Nicaragua), 9
Quadragesimo Anno (encyclical), 63
Quam luxta apistolicum ejjetum, Bull of, 13
Quilalí, 149
Quod Apostolici Muneris, 63

Radio Católica, 181
Radio Mundial, 115
Raiti, town of, 115
Rama Indians, 146
Ramírez, Sergio, 161, 185, 189
Raudales, Ramón, 113
Reagan Administration, the, 202,
    207, 209
Reflection Committee, 197
Rerum Novarum (encyclical), 46, 53, 63
Revolutionary Student Front. *See* FER
Revolutionary Christian Movement,
    the, 128–130, 141
Reyes y Valladares, Canuto (bishop), 16
Riguero Christian Base Community,
    77–79
Riguero, barrio, 77–79, 125; The
    Process of Radicalization in,
    127–135
Río Coco, 115, 145, 147
Río San Juan (province), 6, 142
Rivas (province), 142
Robelo, Alfonso, 165, 202
Roman Synod (1971), 81
Rosario and Light Mines Company, 12
Rosita, 146
Rossel Arellano, Mariano (Archbishop
    of Guatemala), 42
Royal Patronage, 1
Ruben López (bishop of Estelí),
    208–209
Ruíz, Tomás, 5

Sacasa Guerrero, Ramiro. *See* Sacasa,
    Ramiro
Sacasa, Juan Bautista, 22

Sacasa, Ramiro, 98–99
Sacasa, Roberto, 10
Sacred Heart, 172
Salazar y Espinoza, Manuel (bishop of
    León), 165
Salvador, José, 3
San Carlos, National Guard Barracks
    in, 163, 170
San Juda, barrio, 127
San Pablo, barrio of, 70; parish of, 70,
    75, 141–142; Radicalization in,
    141–142
Sandinista army, the, 151
Sandinista Association of Rural
    Workers. *See* ATC
Sandinista Defense Committee. *See* CDS
Sandinista Popular Army, 132
Sandinista student organization. *See* FER
Sandinista Youth 19th of July, 201
Sandinista Workers Federation. *See* CST
Sandinistas. *See* FSLN
Sandino and the Catholic Church,
    21–22
Sandino, Augusto César, 15–16, 112
Sandino, Don Gregorio, 16
Santa Clara, 149
Santa Rosa parish, 206; Church, 207
Santí, Bishop, 208
Schick, René (president of Nicaragua),
    43, 91, 114
Schlaefer, Monsignor Salvador (bishop
    of Bluefields), 84, 155, 161, 208
Schmitz, Pablo (auxiliary bishop of the
    Atlantic Coast), 209
Second Conference of the Latin
    American Bishops. *See* Medellín
    Conference
Second Vatican Council. *See* Vatican II
Segundo, Juan Luis, 61
Sindicato de Radioperiodistas de Managua, 196
Siuna, 146
Social Christian Party, 44, 73, 83,
    99–100, 107, 162, 180, 189
Socialism, The Catholic Church and,
    61–65

Socialist Party of Nicaragua. *See*
  Nicaraguan Socialist Party
Solaun, Mauricio, United States
  Ambassador in Managua, 166
Solentiname, Christian community of,
  68–69, 170–171
Solórzano (president of Nicaragua), 14
Solórzano family, 39
Somocista Liberal Youth, 161
Somoza Debayle, Anastasio (Tachito),
  xiii, 40, 43, 76, 88, 96, 99, 155,
  161, 180
Somoza Debayle, Luis, 40, 43, 91
Somoza García, Anastasio (Tacho), 23,
  36, 40, 43, 99, 102
Somoza, Lilliam, 38
Somoza-Agüero Political Pact of 1971,
  81–83, 101
Soto, Benito, 4
Spellman, Cardinal (Archbishop of
  New York), 41
St. Agnes Congregation, 124
Sumo Indians, 146
Superior Council of Private Initiative
  (Consejo Superior de la Inicitiva
  Privada — COSIP). *See* COSIP

Tachito. *See* Somoza Debayle, Anastasio
Tacho. *See* Somoza García, Anastasio
Terceristas (third force), 124, 187–188, 191
Testimonio, 73–77
Theology of Liberation. *See* Liberation
  Theology
Tipitapa Pact, 15, 17, 24
Todman, Terence, 184
Torres, Father Camilo, 59
Trincado, Joaquín, 18
Triumvirate, 88
Turcios, *Comandante* Oscar, 133
Tyranny, 56

Ubico, General Jorge, 37
UDEL, 97–104, 113, 122, 162–165,
  173, 176–183, 189; Program,
  104–109
Unión Democrática de Liberación. See UDEL
Unión Nacional Opositora (UNO), 43
Union of Popular Organizations —
  UNOP, 180
United Fruit Company, 42
United Provinces of Central America, 5

Valdivieso, Antonio (bishop of León),
  2–3
Vanderbilt, Cornelius, 6
Vanguardia Juvenil, 99
Vasquez, Father Miguel, 157
Vatican Council II. *See* Vatican II
Vatican II, xi, 25, 47, 67, 70, 151;
  documents of, 141
Vega, Pablo Antonio (bishop of
  Juigalpa), 72, 84, 152, 161, 165,
  205, 209–211
Vigil, Father Agustín, 8
Villavicencio, Father Rafael, 8

Walker, William, x, 7
Waspán (town), 125
Well, Samuel, 12
Wiwilí, 23, 149
Workers' Unions, 102–104

Youth Democratic Front. *See* FJD

Zavala family, 39
Zavala, Joaquín (president of
  Nicaragua), 9
Zelaya, José Santos (president of
  Nicaragua), 10, 29; and the United
  States, 11–15
Zelaya (province), 142; Repression in, 148
Zinica, 120; campaign, 120
Zywiec, Father David, 155